HC

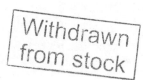

This critical reinterpretation of Proust's *Remembrance of Things Past* offers a fresh, socio-historical analysis of the novel. Departing from the more formalist and rhetorical trends in recent Proust criticism, Michael Sprinker draws upon historical scholarship to assess Proust's portrait of French society, and shows that the novel's account of the class structure and of the rivalry between the landed aristocracy and the bourgeoisie during the first half-century of the Third French Republic was both precise and critically engaged. He argues that in other areas, notably the nature of nationalist sentiment and gender ideology, Proust offers insight into phenomena studied only in fragmentary ways in previous historical writing on this crucial period. His study provides an original approach in its combination of history and literature, and is the most thorough work of marxist criticism on Proust to date.

CAMBRIDGE STUDIES IN FRENCH 50

HISTORY AND IDEOLOGY IN PROUST

CAMBRIDGE STUDIES IN FRENCH

General editor: Malcolm Bowie (*All Souls College, Oxford*)
Editorial Board: R. Howard Bloch (*University of California, Berkeley*),
Terence Cave (*St John's College, Oxford*), Ross Chambers (*University of
Michigan*), Antoine Compagnon (*Columbia University*), Peter France
(*University of Edinburgh*), Toril Moi (*Duke University*), Naomi Schor
(*Harvard University*)

A complete list of books in the series is given at the end of the volume

HISTORY AND IDEOLOGY IN PROUST

A la recherche du temps perdu and the
Third French Republic

MICHAEL SPRINKER

*Professor in English and in Comparative Literature,
State University of New York at Stony Brook*

CAMBRIDGE
UNIVERSITY PRESS

Published by the Press Syndicate of the University of Cambridge
The Pitt Building, Trumpington Street, Cambridge CB2 1RP
40 West 20th Street, New York, NY 10011-4211, USA
10 Stamford Road, Oakleigh, Melbourne 3166, Australia

First published 1994

Printed in Great Britain at the University Press, Cambridge

A catalogue record for this book is available from the British Library

Library of Congress cataloguing in publication data

Sprinker, Michael.
History and ideology in Proust / Michael Sprinker.
p.   cm. – (Cambridge studies in French)
Includes index.
ISBN 0 521 45342 9
1. Proust, Marcel, 1871–1922. A la recherche du temps perdu.
2. Proust, Marcel, 1871–1922 – Political and social views.
3. Literature and society – France – History – 20th century.
4. Proust, Marcel, 1871–1922 – Knowledge – History.
5. Social problems in literature.   6. History in literature.
I. Title.   II. Series.
PQ2631.R63A8921994
843'.914–dc20   93–47273 CIP

ISBN 45342 9 hardback

... art is an unconscious form of historiography, the memory of what has been vanquished or repressed, perhaps an anticipation of what is possible. In art the primacy of the object, understood as the potential freedom of life from domination, manifests itself in the freedom from objects.

T. W. Adorno *Aesthetic Theory*

Now that ain't workin', that's the way you do it
You play the guitar on the MTV
That ain't workin', that's the way you do it
Money for nothin', and your chicks for free
Money for nothing and chicks for free

Dire Straits

Contents

Acknowledgments

It is a pleasure to acknowledge several of the debts owed to various individuals and institutions, without whose support this project would certainly not have been completed so expeditiously – if at all. The bulk of the research and writing was accomplished during two semester-long stints at the Center for the Humanities at Wesleyan University and a one-semester residence in the Center for the Humanities at Oregon State University. To the respective directors of these two worthy institutions, Richard Ohmann and Peter J. Copek, I shall be forever grateful.

Malcolm Bowie, the academic editor of the series, and the staff of Cambridge University Press were immensely helpful and conscientious in shepherding the manuscript through the publication process. I can only hope that they won't regret their efforts in my behalf.

Several individuals read sections of the manuscript in draft, and to them go my sincere thanks for pertinent criticism and advice, not all of which, alas, I had the good sense to follow. My colleagues at the State University of New York at Stony Brook, Sandy Petrey and Gene Lebovics, were especially helpful, the former in pressing me always to make the mediations between history and fictional representation more explicit, the latter in insisting that I meet at least a minimal standard of historiographic accuracy. Whether the final result will satisfy either of them, it is not given to me to determine.

Gregory Elliott and Graham Burchell offered provocative readings of an early version of the entire manuscript. While I could not agree with their conclusions, I have attempted to take their criticisms into account. Similarly, the anonymous reader commissioned by Cambridge University Press provided what every author must prize above all else: a sympathetic but minutely critical reading. I have endeavored to answer the objections posed in every instance where I disagreed, and where I took the point without dissent, the reader's views have been silently incorporated in the text. The present book is much improved as a result of these valuable editorial interventions.

This book contains a large number of diagrams, some rather complicated to realize with computer graphics. For assistance in preparing them I am most grateful to Kristyanne Beenfeldt Sprinker, whose engineering and drafting skills removed all burden from my shoulders.

Most of all, I must thank my students at Stony Brook, who listened patiently while I inflicted different versions of this book's argument on them, and who pressed me continually to precise and strengthen it. The one indispensable ingredient in my own scholarly and critical work has been the sustaining pleasure of teaching, without which I could scarcely have written a single word. I can only hope that what finally resulted from these stimulating encounters may be some small recompense for my students' generosity in helping me to write the present book when doubtless they had better things to do.

Introduction

> If we speak of realism, that is because like all the great
> works of the classical bourgeois novel, like Balzac's *Human
> Comedy,* and Zola's *Rougon-Macquart, A la recherche du temps
> perdu* is also a novel-epic that treats of 'man' and 'society'
> in their mutual relations. More than that, Proust's
> realism is also 'critical,' although his critical spirit has
> nothing in common with the critical spirit of Balzac, of
> Stendhal, of Flaubert, and derives from a completely
> different source.
>
> (N. Rykova, "The Final Stage of Bourgeois
Realism" [1936])

This is a book about Proust and the Third French Republic. It
attempts to recover some of the historical specificity that permeates *A la recherche du temps perdu* and makes it the text that it
is. Why write such a book? In the first place because, as far as I
can tell, it has never been done. In addition, my conviction is
that only by undertaking this type of investigation can we
begin to understand the true complexity and assess the importance and lasting value of those literary works that, for whatever reason, have been enshrined in the European high-culture
pantheon. Proust's reputation is already well established; the
question remains, however, whether and on what grounds his
inclusion in the canon is deserved. I shall, then, be defending
Proust, albeit not uncritically, but for reasons that have only
rarely been urged in his behalf.

The principal – and in the end the only intellectually defens-
ible – reason for pursuing such a study is historical. Eric
Hobsbawm has put the matter well in the "Overture" to his

Age of Empire, arguing that the peculiar contradictions of our own time were born of the period that comes to a climax with August 1914. He characterizes the break as one with the world of liberal capitalism, and opines that "since 1914 the century of the bourgeoisie belongs to history."[1] Whether or not we affirm his judgment about the bourgeoisie's demise, it is difficult to disagree with the view that bourgeois society's familiar institutions reached maturity and found general acceptance in the period just preceding the Great War. Parliamentary democracy (accompanied by universal male suffrage), corporate enterprise, mass-produced consumer goods (along with the modern advertising industry that sustained a taste for them), mass communications – all these now familiar features of advanced capitalism came to fruition in this period. This was the moment when the Euro-American bourgeoisies attained at one and the same time the apogee of their direct global domination in the form of colonial empires, and their greatest prosperity, comfort, and stability in the national domestic sphere. Not without reason has the period been dubbed the *belle époque*. Even as it served for many who survived it as an Edenic memory of a more stable and secure world, so it seemed to many who were living through it to hold out the promise of an eternally bright future that would reproduce the materially virtuous present.[2]

Not everyone held such sanguine views, of course, but to the extent that it makes sense to call this period "bourgeois," it can be said that the dominant ideology of the hegemonic class was certainly optimistic. Even the dominated classes could share in this perspective. The period also saw the growth and consolidation of mass working-class organizations, including political parties which, in at least one incarnation (the Second International led by its largest member party, the German Social Democrats), reproduced bourgeois optimism. They believed that capitalism would evolve into socialism through sheer expansion of the productive forces.

Among those who did not entirely share in this rosy view of liberal capitalism's present achievements and future promise were the titled nobility and landed gentry, those relics of the *ancien régime* that "persisted," as Arno Mayer has eloquently argued, long beyond the formal demise of their political and social hegemony in Europe (and even, in a different way, in the United States, as Faulkner's mature fiction amply illustrates).[3] In the heyday of bourgeois supremacy, the European aristocracy waged a sometimes fierce, but more often quiet and subtle, rearguard action to stave off their ultimate demise, which they certainly felt to be (and perhaps we ought to recognize this too) far from inevitable. [Like the history of all hitherto existing society, that of the *belle époque* was a history of class struggles. This is the history Proust came to chronicle and provisionally explain in his enormous, uncompleted masterpiece, *A la recherche du temps perdu*. My justification for treating this text, therefore, lies in its claim to historical insight and understanding. Proust's novel remains significant precisely to the extent that it illuminates a decisive historical moment in the formation of the modern world.]

I should confess at the outset that the present project did not begin from a desire to study any particular society for the purposes of historical explanation. Its origins lie elsewhere, in a certain dissatisfaction with contemporary literary analysis pursued under marxism's aegis.[4] Taking Marx at his word in the introduction to the *Grundrisse* (or Engels, Lenin, and Trotsky at theirs in various texts on literature and culture), one would have thought that the first task of any consequent materialist criticism would be to study the social conditions under which individual works of art have been produced, for these are, *ex hypothesi*, aesthetic production's causal *prius*. Whatever the limitations and deficiencies in the writings of Lukács and the more orthodox communist critics of the 1930s, their insistence on the ideological character and function of literary texts, their holding to a view of history grounded in the analysis of class structures, and their attempt to demonstrate the ways in which literary texts reveal or expose the historical situations they present – these remain the necessary hallmarks of any marxist literary criticism worthy of the name. And yet all that fell into disrepute during the Cold War, was scarcely revived during the 1960s, and is today, for all intents and purposes, simply forgotten, save as an item of historical curiosity, rarely as a possible model upon which to base future work.

This is surely not the place to engage in a polemic on behalf of something called "vulgar marxism," the vulgarity of which may at times seem almost refreshing in the hothouse climate of our current theoretical hyperspace. What is intended, rather, is to make a modest contribution to the marxist study of litera-ture by considering the principal work of a writer who had no particular sympathy for marxism or socialism in any form, and whose writings, when they have been thought a fit subject for marxist analysis, have generally been denounced as decadent bourgeois aestheticism.[5] And so they were, though one is immediately constrained to observe, as Sartre once famously remarked of Valéry, that if Proust was an aesthete, not every aesthete was Proust. This is an insight shared by Adorno, who observed of Proust's social position and his art: "what Proust saw in Illiers must have happened elsewhere to many children of the same social stratum. But what it takes to form this universal, this authentic part of Proust's presentation, is to be entranced in one place without squinting at the universal."[6] Moreover, it is by no means clear that the *Recherche* is entirely on the side of the bourgeoisie, a point that can only be demon-strated in an exhaustive exposition of the novel. I shall at best give a schematic projection of such a full-scale reading here.

The present study proposes, then, utilizing the classical categories of historical materialism to analyze *A la recherche du temps perdu*. Base and superstructure, class and class struggle, ideology, and revolution – these are the conceptual instru-ments I shall deploy to dissect the narrative structures of Proust's great text, structures that while they undoubtedly possess a formal poetic dimension (authoritatively set forth by Gérard Genette, to whose work I shall have occasion to refer), are not ultimately determined by such considerations. Formal or aesthetic features are themselves a part of ideology, as well as its efficient cause in literary representation. In literature, ideol-ogy can only appear in the presentation of form, so that formal analysis is never a dispensable exercise for materialist criticism.

To say so is not to say anything terribly controversial, but is in a way to repeat what everyone has always known about the *Recherche*: that it is a novel about French society during the first half-century of the Third Republic. But having granted this much, most previous commentary has proceeded as if we know precisely what that means, what the Third Republic was, how the *Recherche* presented it, who were the historical originals of the novel's characters, and so forth. One ought not to belittle previous scholarship in these areas, the more so since without it one's own work would be infinitely more time-consuming and difficult. It should be observed, nonetheless, that the fundamental questions about the nature of society pursued so vigorously by social theory and empirical social science in this century are elided in virtually all literary criticism, be it marxist or not, claiming to study the social origins of literary texts. It's not so much wrong to note, for example, that Charlus seems to have been modelled on Proust's acquaintance, Count Robert de Montesquiou, as it is unhelpful in understanding who or what Charlus is in the novel, and how this character functions as the carrier of certain values and as the site for historically significant ideological conflicts. It is perhaps more useful to say of literary characters what Marx said of the human agents who "make history" but cannot do so "just as they please." Like actual historical individuals, literary characters are ultimately "bearers of structures." [The purpose of this study is to examine some of the structures Proust's characters bear, the better to comprehend how the *Recherche* judges what it takes to be the ultimately determining instance of French history during Proust's lifetime: the ongoing class struggle between bourgeois and aristocrat.]

Why the bourgeoisie and the aristocracy? Once again, only a full exposition can demonstrate what is proposed here as a preliminary hypothesis: that Proust's text advances a model of the Third Republic's class structure which for the most part ignores the still numerous peasantry (with the notable exception of Françoise), and has virtually nothing to say about the increasingly large and politically important urban proletariat. [The *Recherche* presents French society through the lens of a two-class model.⎤ Nor are its principal classes engaged in struggles those (proletariat and bourgeoisie) that have been considered canonical for industrialized capitalist social formations since the *Communist Manifesto*. Nevertheless, I shall claim that Proust's novel, whatever the limitations of its own ideological position – which are real enough, if perhaps too much taken for granted, at the expense of recognizing the genuine historical and sociological insight that the *Recherche* achieves – perspicaciously maps the dominant site of class struggle under the pre-war Third Republic. ⎡The *Recherche* is, in this sense, to be understood as a theory of French society at a decisive moment in its history, an analytical instrument for comprehending the structural conditions that constrained the two major fractions among France's hegemonic classes from the fall of Sedan and the Commune's suppression to the Versailles Treaty.⎤

⎡This is not to suggest that the *Recherche* is entirely exogenous to the domain of ideology. Theories can be at once ideological, viz., products of distinctive socio-historical conditions, and scientific, viz., means for producing knowledge – a point I take in general from Althusser. Be it observed, however, that I differ from him and from Pierre Macherey in attributing a knowledge-producing function to works of art – or at least one highly elaborated work. The delicate relationship between scientific and ideological aspects of a theory cannot be determined in advance of reading; *vide* Althusser's own extraordinary labors over Marx's texts, in particular his contributions to *Reading "Capital"*. My own sense of the theoretical import that literary texts possess is close to the following formulation of the youthful Paul de Man: "if literature cannot be acknowledged as a scientific means of formation, it can still, from a sociological viewpoint, at the very least go together with theoretical research and, in many cases, open up horizons and offer possibilities which otherwise would never have been suspected."[7] Whether my account of the *Recherche* adequately discriminates between the distinctive features of scientific knowledge and those of ideology is left for the reader to judge.⎤

That Proust's novel also forecasts something of the future

that lay beyond its historical horizon, as Walter Benjamin once observed in a much neglected *aperçu*, I hold out as a final possibility, implied but barely argued for here. Proust not only diagnosed the causes for the ultimate demise of the French aristocracy; he also discerned the contradictions in and the historical contingency of bourgeois hegemony. Such is my ultimate hypothesis.

A word about the methodological problems inherent in treating literary texts as windows on the history of social formations. No serious historian would take Proust's *Recherche* to be a wholly adequate account of the structures dominating the social and political world under the Third Republic. Nor would literary historians, on balance, regard the history of Proust's era as an unfailing guide to the poetic specificity of Proust's narrative. At the same time, one regularly encounters in historical writing references to novelists' telling depictions of certain social strata and their typical identities and activities. The question remains, however, about the degree to which fictional representations of social classes – or even historical individuals – are any more than poetically motivated, that is, governed by the constitutive structures of plot and character that the text's aesthetic norms have dictated.

To those in literature who have doubts about the pertinence of historical knowledge to comprehending literary artifacts, one can reply in two ways. First, in even the most astringently formalist accounts of literature, say those of the Russian Formalists or Greimas or Michael Riffaterre, there persists some dimension of historicity, either on the level of literary history itself (in the theory of genres, for example), or in the assignment of cultural values to particular characters or plots. One thinks of Barthes's insistence in *S/Z* on the importance of what he calls the referential or cultural code in *Sarrasine*. This code is grounded in the punctual facts of social life experienced by Balzac in the shifting circumstances of French history from the Empire's fall through the Restoration and into the July Monarchy. In all formalisms, while literary explanation is rarely in the first instance, and never finally, controlled by historical causes exogenous to the text, history invariably creeps in via some back door or other to assert its influence on a given work's specificity.

To say this much already suggests the terms of the second riposte to those who doubt that historical explanation can play a decisive role in literary understanding. For it is clear, even to the most intransigent defenders of literature's aesthetic autonomy, that texts arise from and take their place in history. No one before Jane Austen had written a text like *Emma*, and while others since have perhaps imitated her fictional practice in certain ways (one thinks of *Howard's End* or of Meredith's country house novels, notably *The Egoist*), no one to my knowledge has reproduced the particular brand of social comedy dependent upon a comparatively secure set of socio-moral conventions embraced by a broad spectrum of the propertied and professional classes that is so distinctive a feature of her fiction. Jane Austen is not the sole English novelist to have written primarily about the rural gentry, but the confidence and equipoise with which this world is presented in her novels – the only notable exception being *Mansfield Park*, although even there the ordered society of the well-managed country estate is restored in the end – are scarcely available in English fiction prior to the last decades of the eighteenth century. They survive, if at all, only in some of Trollope's Barchester novels.[8] The point here is not only that the material social facts appearing in Jane Austen's texts are historical – characters who ride on horseback or in coaches, dress and furnishings that evidence a specific period style, modes of speech now archaic or at least stilted to the modern ear – but that the historical situation of the classes about which she writes determines the very form of her fiction. To present the rural gentry in this way after 1832 was all but impossible – as, for instance, George Eliot's major novels from *Adam Bede* to *Middlemarch* amply attest. One could therefore hazard the opinion that there have never been any but historical novels (and poems and plays), whether novelists themselves have always been aware of this fact or not. My strong suspicion is that they mostly are, even if certain modes of literary criticism and scholarship have tried to strip them of just this self-awareness about their craft.

The objections of the historian are, in my view, more consequent, although they are precisely the ones professional
students of literature characteristically ignore or finesse. Is it at
all licit, one might ask, to read off the historical reality of a
given society from one or more of its familiar cultural pro-
ductions? The easy negative answer, which one ought to retain
as a control mechanism over one's research, may, however,
conceal certain methodological problems in the human
sciences that have recently been much discussed in several
disciplines (ethnography most prominently). To some degree
in what follows, it will appear that I have simply deployed
information and hypotheses drawn from political, economic,
and social histories of the Third Republic to explain some of
Proust's novel's salient features. But in other respects, I have
tried to utilize the fictional text to illuminate more fully those
aspects of social life during the *belle époque* and just before that
have remained underdeveloped in standard historical writings
on the period, ideology in particular. On this level of the social
formation, Proust offers perhaps a more reliable, and certainly
a more detailed and nuanced, guide than the historians. But
this is at best a plausible hypothesis. It is, in any event, testable.
⌊Others can compare the work of social and cultural historians
with the *Recherche* to determine whether the latter's account of
ideological conflicts is both warrantable on the evidence and
superior in conception and explanatory power to other explanations of the same phenomena.⌋

No one has ever doubted that Proust observed his society
acutely. I am proposing that he cogently and powerfully theorized its fundamental structures as well. On this account, it
would not be wrong to draw the analogy between Proust's
fictional project and its object that Zola did for his own: the
"experiment" performed by each was, in the first instance, an
empirical scientific one.[9] In both cases the distant objective of
changing the world was made to hinge on the prior and
necessary (if insufficient) condition of interpreting and thereby
understanding it.

Such a view moves in exactly the opposite direction to
standard accounts of Proust's work. J. M. Cocking's summary

observations concerning Proust's relation to contemporary politics are characteristic in this regard:

Apart from [Proust's] comments on class reactions to the Affair, where the interest is sociological in very general terms but not specifically political, there is not much historical reference in the novel; nor is there much to be found in the letters in this selection. He sometimes comments on day-to-day events as any intelligent reader of *Le Figaro* might do. But there is no sign of awareness of the major political changes in the Third Republic: the definitive political victory of the bourgeoisie, the increased influence of the financiers and the industrialists, the establishment of Radicalism as the majority political attitude, with lip-service to the Revolution and the Nation, hostility to aristocracy, Church, and Army, and real interest in wealth and material prosperity. Unlike Balzac, Proust is not much interested in the economic mechanisms of social change, only in the repercussions of such change on social groupings, conventions, and rituals.[10]

That Proust was "aware" of these epochal changes and that the *Recherche* does indeed present "signs" of this fact, I shall endeavor to show in what follows. But Cocking's instinct is nonetheless sure in marking the distinction between the overt representational figures in Proust's text and those in Balzac.

[Are we then to infer, as most readers of the novel have done, that the *Recherche* is not about society at all, save in the most superficial and general sense? All texts manifest silences for which one must account. The *Recherche* is no exception. If it never stops talking about society in terms of snobbery, homosexuality, and manners, it is yet remarkably reticent about the underlying mechanisms that produce the material abundance signified by the leisured classes' salons, dinners, travel, and holidays. We cannot brusquely ignore this massive silence, but neither ought we to dismiss it as simple lack of interest or even ignorance. No text knows everything, but like Marcel, who characteristically conceals the full extent of his knowledge from other characters, the *Recherche* often knows more than it lets on.]

One way to get beyond the novel's presentational surface is to think through its principal ideological coordinates, which derive from what Marx identified as "the fetishism of commodities," or what we might term the ordinary mystifications produced by consumer society. The second epigraph to the present study is meant to foreground this aspect of the *Recherche*. For afficionados of contemporary popular music, it requires little explanation, but for those who are not fans of Dire Straits, it may seem obscure. The song "Money for Nothing" satirizes the commodification of art in late capitalism, for which MTV is as good a symbol as any. It crystallizes, while poking fun at, a working-class fantasy nurtured by contemporary cultural production: the dream of becoming a rock star (or indeed any mass culture icon) and being thereby delivered from the alienating conditions of working-class life, from both its exploitative labor relations and its commodified sexuality.

While social life during the Third Republic's first half-century was not an exact replica of our current consumer society, the fantasy of a life without material care or sexual anxiety was then as much the dominant image of ruling-class existence in the minds of those who were not to the manor born as it is now.[11] Moreover, that one could escape the twin alienations of labor and love, characteristic of bourgeois social relations, through immersion in art is perhaps the most powerful ideologeme mobilized in the *Recherche*. Nor was Proust, I shall be arguing, any less excoriating towards this ideology of art than are Dire Straits. Their demystification of the aesthetic under capitalism is a worthy successor to his. Whether both have thereby merely reconciled their different publics to art (Proust's audience was and is overwhelmingly bourgeois; Dire Straits speak, one surmises, both to working-class and middle-class youth) by utilizing aesthetic instruments to attack capitalist social relations, as Sartre once opined of Proust,[12] is a question I shall for the moment leave open.

Yet, even Proust himself seems explicitly to deny what I am arguing for here. His critical ideology, evident throughout the *Recherche*, programmatically rejects the aesthetic principles I have invoked, erecting an unbreachable barrier between authentically artistic experience and the representation of history and society.[13] The canonical statement of Proust's aesthetic is doubtless the *Contre Sainte-Beuve*, where the "method" of biographical or historical criticism is persistently held up to scorn. In the essay on Balzac, Proust accuses the latter of "vulgarity" in failing to distinguish between "the triumphs of life and of literature," which are illicitly placed "altogether on the same plane."[14] Proust's formalism, his utter disdain for realism, could scarcely be more pronounced: "So in reading Balzac we shall continue to feel and almost to satisfy those passions from which the best literature ought to cure us. A high society soirée as described by ... is dominated by the writer's idea, it purges us of our worldliness as Aristotle would say; in Balzac we feel an almost worldly satisfaction in being present at it."[15]

At the same time, however, Proust recognizes in Balzac the very historical interest that I am claiming can be as readily attributed to the *Recherche*. In some further notes appended to the Balzac essay, Proust goes on to praise the *Comédie Humaine*, not as a work of art but as a historical document:

And since all of this relates to a particular epoch, whose surface trappings it displays and whose foundations it judges most intelligently, once its interest as fiction is exhausted it restarts a new life as a document for the historian. Just as the *Aeneid* may excite mythologists at those very points where it has nothing to say to poets. To us Peyrade, Felix de Vandenesse and many others did not seem very richly endowed with life. But Albert Sorel will tell us that it is in them that we must study the police under the Consulate or the politics of the Restoration.[16]

Proust's novel has by now assumed something of the same status for us, though with one significant difference. Unlike Sorel (and ostensibly Proust as well), who reads Balzac's characters as a naive empiricist does experimental data, one can construe fictional texts less as presentations of punctual facts than as highly elaborated empirical theories. [Their pertinence to historical inquiry derives less from this or that detail of a period's historical experience (say, the costumes or furniture so minutely described in Balzac – or in certain famous scenes in the *Recherche* for that matter), than from the poetic structure that gives the data their significance in the text] The *Recherche* can thus be understood as more than a record of the lived experience of the *belle époque*; it is at the same time, and more profoundly, an attempt to locate and comprehend the underlying structures of French society in that period. Even more broadly, it can be read as a minutely articulated anatomy of the general project and the pathology of bourgeois society. Proust's true companions in arms will prove, somewhat surprisingly, to be his approximate contemporaries, Durkheim and Weber.[17] To put the matter as contentiously as possible, I shall propose that if we translate Proust's key concept of "time" as "history" (something the Narrator himself does on occasion), we can begin to appreciate the *Recherche*'s significance as historical sociology, i.e., as a theory of society in the strong sense. Such is the aim of the present book.[18]]

To consider the *Recherche* as a social novel is not without precedent. A similar reading was first proposed by Alfred Cobban in his essay, "The Historical Significance of Marcel Proust."[19] Anglophone paterfamilias of revisionist historiography of the French Revolution, Cobban reveals in this early text some of the conservative prejudices that would govern his currently fashionable (however historically implausible) reinterpretation of 1789.[20] While sagaciously assessing the novel's depiction of French society from the perspective of the Third Republic's collapse in 1940, he almost certainly overestimates Proust's nostalgia for the bygone era the *Recherche* chronicles. Unbridled enthusiasm for the pre-revolutionary past motivates Cobban's historical judgments, not Proust's.

Symptomatic of how Cobban misconstrues the text's explicit ironizing of its own categories – for a certain privileging of Combray, the country, the world of Marcel's youth is undoubtedly to be observed there – is Cobban's assertion that "nothing happens – nothing ever will happen – to spoil the idyllic almost Rousseauist charm of Combray, which is destined to remain, stored up in the mind of Marcel, like a Platonic idea in heaven."[21] Cobban, one suspects, has silently adopted Combray's own point of view, which is far from Proust's and which, had it prevailed in his life, would have absolutely barred the Narrator from participating in or telling

the story that follows. As Vincent Descombes remarks:
"Combray knows nothing of the external world encircling it
and destined to destroy it during the Great War."[22] The
mature Marcel, by contrast, knows the fate of Combray only
too well – and forecasts it from the novel's earliest episodes.
Walking by Tansonville he first observes Charlus and hears
rumors of Odette's infidelity, and at Montjouvain he is initi-
ated into the intimate relationship of sadism to homoeroticism
that will become a principal feature of those social regions
denominated by Sodom and Gomorrha. The contents of
Marcel's mind, like those in Proust's, encompass a great deal
more than a limited nostalgia for a vanished world.

An even older study is John J. Spagnoli's *The Social Attitude of
Marcel Proust.*[23] Although superficial in many ways (it is short
on the analysis of structures, long on quotations from the
Nouvelle Revue Française edition), the book does recognize
the centrality of social class to the *Recherche* and makes a
number of intelligent observations, in a Lukacsean mode,
about characters as types. Spagnoli asserts three principal
things about Proust's attitudes towards social class: first, that
while discerning in them certain virtues, Proust was generally
critical of the nobility; second, that Proust had nothing but
contempt for the non-Combray bourgeoisie; third, that Proust
exhibited considerable sympathy for the working class. Less
plausibly, as I shall try to show in subsequent chapters, Spagnoli claims that Proust's portrait of the bourgeoisie will not
stand up to historical scrutiny.[24]

J. Canavaggia's *Proust et la politique*[25] is a trenchant little
study of Proust's vestigial attachment to the aristocracy, above
all in its military guise. Canavaggia devotes the bulk of his
analysis, however, to *Jean Santeuil* – for the obvious reason that
its closer relationship to Proust's own life makes the task of
establishing Proust's political views much easier. Things are
less clear-cut in the *Recherche*.

The only recent book-length studies to approach the
Recherche along the lines I propose here are P.-V. Zima's *Le désir
du mythe: Une lecture sociologique de Marcel Proust* and Seth L.

Wolitz's *The Proustian Community*.[26] The former is a Goldmann-ian account of the *Recherche* as the expression of the leisured rentier bourgeoisie's ideology, which Zima sums up in a single concept: snobbism. The book offers some provocative hypo-theses about the relationship between this class fraction and the ancient nobility and contains much interesting material on the *Recherche* itself, but the reduction of the novel's sociological dimensions to this single ideologeme strikes me as overly schematic.

Wolitz, despite his announced conviction that "Proust, not unlike the sociologist, was looking for general laws,"[27] barely ranges beyond the antiquarian and anecdotal in comparing the characters and events in the novel with the society they figure. The one notable exception to this rule is his final chapter on the position of Jews in post-revolutionary French society, which focuses on assimilation. Wolitz never quite says so, but his underlying concern there would seem to be the way Proust participated in the conventional antisemitism of the French upper classes.[28]

If the present study has any merit, it lies in the attempt to present a more analytically nuanced and empirically rich account of "the Proustian world" than any advanced or assumed in the extant Proust criticism. I have few illusions about the reception such a work is likely to receive from readers whose admiration for Proust is primarily aesthetic or ethical. Even those who share my fundamental conviction about litera-ture's historicity are likely to become impatient with the effort expended upon, for example, the constitutive structures of the French economy in the late nineteenth and early twentieth centuries, or upon the characteristic political and ideological institutions of the Third Republic. To them, I can only plead the importance of politics and economy to socio-historical understanding, begging some tolerance at the outset for what may appear an overly long preamble. To comprehend class struggle requires knowing something about the economic con-ditions that constrained its antagonists, and about the political and ideological apparatuses over which they contended. The class struggles in France between 1870 and 1920 were waged on a variety of fronts; not least among them were the economy and the state. The peculiar form each assumed at this period largely determined how the bourgeoisie and the aristocracy would pursue their distinctive class projects on other terrains.

CHAPTER I

Base and superstructure

> In the social production of their life, men enter into definite relations that are indispensable and independent of their will, relations of production which correspond to a definite stage of development of their material productive forces. The sum total of these relations of production constitutes the economic structure of society, the real foundation, on which rises a legal and political superstructure and to which correspond definite forms of social consciousness. The mode of production of material life conditions the social, political, and intellectual life process in general.
>
> (Marx, 1859 Preface)

The bourgeois polity of the Third French Republic arose from the ashes of the twin epochal defeats suffered by its main antagonists: the Bonapartist imperial party whose demise was sealed with the fall of Sedan on September 2, 1870; and the Parisian proletariat who were butchered by General Gallifet's troops when they suppressed the Commune in May 1871. The exact form of the new state would remain undecided until mid-decade, and the bourgeoisie's purchase on power would be contested much longer. But it seems clear in retrospect that the left's decapitation and the delegitimation of the right's most politically significant fraction, consequent upon its humiliating defeat by Bismarck's Prussia, brought to fruition the long process of establishing bourgeois democracy in France that had commenced in 1789.[1] The republic over whose birth Thiers presided would survive all the domestic threats to its existence over the next seven decades and would only expire in the aftermath of another German invasion in 1940.

17

THE SPECIFICITY OF FRENCH CAPITALISM

But what precisely does "bourgeois democracy" connote in this case? We may begin with the first term, which, after Marx, signifies less a political than an economic entity: the ruling class in capitalist society. That France was such a social formation by the second half of the nineteenth century, no serious student of the period disputes. Like its principal political and commercial rivals, Britain and Germany, France had made the transition from predominantly feudal to capitalist social relations and was in tendency, if not yet completely in accomplishment, an industrial power during the Third Republic. Having begun the nineteenth century as the second-ranking commercial nation in the Western world (Britain being the first), France's position had slipped to fourth by 1914, with the rapid industrialization of Germany and the United States during the last third of the century. Economic historians generally agree that French development lagged severely behind its major competitors, although the periodization, pace, and causes of this relative decline remain hotly disputed. A fair summary of the prevailing view is given by Jean-Marie Mayeur:

Even if they differ on the chronology and in their estimation of the breadth and causes of the phenomenon, economic historians are agreed in thinking that in the first decades of the Third Republic the growth of the French economy slowed down considerably. Growth was rapid up to 1860, then it slowed, although it remained higher than the average for the century until about 1880. After 1880 the rate of growth is below the average for the century; between 1883 and 1896 an incontestable "tendency to stagnation" ... is to be observed. It is true that in the world economy as a whole prices were falling from 1873 to the end of the century, but growth was not affected in Germany or the United States as it was in France. France, once the second largest industrial power, slipped to fourth place.[2]

Given this general consensus, two questions arise: first, what were the causes of France's comparative economic stagnation during the early years of the Third Republic; second, what were the characteristic structures of French capitalism between the fall of the Second Empire and the First World

War? Plainly, the two questions are intimately related to each other.

The weight of scholarship since the 1950s has tended to reject various mono-causal explanations of France's relative economic decline: e.g., deficient raw materials resources (coal and ferrous metals, in particular); demographic stagnation; archaic banking practices; the dominance of the rentier mentality combined with lack of entrepreneurial initiative.[3] Instead, it seems that a singular combination of factors held France down, as it were, notably from the 1880s to the end of the century, by which point the residual force of archaic structures more or less doomed the French economy to backwardness for another fifty years.[4] Among these factors, one assumes particular salience, even if its specific causal weight is in dispute: the astonishing persistence of the French peasantry and its structural influence on overall economic modernization. Again, Mayeur's summary makes the point well:

What strikes us then is the rigidity of the working agricultural population and the disproportion between its share of the working population and of the material product. In the decade 1875–84, when the agricultural population accounted for 64 percent of the population employed in productive activities, agriculture furnished only 43.8 percent of the total product. These figures demonstrate how poor agricultural productivity was. The purchase power of the agricultural world "furnished industry with only a poor stimulus to growth." Thus agriculture acted as a brake on growth. This became particularly evident at the time of the big depression which affected the agricultural world from 1873 to 1896. The decline in productivity brought a drop in the demand for industrial products. (Mayeur, "Origins," p. 45)[5]

French capitalism was retarded, at least in part, because it maintained a large (by comparison with other industrial nations) and generally inefficient (again by comparison) agricultural sector, which not only affected the nature of the available labor force,[6] but also, and perhaps more importantly, tended to limit growth in domestic demand. Why did such a situation obtain?

Tom Kemp offers a two-part answer:

In the early twentieth century the French economy was distinguished by the size and resistance to change of its agrarian sector compared with other advanced countries, especially Britain. This was the result of the revolutionary land settlement which made possible the continued existence of a substantial peasant sector ... In France the preservation of the peasantry was seen as a barrier to social revolution; revolutions began in the towns and the large estate owner, as well as the bourgeois, saw in the wide distribution of landed property a safeguard for his own property. (Kemp, *Economic Forces*, pp. 227–8)[7]

I shall have occasion to consider the Third Republic's politics in relation to its economic policies in a subsequent chapter; here it is sufficient to emphasize the basic claim made by Kemp and others concerning the nature of French capitalism in the years prior to the First World War: to wit, that its atrophying after the halcyon days of the Second Empire did not result primarily from an unfavorable international trade conjuncture (viz., the secular depression in world commodity prices that commenced in 1873), nor from the defeat by Prussia (with the accompanying loss of Alsace and Lorraine and the war indemnity), but rather from hypertrophy in the economy's primary (i.e., agricultural) sector, which on the eve of the war still employed some 40 percent of the active workforce (Caron, *France*, p. 33),[8] while remaining stubbornly resistant to modernization.[9] A decade and a half later, Marc Bloch would end his lectures on France's agrarian past with the following testament to peasant society's persistence into the twentieth century:

All the same, it must be admitted that none of the essential features of small peasant farming have disappeared in the course of the nineteenth and early twentieth centuries. Peasant proprietorship, in the full legal sense of the term, has been conspicuously successful in maintaining its ascendancy over much of the soil ... It is trite but true to observe that today peasant farming is still a great economic and social force. The small holding is still landlocked in its antiquated lay-out of field, still stubbornly resistant to change, there is little inclination toward sudden innovation ... and ancestral habits are abandoned only with difficulty; technical improvements have made little headway ... And so the past continues to dominate the present.[10]

If French capitalism's particularity derived in the main from the rural economy's continuing weight, what were the specific structures of capitalist enterprise that were so affected, and how did they respond to the fact of France's non-competitive position in the world market? For as Caron insists, capitalism did prosper in France during the nineteenth century, albeit unevenly. To understand these features of republican France, it is necessary to describe the evolution of French capitalism from its consolidation under the July Monarchy, through its period of dynamic expansion during the Second Empire, its stagnation in the 1880s and 1890s, and its eventual, incomplete recovery during the *belle époque*.

COMBINED AND UNEVEN DEVELOPMENT

In the closing years of the eighteenth century, French capitalism was primarily commercial in nature and orientation and was for the most part badly organized. No significant networks for capital accumulation and distribution yet existed, while legal and other institutions positively hindered these processes. Only with the advent of the Revolution and the overhaul of the legal and administrative apparatuses under Napoleon did France realize the necessary conditions for a fully capitalist development that was by that era requisite for sustained economic growth. One milestone was the founding of the Banque de France in 1800; another was the arrival of James Rothschild in Paris in 1810–11, to set up the French branch of the family banking firm (Palmade, *French Capitalism*, pp. 46–74).[11] Industrialization commenced with the Restoration, but the July Monarchy truly unbound the forces of French capital, creating modern forms of credit and finance and setting in motion the decades-long process of giving the country a modern transport system that would act as an engine of capital accumulation in itself and would also enable the swift and inexpensive delivery of industrial products to mass markets. The undoubted preeminence of the Second Empire's early years in terms of industrial expansion was prepared by the innovations of what Marx called the "aristocracy of the bankers" under Louis-Philippe. If those sometime St.-Simonians, the Péreire brothers, symbolize the political economy of Bonapartism, it is well to remember that they were themselves nurtured in the cradle of the Rothschild empire and that their financial revolution was prefigured in the schemes of Jacques Lafitte (Palmade, *French Capitalism*, pp. 75–115). With the taming of working-class militancy during the June Days in 1848, and finally with the *coup d'état* of December 2, 1851, those entrepreneurs who recognized the future in infrastructural and industrial investment were given virtual free rein to transform the nation into a modern capitalist industrial power. In large measure, they succeeded.

François Caron, drawing on the work of Markovitch, Crouzet, and Lévy-Leboyer, has cautioned against making too much of the growth spurt during the early years of Bonapartism:

There was no real "industrial revolution" or "take-off" in France in the nineteenth century, for the changes which occurred had none of the swiftness and suddenness which such terms suggest. The changes which came about were the result of a series of adjustments. The industrial growth rates which the makers of indices have discovered give us no reason to believe in a sustained acceleration in growth, and the breaks in rhythm which may be observed lead to a slackening-off rather than stagnation. (Caron, *Economic History*, p. 28)

Nonetheless, it is possible to discern a *qualitative* shift in capitalist development under the Second Empire, lasting through the first decade of the Third Republic, which Palmade has labelled "The Great Upsurge."

Perhaps the most enthusiastic fan of France's achievement in this period is Rondo Cameron, who places the French contribution to global capitalist expansion (not excluding the Western hemisphere) at the very forefront of Europe's development:

... Frenchmen contributed more, both directly and indirectly, to the material welfare of Europeans in the century after Waterloo than in all previous history; more, too, than has fallen to the lot of most nations in the span of human history ... France contributed to the economic development of Europe by intellectual, social and legal influences, by the diffusion of technology, and by the export of capital; in combination, these means generated yet another determinant of economic growth, the spirit of enterprise. (Cameron, *France*, p. 306)

In the latter two areas – capital export and the spirit of enterprise – the political economy of Bonapartism was in the European vanguard, helping to shape the industrial, transport, and banking systems across the continent and beyond (in the Levant, for example). But before France could assist in building railways in Scandinavia, Italy, Austria–Hungary, and Spain, factories in Belgium, and the Suez Canal (against fierce British opposition), the nation's own financial institutions had to be transformed. This is precisely what the Second Empire, following up on initiatives begun under the July Monarchy, accomplished.

The year 1852 saw the creation of two pivotal financial institutions: the Crédit Foncier, which financed urban construction and development; and the Crédit Mobilier, which directed national investment on a grand scale, from railways to real estate. In 1863, the Crédit Lyonnais was founded, setting the pattern for modern deposit banks that would mobilize the assets of small investors – a key sector of capital accumulation during the second half of the century and beyond. Such new institutions, along with the massive expansion of the Bourse, not only provided the engine for commercial and industrial growth via their own resources, they dragged older institutions like the House of Rothschild and the Banque de France with them into the speculative frenzy that increasingly characterized the Empire's financial life in the decade before its fall. When upstarts like the Péreires and power brokers like Haussmann eventually overreached themselves, the older institutions gathered up the remains and embarked on a similar, if less spectacular, course to their defeated rivals (Palmade, *French Capitalism*, pp. 124–52; Cameron, *France*, pp. 104–37).

Evidence of French capitalism's continuing vitality throughout the Third Republic's first decade is ample. Not least impressive, no doubt, was the state's capacity to repay the war indemnity ahead of schedule without sacrificing sustained growth. But with the crash of the Union Générale in 1882, the global depression that had commenced in 1873 finally and decisively impacted on France, inaugurating "one of the longest [depressions] in [its] history ..." (Cameron, *France*, p. 134). Nowhere was the pinch felt more severely than in the countryside where, with the phylloxera disaster magnifying its effects, French agriculture plunged into a nosedive from which it would, in essence, never recover. But farmers did survive (although the rural population as a whole declined, largely because rural artisans and women left in large numbers, lured by job opportunities and higher wages in the industrial centers where the need for skilled and domestic labor grew markedly; see Caron, *Economic History*, pp. 124–5). State intervention was a crucial support, imposing a series of protective tariffs, culminating in 1892, to shield non-competitive French products (both agricultural and industrial) from the influx of cheaper foreign goods. The long-term economic effect of this protectionist regime, which put an end to three decades of relatively free trade that had commenced with the Anglo-French treaty of 1860, has been much debated. But its political necessity from the bourgeoisie's standpoint is beyond doubt:

Without protection, the fall in the prices of agricultural products would certainly have been more marked, and the social and political crises which resulted even more intense. Politically there appears to have been no alternative to protection, but there can be no doubt that protection, together with governmental pressure on the railway companies to withdraw differential transport tariffs which favoured imports, had the effect of reducing competitive pressures and facilitated the survival of a large and technically backward section of peasant farming.

This had significant consequences for the development of the whole economy, influencing as it did both the overall use of labour and capital resources and the structure of demand for industrial products. Demand was obviously a key factor determining both the volume of industrial production and the technical forms employed.[12]

With some 40 percent of the workforce still employed in the countryside by 1913 (a figure only slowly attained over the previous two decades), and domestic consumption thus geared rather heavily towards the habits and needs of a peasantry still embracing essentially pre-modern habits of consumption, capital accumulation on a massive scale could never be accomplished by investment in national industries that were – as the demand for protective tariffs from large industrialists made patent – generally uncompetitive in international markets. How, then, did the French bourgeoisie profit from the secular price rise that commenced in the later 1890s and continued up to the First World War? By what mechanisms did the *belle époque* earn its reputation as an era of economic good feeling?

Tom Kemp has drawn attention to the "two-track" nature of French enterprise in this period. Characteristically, small companies still dominated industrial production, even though heavy industry was growing in importance. The causes of this typical – and essentially backward – structure were complex, but its effects can be grasped readily enough. France was compelled to carve out a distinctive market niche in global capitalist trade, excelling in the manufacture and sale of products that could not, with the available technology, be mass-produced. Luxury goods of many varieties (garments and underwear, gloves, jewelry, toys) buoyed up the export economy, while manufacture of two articles (bicycles and automobiles) that would eventually become industrialized but at this period remained within the domain of craft production, was effectively French-dominated (Kemp, *Economic Forces*, pp. 249–59; Caron, *Economic History*, pp. 106–8). Jean-Charles Asselain even claims that the backwardness of French industry held distinct advantages, giving it a competitive edge in certain newer industries (rubber, petroleum, electricity), and a tendency to excel in certain areas through specialization.[13] The extreme fragility of France's comparative advantage in these areas (auto, for instance) would be amply revealed during the inter-war years, as France fell further behind its competitor nations; even prior to the war, its market share in luxury goods was declining (Caron, *Economic History*, p. 108). During the *belle époque*, while French industry recovered some of its vitality and the export economy as a whole prospered by comparison with the previous two decades, the focus of capital accumulation began to change.

During the first decade of the Third Republic, Frenchmen still earned the majority of their income from investments in land; some thirty years later, this would no longer be the case. Guy Palmade summarizes:

If Frenchmen in 1878 earned more than 3,600 million francs from their landed property and their houses and less than 2,500 millions from goods and chattels, these two main categories of income were almost identical by 1903 – with 4,072 million francs for one category and 4,044 for the other. In 1911 the second category was in the lead with 5,300 millions against 4,700. The Frenchman henceforth held more wealth in his share portfolio than in landed property. (Palmade, *French Capitalism*, p. 180)[14]

In shares of what? Palmade and Cameron are unequivocal in their judgment that the decisive shift in investment towards foreign outlets – a shift no one seriously disputes – had disastrous consequences for the French economy. The former criticizes "the over-emphasis on foreign investment," pointing to the paradox

that French capital helped Russia with her development at a time when Belgian capital was contributing to the development of Paris. The weakness of the policy pursued by French capitalists was that national industry was still short of capital in some sectors even if entrepreneurs were not aware of the shortage ... This creditor country had world-wide investments but so many of her loans were never to be repaid, so many of them were not to be honoured and so many other sources of income were to disappear. Already France was not obtaining sufficient income from these distant investments to develop commercial exports to a proportionate extent. (Palmade, *French Capitalism*, p. 210)

Cameron's criticisms are more differentiated – some foreign investments were more productive than others, obviously – but he condemns with equal harshness the most popular form of capital export in the period, investment in foreign government loans:

In a few cases – Belgium, for example – the borrowing governments used a portion of the proceeds of loans for building railways, roads, harbors, canals, and similar public investments; more frequently, however, the loans went to support the extravagance or inefficiency and corruption of court and government, to build fortifications and warships, purchase armaments, and maintain armies ... From the viewpoint of economic analysis ... such "investments" should be looked upon as a form of consumption expenditure – frequently a pernicious form, at that. Not only did they fail to create new wealth, but in many cases by allowing the borrowing government to withdraw resources from productive occupations and devote them to uneconomic or destructive uses they actually retarded the increase in wealth. (Cameron, *France*, p. 243)

Putting aside the effect such investments had on the economy of the borrowing nation – for this would not be likely to enter into the calculations of the French lender, concerned only to maximize his own return – was it the case that increased foreign lending significantly starved French industry of capital and thus contributed to the nation's competitive decline?

Recent studies have generally tended to contest the hitherto dominant view, acknowledging the increase in foreign investment during the *belle époque* but denying that it significantly retarded domestic industrial expansion. Caron minimizes the extent of capital export, and notes that after 1911 the trend seemed to reverse itself (Caron, *Economic History*, pp. 114–15). Maurice Lévy-Leboyer cautions against confusing cause with effect. If French capital migrated abroad between 1895 and 1910, its flight was more to do with changes in the level of infrastructural investment, which tended to soak up capital in domestic enterprise and was dependent on other factors than the eagerness of French financiers to subsidize reactionary regimes in Europe and the Middle East.[15] Or seemingly wasteful colonial adventures. Tom Kemp notes that France's overseas empire remained always a marginal factor in the economy as a whole – in contrast to Britain's increasing dependence on revenues from India in the same period – benefitting only certain sectors. But he also allows that its provision of a small extra market for goods could mean in a given case the difference between achieving an acceptable profit rate or not (Kemp, *Economic Forces*, pp. 270–5).[16]

French capitalism entered the war lagging significantly behind other advanced industrial nations, both in gross indus-

trial output and in its basic structures of capital accumulation
and large-scale industrial expansion. The war, of course,
affected industrial production enormously – not least because
much of the industrial heartland remained occupied by
German troops throughout. But not all the effects were
adverse, as the comparatively rapid and sustained post-war
recovery evidenced (Caron, *Economic History*, pp. 177–81). If
the French bourgeoisie had been unadventurous – save in
speculating on the security of foreign governments – during the
last quarter of the nineteenth century and the first decade of
the twentieth, it was far from moribund or uninnovative
during and after the war. Saddled with a still archaic agricultural sector – which would only achieve effective modernization after the Second World War (Caron, *Economic History*,
pp. 220–2) – French industry nonetheless led all Europe in rate
of industrial growth up to 1929 (Caron, *Economic History*,
p. 179). The economy, in short, though still laboring under the
legacy of certain anachronistic structures, hampered by the
century-long demographic crisis, and only marginally better
off (with the recovery of Alsace and Lorraine) in terms of raw
material resources, was clearly a dynamic one with considerable long-term growth potential, particularly when compared
with its ancient rival, Great Britain.[17] In retrospect, it is not
difficult to recognize that French capitalism, an early starter in
the eighteenth century and a slow developer throughout the
nineteenth, had finally attained maturity and increased self-
confidence by the Treaty of Versailles. That it had done so was
in no small measure due to transformations in political and
social life over the preceding half century. It is to those key
elements in the superstructure of French society that we must
now turn.

THE REPUBLICAN COMPROMISE

Daniel Halévy, Proust's contemporary and schoolmate, gave
to the birth and early years of the Third Republic their
enduring image in history. The parliamentary democracy that
Thiers helped to found and over which he presided for nearly

two years marked "the end of the notables." Halévy's hostility towards the political system that finally triumphed, after the failed restoration of Seize Mai, is well known. His critical appraisal of the regime has been seconded by other commentators on the history of the Third Republic, notably Stanley Hoffmann, who dubbed the republican synthesis that emerged definitively at the end of the 1870s "the stalemate society."[18] Hoffmann emphasizes the peculiarly defensive nature of this first French parliamentary democracy of significant duration, arguing that its power derived from exercising ideological hegemony, in marked contrast to the *dirigiste* character of the imperial state it supplanted: "The organization of this state was such that an effective executive, clear-cut economic or social alternatives, and a strong party system could not emerge."[19] The constitutional settlement established by the National Assembly in 1875 to stave off the Bonapartist revival was a product of compromise among essentially warring factions; as the history of the next four decades would prove, the stability of any government formed under this system was tenuous at best. The period from 1876 to 1914 saw fifty-two changes of cabinet, with only eleven of these surviving as much as one year.[20] Was this notoriously fissiparous parliamentary regime incapable of political action, as many of its critics have contended?

Jean-Marie Mayeur, summarizing the views of René Rémond, among others, contends that the state form realized by the National Assembly, appearances to the contrary, was in fact a triumph of quite distinct principles, ones that had a far from negligible heritage in French political history: "The laws of 1875 established a representative form of government without sovereignty of the people, a parliamentary régime in conformity with the Orleanist ideal and accepted by the new republican generation, now converted to reality, but not by the intransigent republicans" (Mayeur, "Origins," p. 25). These latter would attempt to make trouble for the state, particularly during its first several years, but they would never seriously threaten its ultimate viability. On the contrary, from the mid-1880s they would be its indispensable bulwark. Moreover, as Mayeur goes on to observe, the strength of the bureaucracy, conceived by Napoleon I and firmly entrenched under the Second Empire, would remain untouched by the advent of parliamentarism: "[The Conseil d'Etat], under threat after the collapse of the Empire, now reassumed all its old importance. Nothing was said about its powers: the new régime did not touch the administration, its traditions or its legal status. The parliamentary Republic upheld the powers of the administration" (Mayeur, "Origins," p. 25).[21] Why should this have been the case?

The answer lies in the peculiar class compromise that the Third Republic incarnated. Arno Mayer has argued that the continuing vitality of the European landed aristocracy well into the twentieth century derived in large measure from its capacity to hang on to key sectors in the state apparatus, to continue "reproducing a governing class that not only staffed the state bureaucracy but also kept replenishing the higher echelons of political leadership."[22] As he goes on to show, France was the partial exception to this rule. The Third Republic, with its ostensible blocking mechanism for popular ambitions in the Senate, did not altogether favor large landlords (as did, for example, the House of Lords in Britain). Rather, it incorporated the mass of smallholders effectively hegemonized by the Radicals, who thereby benefitted from the countryside's over-representation in the Chamber. The dominant fact about the parliamentary state in France was that it was a *conservative republic*, founded upon certain traditional values (including, despite the force of anti-clericalism, the resilient ideological power of the Roman Catholic Church), but not in any useful sense empowering or giving significant advantage to the landed aristocracy, save in the army and in the diplomatic corps.[23] As Mayeur succinctly puts it: "It was in fact in this alliance between a section of the upper middle class, the 'new strata' and the working people of the towns and the countryside that the secret of the republican victory lay." It should be emphasized, however, that workers were not significantly empowered in this arrangement. Mayeur shortly adds: "In the republican bloc the workers formed only a contributory element" (Mayeur, "Origins," p. 39).[24] Republican in form, the parliamentary state was nevertheless far from democratic in substance. To the degree that it denied workers access to the apparatus itself,[25] it belied its own rhetoric, which claimed lineage directly from the revolution of 1789. How, then, did the regime maintain popular legitimacy and the overall stability consequent upon it?

The republicans, above all those dubbed Opportunist by their contemporaries, sustained parliamentary majorities over the first quarter-century of the Third Republic's existence, sometimes in alliance with the Radicals, sometimes with conservatives of various stamps. They effectively prevented any resurgence of the anti-republican forces that had presided over the Republic's birth. At the same time, they were unable to extinguish royalism and Bonapartism entirely, either in the Chamber or in the country at large, as the Boulanger fiasco would soon make plain. This resilience of the right, was, it was realized, the most dangerous enemy, not just of parliamentary democracy, but ultimately of bourgeois hegemony. Utilizing their solid majorities in the Chamber, the representatives of the bourgeoisie set about consolidating social power in other key institutions. The army remained, as both the Dreyfus Affair and the continuing struggles over conscription would show, an ideological bastion of the *ancien régime* that the republicans dare not assault openly.[26] Their inroads into the state apparatus focused, instead, on the administrative bureaucracy and on the educational system.

FREE, COMPULSORY, SECULAR

The republican triumph in the 1879 elections ushered in a period of optimism soon to be undermined by the economic reversals that followed hard upon the Union Générale crash in 1882, leading directly to the revanchism embodied in General Boulanger. But while astride the unpredictable parliamentary beast, Jules Ferry and his associates began to create the bases for long-term confidence in and loyalty to the republic. Adopting the *Marseillaise* as the national anthem and declaring

Quatorze Juillet a national holiday, they strove to inculcate
patriotism and regard for the traditions of republican France
among the popular masses. Republican ideological work
sought a definitive break with the old regime's clerical tradi-
tionalism – royalism and Roman Catholicism were, if not
synonymous, often closely intertwined in this period.[27] In
addition to the series of laws limiting the prerogatives of the
Church itself, the crux of the republicans' legislative program
was its educational reforms. Ferry's own statement, published
in the *Revue pédagogique* in 1882, offers the clearest picture of the
aims of the reforms that have borne his name ever since.
Laicization would achieve

> the greatest and most serious of social reforms and the most lasting of
> political reforms ... when the whole of French youth has developed,
> grown up under this triple aegis of free, compulsory, secular edu-
> cation we shall have nothing to fear from returns to the past, for we
> shall have the means of defending ourselves ... the spirit of all these
> new generations, of these countless young reserves of republican
> democracy, trained in the school of science and reason, who will
> block retrograde attitudes with the insurmountable obstacle of free
> minds and liberated consciences. (Quoted in Mayeur, "Origins,"
> p. 85)[28]

The goals of "free, compulsory, secular education" were
two-fold: "to strengthen 'la patrie'" and "to liberate con-
sciences from the 'retrograde spirit'" (Mayeur, "Origins,"
p. 86). At all levels, but most vigorously in the primary schools,
the republicans pursued these aims, dismantling the religious
bases of instruction, extending the term of study, and eliminat-
ing the prohibitive fees that had prevented many from receiving even minimal education.[29] Perhaps most dramatic of all,
the Third Republic introduced secondary education for
women and created the only career opportunity open to female
bourgeois in this period: schoolteacher.[30] Higher education
was also affected, as the foundation of the Catholic universities
in 1875 was challenged by the reorganized and modernized
state schools. While the center of higher education, both in the
universities and in the *grandes écoles*, remained Paris, regional
faculties were empowered to receive local subsidies, so that a

truly national system began to emerge.[31] Not for nothing did
Louis Althusser, in his massively misunderstood essay on Ideological State Apparatuses, locate the shift from the *ancien régime*
to bourgeois democracy in the school's replacement of the
church as the principal locus for ideological reproduction.[32] In
republican France, bourgeois hegemony may have been
secured initially (and would be guaranteed periodically) by
calling out the repressive state apparatus, but its ultimate
legitimacy and viability, reaffirmed continually in parliamentary elections for some six decades, was achieved by colonizing
the frontiers of education. Mayeur's summary of this latter's
effects seems balanced and just:

> the influence of the school did not make itself felt immediately, but
> the fact remains that in this domain schoolteachers were able to shape
> attitudes and to reinforce developments. The textbooks of history,
> geography, reading and morality developed national feeling and
> crystallized the legendary symbols of patriotism from the Grand
> Ferré to Jeanne d'Arc, from the chevalier d'Assas to the drummer-
> boy Bara. The image of France projected by books like *Le Tour de la
> France par deux enfants* is that of a country with well-balanced resources
> and climate dominated by a rural, craft economy. Good house-
> keeping and thrift are the virtues praised above all others. (Mayeur,
> "Origins," p. 116)[33]

One must never forget, however, that the introduction of
free, compulsory, secular education did not produce – nor was
it intended to produce – a functionally egalitarian society.
Reforming primary education ensured that the entire citizenry
would possess certain rudimentary skills, and also that they
would be taught respect for the institutions and traditions of
republican rule; genuine equality of opportunity was neither
its aim nor its result. Real economic advantage accrued only to
those who passed beyond the compulsory limit (age eleven),
since higher primary education was the prerequisite for such
petit bourgeois careers as railway or postal clerk and primary
school teacher. In the two former cases, it was required to be
able to sit for competitive examination; in the latter, it was
necessary for admission to teacher training colleges (Mayeur,
"Origins," p. 115). The further one climbed up the edu-

cational ladder, the narrower the rungs. The bourgeois ideal of the "career open to talents" meant in practice better careers for those few whose class background prepared them to fare well in the educational competition that was the indispensable entrance ticket. Again, Mayeur's summary tells the story nicely:

> there were two school systems with practically no communication between them. The primary school was the school of the people; the *lycées* and *collèges*, with their fee-paying elementary classes, were the schools of the bourgeoisie. The children of the lower middle classes, even the most brilliant pupils of the primary school, could gain entrance to [secondary education] if they had a scholarship. This fact was reckoned to give the system a democratic character. During the period which concerns us [1871–98] the number of pupils who passed the *baccalauréat* did not increase any more than did the number of children attending the *lycées*; the figure varied between 6,000 and 7,000 per year from 1873 onwards. This total was not exceeded until 1891 with the creation of the modern *baccalauréat* and many dropped out during the course, partly owing to the high cost of the fees.
>
> The *baccalauréat* formed a certificate of entry to the bourgeoisie; it became, as the liberal economist Courcelle-Seneuil observed as early as 1872, a sort of "mandarin's diploma" (Mayeur, "Origins," pp. 109–10).[34]

Even later, when the reforms of 1902 would end the exclusiveness of the classical requirement for the *baccalauréat* and thus turn the universities into training grounds for professions other than the traditional liberal ones, the distinctive class character of higher education in France would be maintained (Rebérioux, "Radical Republic," pp. 234–5).[35]

The contradiction in the bourgeoisie's educational program, which proclaimed equality of opportunity for all while enforcing strict separation between classes and fairly rigid stratification within them, is neatly captured in an observation by a future President of the Fifth Republic who was himself a product of this very class-ridden bourgeois educational apparatus codified under the Third Republic. A graduate of the Ecole Normale Supérieure, Georges Pompidou once remarked of that most emblematic of French elites: "One is a *normalien* as one is a prince by blood."[36] We shall often have occasion in the

following pages to observe the infection of bourgeois ideology
by images and ideas borrowed from its aristocratic forebear –
ample confirmation of Marx's tart judgment that "the bourgeois of our days considers himself the legitimate successor to
the baron of old."[37]

BOURGEOIS STATE POWER

Other state apparatuses were used as instruments to forge a
political consensus favorable to bourgeois interests, of course,
notably those comparatively permanent sectors of the administrative bureaucracy staffed by a combination of political
appointees and meritocratically selected candidates. On the
eve of the war, Madeleine Rebérioux writes, political continu-
ity in the state

was ensured by a few great crops whose recruitment betrayed a
political favouritism that was sharply denounced and the compro-
mises swallowed by the Republic. The Council of State – after 1910 it
had 114 members – the Inspection des Finances – to which Joseph
Caillaux belonged – and Foreign Affairs still recruited only partly by
competition. A quarter of the appointments as appeal judges and all
those councillors of State remained in the government's gift. As for
the competitions, candidates prepared for these at the Ecole Libre des
Sciences Politiques, founded in 1871. From the start the organization
of the work in *écuries* (stables) eliminated those who were not heirs in
the most restricted sense of the term. The requirements in the way of
elegance and "presence" led the nobility and the top ranks of the
bourgeoisie to occupy a far superior position relative to their number
and moreover to their real ability. Real dynasties administered
France at the highest level and influenced governmental decisions by
the information they assembled, the reports they presented and the
policies they suggested. (Rebérioux, "Radical Republic," p. 322)[38]

If the Third Republic attained a measure of social stability
during the *belle époque*, this was due less to a wise generosity
towards the working classes (which it most certainly did not
exhibit), than to an effective collaboration between leading
sectors of the previously competing classes, bourgeoisie and
aristocracy, in the principal organs of the State.
One sign of this collaboration was the consensus achieved

over economic and fiscal policy, which welded together different fractions of landed and industrial wealth in a broad con-
cordat over tariffs, social legislation, and state fiscal exactions.[39] Punctuated by the ideological scorched earth
campaigns during the Dreyfus Affair, this solid foundation of
class compromise was laid in the early 1890s and lasted
through the war, from which the French bourgeoisie emerged
more vigorous and capable than ever, poised to reap the
benefits of post-war recovery and fully armed to meet the
challenge of its newest class antagonist, which had emerged
with some organizational clarity in the decade before 1914. But
that struggle properly belongs to the "future" forecast by
Proust's *Recherche*, not to its own historical moment, and so we
shall defer discussing it until the chapter on "Revolution"
below.

A COMMON NATIONAL CULTURE

Not all ideological apparatuses are officially connected to the
state, although even in such institutions of "the public sphere"
as the periodical press, the salon, or the social club, the influence of state power is never negligible. Freedom of expression
came slowly to France, as the *procès* Zola amply illustrated and
press censorship during the First World War would confirm.
Mayeur asserts that the general culture of the early Third
Republic "was profoundly political" (Mayeur, "Origins,"
p. 118), and Eugen Weber is even more emphatic in claiming
for the press a decisive role in shaping and controlling the
Republic's political life during the *fin de siècle*:

The 1880s and 1890s saw the press replace Parliament as the chief site
and instrument of public debate, frightening politicians even more
than it impressed the general public, but affecting the public by its
capacity to communicate, magnify, and manipulate the notions,
scenes, and bits of information that it brought very close to home.[40]

This was the period, in fact, when mass circulation newspapers
became a staple of everyday life across the capitalist world.
Eric Hobsbawm comments: "The mass press, which began to
reach circulations of a million or more in the 1890s, trans-

formed the environment of print, but not its content or associations – perhaps because men who founded newspapers were probably educated and certainly rich, and therefore sensitive to the values of bourgeois culture."[41] In France, the *Petit Journal* achieved unchallenged dominance in the field, more than trebling its circulation between 1872 and 1882, and reaching the million mark by the first decade of the twentieth century.[42] Its conservative republicanism thus served powerfully to reinforce the values promulgated more directly under the state's aegis in the schools. As the standard history of the French press observes: "in these little papers ... the people learnt to read and, thanks to them, were prevented from forgetting the lessons they had learnt at school."[43] The novel institution of the regional paper, with few exceptions, reproduced this same ideological current (Mayeur, "Origins," p. 117). By the *belle époque*, the social conservatism of the dailies was firmly entrenched. They conveyed this worldview to an ever larger public across the nation (Rebérioux, "Radical Republic," pp. 287–8). The French bourgeoisie thus prosecuted its class ideological project on this front as well, over time securing the loyalty of the mass of the population by integrating them into a common national culture.[44]

There is much more to be said about the ideological apparatuses conquered, controlled, or significantly influenced by the bourgeoisie during the Third Republic's first half-century. But since this is the very arena where Proust's *Recherche* is most explicit, it may be well to turn to the novel itself to continue our account of this bourgeois society's superstructural edifice. At the same time, it will be necessary to consider some implications of the preceding discussion of the state and the economy in relation to certain elements in the *Recherche*. These latter reveal Proust's rather acute understanding of those aspects of bourgeois society that seem at first marginal to his fictional project.

PROUSTIAN SUPERSTRUCTURES

Eugen Weber concludes his study of social life in the early Third Republic by citing Proust's *Recherche* as an appropriate

model for historical inquiry into the period. With only mild
hyperbole, he writes:

What is *Remembrance of Things Past* but the profound account of a
profoundly frivolous world? A fin de siecle history of the fin de siecle,
always remembering Proust's view that Clio was the muse who
gathered in everything that the loftier muses of Philosophy and Art
rejected, everything not founded on truth – contingent, uncertain,
accidental, incidental, and ultimately dependent on the evanescent
impressions and the distorting memories of men. In history, as in
Proust, observation depends on the observer's point of view, claims to
objectivity can be misleading, all we can do is to suggest connec-
tions.[45]

This anti-theoretical or anti-scientific view of historical writing
accords well with the received image of Proust's novel, which
has often enough been taken to be a critique of objectivity and
a celebration of the subjective insights gained from or in art. It
is profoundly at odds with the type of historical investigation
pursued here, and, I shall be arguing, with the historical
project of the *Recherche* itself. But for the moment we may take
our cue from Weber and consider some of the specific forms of
historical existence manifested in Proust's text. In particular, I
shall briefly survey the ideological positions presented in different characters and their connection to the forces and relations
of production which, as Walter Benjamin observed, Proust did
everything in his power to occult. If the economy does indeed
appear in the *Recherche*, it does so only under the guise of social
relations that are not in the first instance economic.

What are the principal state apparatuses portrayed in the
novel? In the first place, there is the military, which is carefully
presented in the Doncières section of *Le côté de Guermantes* and is
present on society's margins in the several discussions of the
Dreyfus Affair. Its most important representative is Robert,
Marquis de Saint-Loup, who dies heroically in the First World
War. The military also inflects the lives of several other characters, notably Françoise. She is much disturbed by the sight of
soldiers in Combray and engages the family gardener in a
discussion about military service. Their differing opinions echo
debates that raged in the National Assembly during the Third

Republic's early years and were revived in the Chamber on the eve of the war.[46] In addition, there is the somewhat incongruous figure of Swann, who at the height of the Dreyfus Affair insists on wearing the medal he had won fighting in the Franco-Prussian War, signifying that his support for Dreyfus does not denote any anti-militarist or anti-patriotic sentiments. At the same moment, he appends "a codicil to his will asking that, contrary to its previous provisions, he might be buried with the military honours due to his rank as Chevalier of the Legion of Honour" (II:739). [à son testament un codicille pour demander que, contrairement à ses dispositions précédentes, des honneurs militaires fussent rendus à son grade de chevalier de la Légion d'honneur] (III:111). Doubtless some of Proust's own ambivalence towards the military at this period creeps into this portrait of the quintessential dilettante and socialite who is nonetheless a fervent patriot. Proust had willingly done his obligatory year's service, although he might well have avoided it, and there is every indication, both in the biographical record and in the portrait of barracks life at Doncières, that he considered his soldiering a pleasurable experience. At the same time, his active support for revision of Dreyfus's conviction is well known. In the novel one encounters considerable distaste for the jingoistic nationalism that dominated French political and intellectual life before, during, and after the First World War (see III:747–51; IV:304–8).

We know that Proust closely followed the war's progress in France, an attentiveness that appears directly in Marcel's correspondence with Gilberte in *Le temps retrouvé*. His fascination with these events is even more prominent in Marcel's wartime discussions of strategy and tactics with Saint-Loup (see III:782–4, 1029–30; IV:338–40, 558–9). As becomes clear in the first of these passages, Proust well understood von Clausewitz's famous aphorism about war and diplomacy; the ultimate horizon of military thinking and, *a fortiori*, the prosecution of war, is politics. When Saint-Loup rails against the French policy towards Italy, Marcel responds:

"How shocked your uncle Charlus would be to hear you!" I said. "The fact is that you would be only too pleased to give the Pope another slap in the face, while your uncle is in despair at the thought of the damage that may be done to the throne of Franz Josef. And in this he says that he is in the tradition of Talleyrand and the Congress of Vienna."

"The age of the Congress of Vienna is dead and gone," [Saint-Loup] replied; "the old secret diplomacy must be replaced by concrete diplomacy. My uncle is at heart an impenitent monarchist, who can be made to swallow carps like Mme. Molé and scamps like Arthur Meyer provided that both carps and scamps are *à la Chambord*. He so hates the tricolour flag that I believe he would rather serve under the duster of the Red Bonnet, which he would take in good faith for the white flag of the Monarchists." (III:784)

["Si ton oncle Charlus t'entendait!" lui dis-je. "Au fond tu ne serais pas fâché qu'on offense encore un peu plus le pape, et lui pense avec désespoir au mal qu'on peut faire au trône de François-Joseph. Il se dit d'ailleurs en cela dans la tradition de Talleyrand et du Congrès de Vienne." "L'ère du Congrès de Vienne est révolue," me répondit-il; "à la diplomatie secrète, il faut opposer la diplomatie concrète. Mon oncle est au fond un monarchiste impénitent à qui on ferait avaler des carpes comme Mme. Molé ou des escarpes comme Arthur Meyer, pourvu que carpes et escarpes fussent à la Chambord. Par haine du drapeau tricolore, je crois qu'il se rangerait plutôt sous le torchon du *bonnet rouge*, qu'il prendrait de bonne foi pour le drapeau blanc.] (IV:339–40)

What is glimpsed here is the intra-class struggle between distinct fractions of the titled nobility: the one, represented by Saint-Loup, embracing (or at least making their peace with) the bourgeois republic; the other, figured in the Baron de Charlus, unregenerate to the end, their ultimate loyalty defined not by the nation but by class and lineage.

That Charlus is an anachronism by this point in history scarcely needs emphasizing; the novel explicitly asserts it. Nevertheless, it is worthwhile noting here that the ideological position he represents, while it retained some purchase over a small sector of the French population even during the war, was effectively disarmed in the parliamentary elections of 1876. It was given its ultimate quietus with the passing of the Comte de Chambord, last direct descendent of the Bourbon monarchy, in 1883.[47] To the extent that the French aristocracy continued to exercise any influence in social and political affairs after the constitutional settlement of 1875, it did so by following the path indicated by Saint-Loup, not that of Charlus. The former's death in the war (Charlus survives, albeit feebly, well into the 1920s) signals what was for Proust French society's definitive structural feature at this period: the nobility's final exit from the stage of history.

The police make some brief appearances in the *Recherche*, but for the most part the state's repressive apparatus is entirely mute. The army's function for Proust is less to ensure civil peace,[48] than to defend the nation against foreign aggression and prosecute imperialist policies. Saint-Loup is posted to Morocco, it will be recalled, which the French had only recently conquered and which would become a site of political tension with Germany in the run-up to the war. With the notable exceptions of Norpois, representative of the older aristocratic corps in the Foreign Ministry, Marcel's father, who is an under-secretary there, M. Bontemps, who sits in the Chamber and ultimately sponsors the law increasing the term of military service from two to three years (III:747; IV:305), and more distantly the Duc de Guermantes, who had once served in the National Assembly (II:246,480; II:536,754),[49] the republican state does not figure prominently in the novel, save as a backdrop to the narrative. And yet, politics is everywhere in the *Recherche*. Its presence is mediated through a whole series of institutions, some few state-controlled, but most occupying that fluid domain famously defined by Habermas as "the public sphere."

One ideological state apparatus that does appear in the foreground is the schools. Brichot is a professor at the Sorbonne, and Cottard holds a post in the medical faculty. Since both are more or less fools – although the latter proves to be an entirely competent physician – one can surmise Proust's general attitude towards the system of higher education that emerged in the wake of the Ferry reforms. On another level, however, the novel manifests a quite different attitude towards the republicans' educational program.

Near the end of *A l'ombre des jeunes filles en fleurs*, Marcel recounts an episode in his relations with the little band of girls

composed of Albertine and her friends involving school examinations.[50] Albertine has recently received a letter from Giselle
that includes the latter's "composition qu'elle avait faite pour
son certificat d'études" (I:972; II:264). A discussion of the
essay's merits ensues, with Andrée roundly criticizing Giselle's
rhetorical strategies and Albertine hanging on every word,
since she herself will shortly be sitting for the same examination
and hopes to pick up some useful advice. The episode is brief
and is probably intended as a prelude to later scenes in which
Marcel is said to act as Albertine's mentor, introducing her to
literature and the arts and cultivating her taste, manners, and
dress. The point here is to indicate both Albertine's naïveté (or
comparative ignorance) and her cunning in eliciting helpful
knowledge from her friend, at the same time as it gives the
Narrator occasion to establish Marcel's superior cultural credentials at that period in his life. The latter is slightly older than
the girls and has, we presume, already passed his own school-
leaving examination.

It may go all but unnoticed, however, that this scene could
not have taken place at any prior moment in French history
(the first visit to Balbec must occur sometime in the mid-1890s,
before the public outcry over the Dreyfus Affair). Until the
Ferry reforms of the 1880s (specifically, prior to the *loi Camille
Sée* of December 21, 1880), women generally would not have
had access to public secondary education. Patently all the
middle-class girls in the little band have.[51] If one considers
other female characters in the novel, Marcel's mother, the
Duchesse de Guermantes, Mme. de Cambremer, or even
Odette, the contrast is striking. With the exception of Odette,
whose "education" has scarcely been formal and whose taste in
literature and the arts is a constant source of amusement for
Swann (when it isn't just an annoyance), women of the previous generation will have acquired some acquaintance with
literature, music, and painting. But nothing in the novel indicates that their cultural preparation has been anything but
desultory. Given their class background, it is safe to assume
they have been educated either by private tutors (customary
among titled nobility like Mme. de Guermantes – although at

what point this individual instruction was suspended is left suitably vague) or, more probably, in convent schools.[52] The new generation of women from the middle classes, by contrast, is the first to pass through the national system of secondary education and thus to be more nearly on a par with men.[53] This, too, is an aspect of what made France at this period a bourgeois republic. Extension of the educational franchise was part and parcel of the republican bourgeoisie's democratic ideology, which held that women were citizens quite as much as men. Indeed, republican ideology placed great emphasis on women's special role in securing loyalty to *la patrie*.[54] In the *Recherche*, no better example of this specifically female function to secure republican hegemony can be found than the ubiquitous Mme. Verdurin, violently anti-aristocratic when we first encounter her, a passionate Dreyfusard later on, and a tireless patriot during the war.

Among the epic struggles during the Third Republic's first thirty or so years was that over the status of the Roman Catholic church. Radical republicans consistently branded it the republic's chief ideological enemy. The shifting positions and legislative initiatives culminated in a series of laws promulgated during the Combes ministry from 1901–5, finally achieving formal separation of Church from State (Rebérioux, "Radical Republic," pp. 227–32).

In the *Recherche* itself, these struggles are only hinted at – in the rivalry between Brichot and the curé from Combray over the etymology of French place-names, in Françoise's horror at the government's persecution of the Church, and at various moments when the Dreyfus Affair is foregrounded. Proust himself was extremely ambivalent about the Church's power and influence in a secular democratic republic. A Dreyfusard, he was not insensitive to the clergy's role in promoting the military's agenda and in spreading antisemitism. But in a remarkable letter to Georges de Lauris dated July 29, 1903, he demurred from the extreme anti-clericalism then dominant in the government. Citing the local priest's exclusion from the school prize-giving ceremonies in his family's home town of Illiers consequent upon Ferry's decree of March 29, 1880 (which had called for the dissolution of the Jesuit teaching order), Proust attacks the anti-clerical laws then being enacted. He does not hold that the Church is in any sense a progressive institution, but he insists that anti-clericalism can only further divide Frenchmen from each other. Moreover, the Church itself stands for certain values, embodied in its monuments, that are the lifeblood of rural communities like Illiers:

... I don't think it's right to have stopped inviting the old priest to the prize-giving, since in the village he stands for something more difficult to define than the social function symbolized by the pharmacist, retired tobacco-monopoly engineer and the optician, but which is every bit as worthy of respect, if only because of the intelligence of the pretty, spiritualized steeple, which points towards the setting sun and melts so lovingly into its pink clouds and which I am sure, to the stranger arriving in the village, looks finer, nobler, more disinterested, more intelligent, and, what we want most of all, more loving, than any of the other buildings, including those decreed by the most recent laws.

[il me semble que ce n'est pas bien que le vieux Curé ne soit plus invité à la Distribution des prix, comme représentant dans le village quelque chose de plus difficile à définir que l'office social symbolisé par le pharmacien, l'ingénieur des tabacs retiré, et l'opticien, mais qui est tout de même assez respectable, ne fut-ce que par pour l'intelligence du joli clocher spiritualisé qui pointe vers le couchant et se fond dans ses nuées roses avec tant d'amour et qui tout de même, à la première vue d'un étranger débarquant dans le village, a meilleur air, plus de noblesse, plus de désinteressement, plus d'intelligence et, ce que nous voulons, plus d'amour, que les autres constructions si votées soient-elles par les lois les plus récentes.][55]

Proust's well known devotion to Ruskin at this period sustains the argument here. He bases his defense of the Church as a productive social force primarily on ethico-aesthetic grounds. No reader of the *Recherche*, in particular of the famous section in "Combray" on the steeples of Martinville, will fail to register this ideology's continuing force in the novel. Neither the Narrator nor Proust himself could in any meaningful sense be declared anti-religious, while Brichot's unremitting anti-clericalism (along with Mme. Verdurin's) seems scarcely more than a ridiculous affectation, to be taken no more seriously than his pedantry (or her social pretensions).

Still, nothing could be more misleading than to identify Proust with conventional religiosity, much less with any of the several manifestations of right-wing Roman Catholicism that had emerged in France at this period. He is entirely lucid in this same letter about clerical antisemitism and the general illiberality of many priests. But he is equally convinced that suppressing the clergy cannot possibly accomplish its avowed aim. The elimination of the religious spirit in France cannot be "killed by laws, [it] will die when [its] content of truth and social utility is corrupted or diminished ... [ce n'est pas par les lois que les idées et les croyances dépérissent mais quand ce qu'elles avaient de vérité et d'utilité sociale se corrompt ou diminue ...]" (*Letters*, p. 344; 384). The real menace to social peace, in Proust's view, is not the Church but that more characteristically modern institution for promulgating ideology – the press:

Moreover, it's not teachers, even bad ones, who shape young people's opinions ...; it's the press. If it were possible to restrict the freedom of the press, rather than of education, the ferments of division and hatred might be somewhat diminished. But *intellectual protectionism* (and the present laws are a form of Mélinism a hundred times more odious than Méline) would also have its drawbacks.

[D'ailleurs les maîtres (professeurs des écoles) fussent-ils mauvais, ce n'est pas l'influence des maîtres qui forme les opinions des jeunes gens ... c'est la Presse. Au lieu de restreindre la liberté de l'Enseignement si l'on restreindre la Liberté de la Presse on diminuerait peut'être un peu les ferments de division et de haine. Mais le *protectionnisme intellectual* (dont les lois actuelles sont une forme méliniste cent fois plus odieuse que Méline) aurait bien des inconvénients aussi.] (*Letters*, p. 344; 384; Proust's emphasis)[56]

The passage exhibits an interesting mixture of ideologies. Its purpose is precisely to argue against anti-clericalism, but it does so by appealing to some of the most familiar canons of Enlightenment free-thinking and classical liberalism, i.e., the very systems of thought that gave rise to anti-clericalism in the first place.

When Proust goes on to criticize the venality and ideological influence of the periodical press in detail, he contrasts the narrow-mindedness this latter encourages with the liberality fostered by the very secular education that opposes the institution he is ostensibly defending:

Minds that will never open have *L'Écho* or *L'Éclair* as their teacher, these are the newspapers of their social group, which in turn feed and form their conversation and ideas, if such words are applicable to them. Whereas the opening mind has a Sorbonne professor (or an abbé with *modern ideas*) as its teacher ... Rest assured, the fact that a *licence* in literature is required for military service has done more for the cause of the advanced liberal Republic than any expulsion of monks. The others, those who haven't been to university, Pâris, Albu, [Muller], stick to the political ideas of their social group, that is, *of their newspapers*.

[Voyez que pour les intelligences qui ne s'ouvriront pas le Maître, c'est l'*Echo*, c'est *L'Eclair*, c'est le journal de sa société qui à son tour alimente et forme les conversations, les idées si cela peut s'appeler ainsi de cette société. Et pour l'intelligence qui s'ouvre c'est le Maître en Sorbonne (ou l'abbé *à des idées modernes*) ... Soyez sur que le fait d'exiger la Licence ès lettres pour le Service militaire a plus fait pour la cause de la République libérale avancée, que toutes les expulsions de moines. Les autres, ceux qui n'ont pas "travaillé," Pâris, Albu, (Muller), en restent aux idées politiques de leur société, c'est à dire *de leurs journaux*.] (*Letters*, p. 345; 385; Proust's emphasis)

Of course, Proust believes that enlightened clerics can be quite as progressive as the most advanced secularists. He therefore sees no contradiction between defending the Church's temporal role and his general affirmation of secular liberalism. But in the political climate of the day, these were two entirely distinct, indeed incompatible, positions. Proust's commitment to this manifestly self-contradictory view is not unlike Swann's claim to be at once a Dreyfusard and a patriot.

Of the periodical press itself, little is made in the *Recherche* – save that we know both Marcel and the Duc de Guermantes are regular readers of *Le Figaro*, then as now, the principal organ of mainstream French conservatism. Marcel's first publication appears there, and Proust himself contributed to its pages on occasion. At all events, Proust's letter to de Lauris makes it clear that the press's power lay in its appeal to the well-established opinions of its readership, defined by their social position. The press would therefore be less the promulgator of ideologies than their mundane repository.[57] People read newspapers, Proust avers, to confirm what they already believe. For Marcel in the novel, *Le Figaro* is scarcely a source of political information at all (the Narrator's ultimate political identifications pose a nice question); rather, it serves as another means to promote his social ambition. That newspaper's readership includes many, even most, of those whose salons he wishes to enter.

Which brings us directly to the quintessential institution for ideological elaboration and social stratification in the *Recherche*: the salon itself. At the outset of the novel, we encounter the class-divided world of upper-crust French society in the story of Swann's love for Odette. Among the narrative's dominant strands, none will prove more crucial to its socio-historical significance than the competition for social prominence waged by the three principal hostesses: Mme. Verdurin, Odette, and the Duchesse de Guermantes. No other site in the novel so immediately signifies "society" as do the numerous entertainments, dinners, and other social gatherings. Proust's upper-class characters (with some few exceptions discussed in the following chapter) measure their own value and understand their rank in the world exclusively in terms of the houses they are privileged to visit and those from which they are excluded. The point is familiar to anyone who has read the *Recherche*, but it has perhaps been insufficiently emphasized how decisive are shifts in the social hierarchy for the novel's ideological trajectory as a whole, and for its continuing importance as a map of the *belle époque*'s socio-political history. If the *Recherche* narrates the tale of Marcel's maturing into the Narrator who has told it, the matter of that tale has as much to do with his coming to understand the structures and determinants of social life as it does with his having gained insight into the nature of authentic aesthetic creation. We shall return to this topic in discussing *Le temps retrouvé*, where the opposition between society and art, in many ways the dominant one in the *Recherche*, is posed most starkly.

Mention of the Narrator's aesthetic education suggests another group of ideological apparatuses that play a significant role in the novel: the arts. Each of the major art forms to which Proust closely attended is represented primarily by a single figure: Berma for the theater; Vinteuil for music; Elstir for painting; and Bergotte for literature. All these characters function not only as occasions for aesthetic speculation, but also as instruments for attaining social distinction and for political maneuver. Mme. Verdurin is the manipulator *par excellence* of aesthetic value. When we first encounter her she is mistress of a bohemian salon devoted to Wagnerism (before this latter was fashionable). Later on, she cultivates talented performers like Morel, and ultimately she becomes the patroness (after marrying the Prince de Guermantes) of the rising theatrical stars, Rachel and Bloch. But Odette, too, having received her earliest lessons in social distinction from Mme. Verdurin, cultivates aesthetic value for social gain. In her drawing room Marcel first encounters Bergotte, who is among its *habitués* for a certain period. Even a figure like Mme. de Villeparisis (socially speaking, she has been marginalized by the time Marcel first meets her) eagerly grasps at cultural attractions that might aid her in reclaiming some portion of the social eminence she has forfeited due to her scandalous life. Finally, as is still true of certain cultural occasions today (gallery openings, first nights at the opera and theater, and so forth), the theater is a place where social hierarchies are reinforced by the very spectacle of visibility. Marcel's real grasp of the divisions and nuances within society commences when he observes the Princesse and Duchesse de Guermantes at an opera gala near the beginning of *Le côté de Guermantes*.

Other institutions operate on the text's margins: social clubs like the Jockey or honorary societies like the Académie Française (to which Marcel's father aspires unsuccessfully). But they remain largely ornamental, confirming signs of social power rather than arenas where it is seriously negotiated. When the Duc de Guermantes is denied the presidency of the

Jockey, his vanity is sharply wounded, but his social position is scarcely affected. Society in this novel just is the composition of one's list of invitations, the places where a person can or cannot be seen. While those in the Faubourg Saint-Germain are generally pleased to think that its rules, its membership, and its boundaries are more or less fixed for all eternity, nothing is more certain in the *Recherche* than that the structures of social power are always in danger of eroding or vanishing altogether. One of the last bastions of the *ancien régime*, the Faubourg found itself during the *belle époque* perpetually besieged by a bourgeoisie not only desirous of entering its drawing rooms, but frankly set upon wresting control of the levers of social power from its putative masters among the titled nobility. This is simply to say that in the *Recherche*, as in the society it aims to present, the ideological apparatuses, state and otherwise, always exhibit, in however mediated or distant a form, the conditions of the class struggle. Those conditions, of course, are determined in the last instance by the structure of economic relations, that is, by the balance of economic power in the social formation. In the *Recherche*, it is characteristically unclear how most of the upper-class characters earn their money. We know, for example, that Swann is immensely rich, as is the Duc de Guermantes, and that both inherited their fortunes (the former derived largely from stocks, since his father was an "agent de change"). We know, as well, that while Robert de Saint-Loup has a large fortune when we first encounter him, he is compelled to make an otherwise unsatisfactory marriage to Gilberte Swann in order to replenish the family coffers. Other instances of the aristocracy's appropriating bourgeois wealth abound – in the Cambremers, notoriously, and, we may surmise, in the late marriage of the Prince de Guermantes to the former Mme. Verdurin. But in none of these cases is any close attention – of the sort that Balzac would have paid – given to the nitty-gritty business of economic activity itself. In the absence of any evidence to the contrary, it is probably fair to assume that Proust's upper-class characters are mostly rentiers with holdings in land (like the Guermantes' country estates or Swann's Tansonville) and, equally likely, considerable investments in securities. While ideological power is still being contested on the social battlefield, economic relations have entirely been subsumed, for the upper classes at least, under the mantel of capitalism. Bourgeois marry aristocrats to gain entry into their social world; aristocrats marry bourgeois for their money. Thus the economy appears in this text most directly in the marriage market that dominates the action just prior to the final volume, when the titled nobility's economic viability has begun to totter once and for all, and when their purchase on even a modicum of political and social power was slipping rapidly away. The efficient cause of this eclipse was the First World War, which showed up the glaring inadequacies of a French economy still tied to its comparatively vast and generally inefficient agricultural sector; its sign in the novel is the progressive *embourgeoisement* of the Faubourg Saint-Germain. In the *Recherche* we discover the economic foundations of society only by burrowing through the superstructural manifestations that are the novel's clearest markers of class divisions and are the site of and the stake in its portrayal of class struggles.

CHAPTER 2

Class and class struggle

The bourgeoisie has subjected the country to the rule of the towns. It has created enormous cities, has greatly increased the urban population as compared with the rural, and has thus rescued a considerable part of the population from the idiocy of rural life.

(Marx and Engels, *The Communist Manifesto*)

Considered demographically, France on the eve of the First World War was predominantly a rural nation. In 1911, some 56 percent of the population still lived in and around towns and villages with fewer than two thousand inhabitants. Nor was the rural population's rate of decline precipitous: only 10 percent since 1880.[1] The tendential processes of urbanization, industrialization, and proletarianization, remarked by Marx and Engels in the 1840s and visibly manifest in all the other major capitalist powers by the end of the nineteenth century, remained at best unevenly realized in France by the *belle époque*.

Jean-Charles Asselain has emphasized the variegated nature of the nineteenth-century French economy. We may conclude from this fact that France's class structure was differently inflected from that in Great Britain, Germany, and the United States. Perhaps the most important feature of France's uneven development was the industrial concentration – hence, the rapid capitalist growth – in the Northeast, roughly above the line stretching from Cherbourg to Marseille. The overwhelming preponderance of Paris and the Seine region was a given: "The Parisian pole captured, in the France of 1913, an absolute preeminence in the political, administrative, and cultural

51

note

order, but also economically, in marked contrast with both
Great Britain and Germany ... [the] department of the Seine
included a total of 1.1 million workers employed in industry,
i.e., one-sixth of the French industrial working force."[2] And
yet, throughout the Third Republic, the industrial regions of
concentrated population continued to be comparatively
under-represented in the parliamentary system. This contradiction between parliamentary political power and economic
preeminence would have significant consequences for the
conduct of class struggle between nobility and bourgeoisie. To
understand the conditions of this struggle and the course it
followed, it is necessary to establish the lineaments of each
class. First, however, a brief excursus on the concept of class as
it is used in the present study is required.

No topic in the modern social sciences is more vexed than
that of social class. Even within the marxist tradition, its
definition is far from settled, either in the sociology of contemporary society or in historiography proper.[3] The insuffi-
ciency of Marx's theoretical elaboration is notorious. Chapter
52 of *Capital* volume III, entitled "Classes," breaks off after a
few paragraphs, having barely opened the question. Still,
Marx's preliminary definitions are worth pondering: "The
owners of mere labour-power, the owners of capital and the
landowners, whose respective sources of income are wages,
profit and ground-rent – in other words wage-labourers,
capitalists, and landowners – form the three great classes of
modern society based on the capitalist mode of production."[4]
As capitalism matures, the overwhelming majority of the
population will be transformed into wage-laborers, a process
that is inaugurated, Marx ceaselessly insisted, by altering
property relations on the land:

the monopoly of landed property is a historical precondition for the
capitalist mode of production and remains its permanent foundation,
as with all previous modes of production based on the exploitation of
the masses in one form or the other. But the form in which the
capitalist mode of production finds landed property at its beginnings
does not correspond to this mode. The form that does correspond to it
is only created by it itself, with the subjection of agriculture to
capital ... (Marx, *Capital*, III:754)[5]

Private property in land is the precondition for the emergence
of the capitalist mode of production, but only with the im-
position of new agrarian relations of production – viz., by "the
expropriation of the rural workers from the soil and their
subjection to a capitalist who pursues agriculture for the sake of
profit" (Marx, *Capital*, III:751) – does landed property assume
its distinctively capitalist form.

As Marx argues at length elsewhere, capitalist farming and
industrial capital both participate in a single historical process
(the genesis of the capitalist mode of production), but each
develops from different sources and possesses a distinctive
trajectory.[6] This is the reason for his differentiating between
landowners and capitalists, just as it is the ground of their
antagonism in modern society. In Britain, famously, the
antagonism was resolved in favor of the landowners, who
subordinated the nascent industrial capitalist class to its interests.[7] France, by contrast, had a classical bourgeois revolution,
although, as has already been noted, the consolidation of
bourgeois class power took more than a century to be achieved.
The Third Republic witnessed the final stages in this struggle,
as the titled nobility, historically the preeminent landowning
class, saw its political fortunes decline after the mid-1870s, its
economic stability waver during the global depression from the
1870s to the 1890s, and its ideological hegemony wane in the
aftermath of the Dreyfus Affair.

In the *Recherche*, only rarely is the class struggle between
bourgeois and aristocrat (or capitalists and landowners) staged
as open economic or political warfare. Characteristically,
society (*le monde*) refers to the diurnal round of public and
private intrigues that characterizes salon life; it is concerned
with the people and events reported in the society pages of
major newspapers. Class struggles thus appear in the novel in
the guise of the major characters' anxieties about and their
changes in social status. Proust's novel is a veritable encyclo-
pedia of what Piere Bourdieu has termed "distinction."[8]

A character's class position, in the technical, economic sense
in which Marx understood the term, need not, of course,
coincide with his or her status. Swann, for example, springs
from impeccably bourgeois origins and is, during the period of

the novel, a capitalist rentier. Yet, his social position (prior to the Dreyfus Affair anyway) approaches that of the bluest bloods, with whom he has long been intimate, and it patently surpasses that attained by many of the titled nobility, for example, his erotic rival, the Comte de Forcheville. Class and status are theoretically distinct but empirically intertwined. The struggles over the latter result from the structural contradictions that define the former's existence. Bourdieu captures the essence of this relation:

> A class is defined as much by its *being-perceived* as by its *being*, by its consumption ... as much as by its position in the relations of production (even if it is true that the latter governs the former) ... the individual or collective classification struggles aimed at transforming the categories of perception and appreciation of the social world and through this, the social world itself, are indeed a forgotten dimension of the class struggle. But one only has to realize that the classification schemes which underlie agents' practical relationship to their condition and the representation they have of it are themselves the product of that condition, in order to see the limits of this autonomy. Position in the classification struggle depends on position in the class structure ...[9]

Proust's narrative presents competition for social pre-eminence as a reliable index of the ongoing class conflict between landowners and capitalists. The loss of social exclusivity that the novel progressively discloses, indicates the definitive, final triumph of capitalist social relations and the bourgeoisie's undisputed ideological hegemony over French society as a whole.[10]

THE PERSISTENCE OF THE OLD REGIME

George Weisz puts the case too strongly when he asserts that "surprisingly little [is known] about the class basis of the Third Republic beyond the fact that it represented the influx into political life of many groups that had previously been excluded."[11] It is true, however, that some classes have been but little studied, in particular the nobility. This comparative neglect (workers have, by contrast, received voluminous attention) is probably due in large measure to the residual republican prejudices among French intellectuals, one consequence of the bourgeoisie's successful ideological program during the Third Republic and after. Casting itself as inheritor of the traditions of 1789, the republican bourgeoisie effectively demonized both throne and altar, playing upon popular fears that support for the nobility risked a possible return to the economic relations of the *ancien régime*.[12] While it is clear in retrospect that there was little prospect of such an eventuality, the French nobility continued to see itself as a distinct class and to act in class ways through the First World War. Ralph Gibson makes the point well:

The nobility was therefore an objective reality, right through the nineteenth century. It had its own patterns of residence and marriage, its own professional activities, and (in many cases) its own politics. As a group, it doubtless diluted itself by welcoming new recruits whose credentials did not extend back to the Ancien Régime. It is not possible, however, to go so far as to say that it simply dissolved itself in the world of the *grands notables*. The nobility remained an identifiably separate and self-conscious element of French society. Social and political necessities may have forced it to make alliances – particularly in defence of "order." But alliances they remained, and not amalgamations. (Gibson, "French Nobility," p. 11)

Who were the nobility and how did they continue to act as a distinct class? The answer to the first question is by no means straightforward. Gibson defines nobles as descendants of the people who voted with the nobility in the 1789 Estates General ("French Nobility," p. 6). Philippe du Puy de Clinchamps estimates their number at that moment as approximately 12,000 families and 60,000 persons.[13] Such figures are, however, notoriously unreliable.[14] Things become more complicated still during the nineteenth century, with the creation of new titles under both empires and the acquisition of the *particule* by wealthy bourgeois. Definitional problems and determination of precise numbers aside, one is inclined to concur with David Higgs's judgment that the "vital element for the study of nobles in modern France is *the desire to become noble*" (Higgs, *Nobles*, p. 5; emphasis in the original).

While it is surely correct to insist upon the nobility's absolute decline both in numbers and in direct political and economic power during the nineteenth century, more noteworthy still was their remarkable resilience. Theodore Zeldin, whose sweeping judgments one is otherwise inclined to mistrust, puts the matter succinctly: "This survival and re-creation of the nobility would not have been very significant if it had not been allied with a preservation, and in many cases a reinforcement, of the nobility's wealth. The nobles lost land at the Revolution but apparently far less than is popularly assumed."[15] Gibson concurs, and Higgs, who contends that the nobility did suffer an inexorable decline throughout the century, nonetheless chronicles, in his chapters on "Noble Landholders" and "Noble Wealth," the various strategies they pursued to remain well-to-do, hence, noble (Gibson, "French Nobility," p. 24; Higgs, *Nobles*, pp. 33–69, 102–29). Moreover, as Higgs observes (following Zeldin), during the *belle époque*, even the absolute numerical decline may have been temporarily reversed (Higgs, *Nobles*, p. 27). Politically, of course, the nobility signally failed to achieve the monarchical restoration so many desired (and some actively schemed for) during the Third Republic. But this overt defeat at the national level should not blind us to their continuing social power and cultural prestige, their capacity to dictate the terms on which the bourgeoisie would struggle to obtain the outward signs of social acceptance. And, while the revanchism that characterized the Dreyfus Affair was not an aristocratic monopoly, the nobility's identification with the officer corps was general – reinforced no doubt by their comparative over-representation in its higher ranks (Gibson, "French Nobility," p. 28). It would scarcely be an exaggeration to characterize the ideological split evident in the Affair as a belated manifestation of the century-long struggle between royalism and republicanism, which was the political expression (currently fashionable revisionism notwithstanding) of the class struggle between aristocracy and bourgeoisie.

The French nobility successfully sustained its self-image and fought a desperate rearguard action against its ultimate demise up through the First World War. They could do so not only

because their major class antagonist accepted their terms for
signifying social distinction, but also because they quite
cleverly accommodated themselves to the French economy's
changing nature. Higgs remarks how the nobility's increasing
distaste for *des affaires* sealed their fate (Higgs, *Nobles*, pp.
105–7, 129), while granting that by the *belle époque* they had
managed to overcome a measure of their natural disdain. In
addition, those whose agricultural properties lay in the north
did very well for a reasonably long time, enabling them to
concentrate in the Paris region and retain sufficient capital to
reinvest prudently in urban real estate and state bonds (Higgs,
Nobles, pp. 34–41, 59–67; Gibson, "French Nobility," p. 17).
The nobility supported, because it would benefit directly from,
the tariff restrictions passed by the Opportunists,[16] and it made
extremely shrewd purchases of and found profitable uses for its
houses in town.[17] At a pinch, they could even resort to advan-
tageous marriages with the *haute bourgeoisie*, both native and
foreign, to shore up the less stable wings of their stately edifice
(Zeldin, *Politics and Anger*, pp. 41–2). Up to the war, the French
nobility remained rich, powerful (if decreasingly so in parliamentary politics), and unassailably self-confident. Nothing
that is known about this class contradicts what can be learned
from Proust's *Recherche*.

One clear indication of continuing aristocratic power is the
extent to which the bourgeoisie conceded the nobility's monopoly over social distinction. Higgs is unequivocal on this point:

Nineteenth-century nobles and particularly aristocrats found their
last redoubt of social power in control of the criteria of elegant
behavior. No sooner had an erstwhile M. Jourdain carefully learned
the current forms of good manners than his patient mimicry was
derided. It was in this sense that Marx scornfully said of the nobility
of his time that they had become the dancing masters of Europe.

Nevertheless, the ability to set the tripwires that marked social
boundaries was one that inspired healthy respect and fear in the
social climbers – that is, the newly successful – in France. (Higgs,
Nobles, pp. 181–2)

Daniel Halévy's "republic of dukes" persisted on this level long
after its political demise in the late 1870s. In command
economically from the July Monarchy onwards, unchallenged

politically after the failed restoration of Seize Mai, the bourgeoisie struggled for ideological hegemony, but unevenly.

THE SOURCES OF BOURGEOIS HEGEMONY

Gibson argues that the bourgeoisie's ultimate triumph was
achieved politically because it waged a successful campaign to
capture the hearts and minds of a majority among ordinary
people, the rural masses in particular (Gibson, "French
Nobility," pp. 31–7). It could do so in large measure because
by the early 1880s it had obtained the means to dictate the
terms of political struggle on the national level, consolidating
its control over the state apparatus (national and local) and
reproducing itself in the key areas from which political power
could be exercised.

Pace Alfred Cobban, François Furet, *et alia*, the Revolution
of 1789 provided the commercial and professional bourgeoisie
with its entrance ticket to France's national political arena.
The Napoleonic defeat opened the door for the aristocracy to
eject them again, but the Restoration signally failed to consoli-
date the nobility's position in any permanent or stable structures. The exact form of bourgeois political power would
require nearly half a century to realize, but during the entire
period from 1830 to the mid-1870s, the steady, occasionally
rapid expansion of French capitalism effectively ensured that
the ruling class in France would never again derive its wealth
from feudal prerogatives or seigneurial exactions. Once definitively astride the state apparatus, the French bourgeoisie consolidated and extended its economic domination and set about
making its services indispensable to the smooth functioning of
the state apparatus as well. The bourgeoisie's class project
under the Third Republic constructed a new definition of and
constituted new cadres for the social elite bearing its own
stamp.

One should not summarily dismiss Zeldin's claim that the
republican state preserved much from the imperial state it
replaced (Zeldin *Politics and Anger*, pp. 239–40). But to the
extent that this was so, it can also be read as a sign of the

bourgeoisie's already powerful position within the Napoleonic administration. What did change, however, in addition to the precipitous decline in the nobility's parliamentary representation, was the institutional basis for elite recruitment that would guarantee the bourgeoisie's political preferment. The class struggles of the Third Republic were predominantly over the means to secure ideological hegemony; their site was the state apparatus.

Zeldin makes the point that from 1881 onwards, the Chamber was dominated by the upper and professional bourgeoisie (Zeldin, *Politics and Anger*, p. 213). He further asserts that parliamentary preeminence over the ministries was produced by the latter's frequent dissolution, although he concedes that ministerial changes characteristically did not produce major policy shifts (Zeldin *Politics and Anger*, pp. 220, 225–6). Madeleine Rebérioux's judgment previously cited (see above, "Base and Superstructure," p. 35) bespeaks the underlying truth of the matter: to wit, that the republican state apparatus on the eve of the First World War was a bulwark of bourgeois hegemony. How was this structure created?

The literature on France's elite formation is too vast for effective summary here. I can, however, highlight the principal features of the process that bear on the world Proust knew and chronicled. As is well known, the core of elite recruitment was (and is) the *grandes écoles*, institutions that first emerged in the eighteenth century and were expanded from the revolution onwards. The Ecole des Mines and the Ponts et Chaussées were joined by the Polytechnique and the Ecole Normale, later by the Ecole Pratique des Hautes Etudes, and ultimately by the Ecole Libre des Sciences Politiques. Separate from the archaic university system of the faculties, they "were entered by competitive examination (unlike the universities, which were open to all who had very elementary paper qualifications), and they offered scholarships, long before the universities did."[18] Under the Third Republic, *normaliens*, *polytechniciens*, and graduates of "Sciences Po." were especially prominent and powerful; they produced what was in effect a mandarinate that dominated policy and shaped civil society. While the first gravitated

towards the Socialist Party, the second towards big business,
the upper levels of state administration came increasingly to be
staffed by products of the Ecole Libre, which had been created
in the early years of the Third Republic: "In the period
1901–35, of 117 successful candidates in the competition for
entry into the Conseil d'état, 113 were from Sciences Po., 202
out of 211 admissions to the Inspection des Finances, 82 out of
92 to the Cour des Comptes, and 246 out of 280 to the ministry
of foreign affairs" (Pierre Rain, *L'Ecole des Sciences Politiques*;
cited in Zeldin, "Higher Education," p. 79). Egalitarian in
principle, the *grandes écoles* were far from being so in fact:

A sizable proportion of the country's intellectual and technical
leaders passed through them, but perhaps for this very reason their
general structure and organization remained largely unchanged. The
esprit de corps of their graduates and the conservatism (in professional, as distinct from political matters) of most of their teachers
preserved their privileged, almost oligarchical, character. They
claimed they were democratic because the elite they created was
recruited by examination, but there was no real equality of opportunity to pass the examinations. They drew the vast majority of their
pupils from the middle classes, because secondary education was not
yet freely available to the poor. (Zeldin, "Higher Education," pp.
79–80)

The point is crucial. Entrance by competitive examination
made *lycée* training indispensable; only the well-to-do could
aspire to it.[19] In addition, the separate structures and curricula
of women's education made the *grandes écoles* an exclusively
male preserve.[20] When the republicans recognized the necessity of educating middle-class women for citizenship, they
established a separate institute (the Ecole Normale at Sèvres)
to train teachers for women's *lycées* and *collèges*. The school was
staffed and attended by women and had a distinctive curricu-
lum aimed at preparing its graduates to educate female ado-
lescents for service to home and family, the sites on which it was
believed they were uniquely qualified to reproduce republican
subjects.[21] As in the division between secondary and primary
education – the former for the middle and upper classes, the
latter for "the people" – women's education under the Third
Republic was separate and unequal. We shall have occasion

later on to deal more fully with gender distinctions in republican France. These had economic consequences (the only respectable profession to which middle-class women could aspire through the First World War was that of schoolteacher), but they were first and foremost ideological.

If I have dwelt on the educational apparatus, this is because it was arguably the decisive instrument for securing bourgeois hegemony. It inculcated republican values among all classes (save the nobility, who long resisted public education), and it sorted out candidates for different social strata through a system of ostensibly meritocratic but in fact materially exclusive funneling. Capitalism produced a ruling class whose economic imperative was to buy cheap and sell dear. This class reproduced itself by establishing a set of institutions that would guarantee its preponderance within the state and throughout civil society by denying peasants and workers significant access to the levers of power, while interpellating them to the republican ideology that the bourgeoisie claimed as their own. The bourgeois class project was therefore double: defeat the nobility and co-opt "the people." That the project succeeded, at least temporarily, was demonstrated during the First World War: no significant fraction of French society bolted from the national coalition, not even when it appeared that the system itself was blundering from one disastrous policy to another.[22] By 1914, the bourgeoisie had secured not only the capacity to rule, but the quite general belief that it was in the best interests of all that they should do so. Less than half a century earlier, such a consensus had been unthinkable.

A COMPLEX, OVERDETERMINED SUBJECT

What class did Marcel Proust represent? Walter Benjamin's brief remarks on the subject will later provide a crucial directive concerning the identifications the *Recherche* as a whole aims at. For the present, let us simply delineate the class position into which Proust himself was born, as well as the ones with which he would identify during the course of his life prior to composing his novel.

Proust's father Adrien sprang from *petit bourgeois* origins.

Marcel's paternal grandfather had been a shopkeeper in the small rural town of Illiers not far from Chartres. His pious ambition was for his son to take holy orders, but Adrien followed a different path, studying physical sciences and eventually moving to Paris to become a successful physician with a particular interest in public health and sanitation. Adrien was to become a central figure in the campaign to establish a *cordon sanitaire* to prevent the spread of cholera in Northern Europe. For his efforts, he was awarded the Legion d'Honneur's red ribbon in the Second Empire's last days. At the same moment, he married Jeanne Weil, daughter of a wealthy Jewish stockbroker.[23] Her brother Georges was a lawyer, her uncle Louis a well-heeled pleasure-seeker whose various liaisons included at least one with a famous cocotte. After his mother's death, Proust inherited a share and occupied one of the apartments in the latter's townhouse at 2 boulevard Haussman (Painter, *Proust*, I:85, 192; II:61).

Proust's spendthrift habits are legendary – and more than once occasioned quarrels with his parents – but nothing he could do seemed capable of seriously endangering his sizable income. We can guess at its extent by recalling that he could gamble some 300,000 francs on gold futures during 1911–12 and lose 40,000 without necessitating significant economies (Painter, *Proust*, II:174). Painter puts the matter tersely: "he would always remain wealthy" (Painter, *Proust*, II:97). A scion of the upper bourgeoisie, Proust was never under material necessity to earn his bread. He lived not merely comfortably but extravagantly on revenues from inherited property and capital. In this he resembled no one so much as Swann in the *Recherche*. (And Marcel also, although the latter's extravagance, notably over Albertine, tends to pinch more than seems to have been the case for Proust himself.)[24]

But plainly Proust's personal commitments were not to the values and habits characteristic of the majority of his class. For as a class, even wealthy rentiers tended to engage in business or take a profession, lest their income be seriously impaired. During the majority of Proust's lifetime, at least up to the war, the French bourgeoisie enjoyed a comparatively untroubled period of expanding horizons. There were crises, of course, and the long depression that lasted from the 1870s to the mid-90s significantly affected those whose income derived largely from agriculture. But on balance the business climate during the Third Republic's first half-century of existence was extra-ordinarily favorable, and the bourgeoisie collectively did not fail to take advantage of it. Proust, by contrast, was at best a desultory participant in the immediate economic activities of his class. He totally ignored the duties of the only post he ever held – that of librarian – and was in the end summarily dismissed from it. While he did earn some money by writing, particularly in the last years of his life, unlike Balzac, Zola, Conrad or even Henry James, he was never seriously dependent on his pen for income. He thus lacked that to which, as a typical bourgeois, he might otherwise have aspired: a profession.

What, then, were Proust's primary class identifications? To call them aristocratic is not wrong, but it remains to precise this term's meaning as it came to be understood during Proust's lifetime, when the French aristocracy would lose virtually all its purchase on direct political power. Towards that end, we can do no better than recount the broad outlines of aristocratic manners and predilections sketched by Arno Mayer.

Mayer's account of the landed aristocracy's economic transformation emphasizes increasing inter-class collaboration. The nobility tended to invest more heavily in urban real estate (while retaining their country estates for fashionable social activities), and also to obtain important positions on boards of directors in banking, industry, and trade. At the same time, wealthy bourgeois gained entry to the formerly exclusive realm of aristocratic society through marriage (Zeldin, *Politics and Anger*, pp. 41–2). What resulted was a class compromise that stabilized the political and social situation among the upper classes, particularly after the Dreyfus Affair.[25] At the level of social prestige, however, the bargain struck was an unequal one, for here the aristocracy maintained its hegemony long after its economic and political power had begun to wane:

Although relegated to the margin of the republican polity, the
French aristocracy maintained its social and cultural pre-eminence.
As if to compensate for its absolute political fall and relative economic
decline, it became more self-consciously mannered and proud-
minded than any other European nobility. Old highborn families
learned to valorize their renowned names and ancestries ... rather
than standing out as decadent, corrupt, idle, and vain, the French
nobility dazzled Paris and foreign notables with its charm, elegance,
and finesse. (Mayer, *Persistence*, p. 105)

Its bourgeois compeers for the most part accepted this standard. As Mayer writes some pages earlier:

Even under the Third Republic dukes, marquises, counts, and barons
occupied such prominent economic, social, and cultural positions
that the *grands bourgeois* never ceased to revere and emulate them. The
aristocratic world remained so seductive that many bankers, entrepreneurs, and professionals who failed to marry into it sought to pass
themselves off as nobles by simply attaching the particle *de* to their
names. (Mayer, *Persistence*, p. 102)[26]

On Mayer's view, which squares nicely with the *Recherche* (he
refers to the novel *en passant*, and it would appear from the list
of aristocrats he mentions that the world he is describing was
precisely the one where Proust circulated; see Mayer, *Persistence*, p. 107), four aspects of aristocratic life dominated the
Third Republic's social landscape: first, the maintenance of old
and construction of new chateaux, which "were prime badges
of seignorial status or pretension and provided rarefied space
for socializing during the summer and shooting seasons"
(Mayer, *Persistence*, p. 106); second, the continuing vitality of
salon culture; third, the persistence of dueling; and, fourth,
the revival of dandyism (Mayer, *Persistence*, pp. 106–8).
Economically preeminent from the Second Empire onwards,
politically dominant after 1875, the upper bourgeoisie sought
social prestige by imitating aristocratic manners and practices
and by gaining entry to those institutions over which the titled
nobility still ruled, including their clubs (like the Jockey and
the Union) and their homes.
    Proust's insertion into this milieu is well known. Like his
fictional protagonists, Swann and Marcel, Proust self-

consciously strove to scale the highest reaches of the Faubourg Saint-Germain, successfully trading on his wit and his knowledge of the arts to enter the ostensibly closed world of the *gratin*. His schemes to secure otherwise unobtainable invitations to dinner parties and receptions hosted by the great mistresses of Parisian salons are legendary, chronicled both in his extensive correspondence and in Painter's biography. In the *Recherche* itself, ample evidence remains in the parallel careers of Swann and the Narrator to suggest how deeply Proust drank at the well of aristocratic manners, how thoroughly he assimilated the nobility's self-understanding and its innumerable foibles.

This is not to say that Proust remained an uncritical admirer of the Faubourg. One cannot read his massive novel without catching the considerable scorn heaped on the shallow egotism and essential heartlessness of characters like Oriane de Guermantes and her husband Basin, not to mention the text's utter lucidity about snobbism evident in figures like Legrandin, Bloch, and Mme. de Cambremer. The *Recherche* thoroughly demystifies the very vice to which Proust must himself have been inclined. As with so many of the novel's principal themes, Walter Benjamin is brilliantly incisive about Proust's critique of aristocratic pretension: "it was to be Proust's aim to design the entire inner structure of society as a physiology of chatter. In the treasury of its prejudices and maxims there is not one that is not annihilated by a dangerous comic element."[27] One might say that in the *Recherche* conversation is at once everything and nothing, that in certain scenes (generally the great receptions and the dinner parties up to the climactic one given by the Prince and Princesse de Guermantes in *Le temps retrouvé*) it occupies much space without offering significant insight. Characteristically in Proust, what counts is what the Narrator says about the talk he reports; the talk itself remains almost entirely vacuous.[28]

While it might be profitable to speculate on the reasons for Proust's ultimate disillusionment with the aristocratic social world he cultivated so assiduously and energetically, of more immediate moment is to understand how this affected – indeed

produced – the monumental funerary edifice to that world that
is the *Recherche*.[29] If we accept Arno Mayer's characterization
of the Third Republic's dominant social forces up to the First
World War as an effective class compromise between bourgeoisie and aristocracy, it is possible to see Proust's career as
virtually a textbook illustration of this dynamic. *A fortiori*, his
novel will represent the history and ideology of this social
formation from the point of view of its rulers. Proust's significance derives from his contradictory class position, which
caused him to identify equally with the ideology of the upper
bourgeoisie into which he was born, and with that of the
nobility whose favor he sought. Proust could disclose the inner
workings of French ruling-class politics in this period because
he was situated at the conjuncture, which was the decisive site
for the Republic's class struggles prior to the Great War, of
aristocratic social power and bourgeois social ambition.
Proust's interpellation into subjectivity was, we may safely
assert, overdetermined.[30]

WHY SWANN DREAMS OF NAPOLEON III

Before proceeding to an overview of the classes represented in
the *Recherche* and the struggle for hegemony in French society
between bourgeoisie and nobility that it narrates, I shall consider a single brief episode that exemplifies how Proust's novel
talks ceaselessly about social relations and political events
while not appearing to do so. The scene I propose to examine
comes at the close of "Un amour de Swann"; it has received
scant attention in the vast secondary literature on the *Recherche*.[31] At the end of his infatuation with Odette, when he is
convinced he is so thoroughly indifferent to her that his discovering proof of her having been Forcheville's mistress
"caused him [Swann] no pain, for that love was now far
behind" (1:411) [il n'en ressentait aucune douleur, que l'amour
était loin maintenant] (1:372), Swann has a most peculiar and
arresting dream.[32] The exposition is lengthy, but since the
dream representation's intricacies are crucial to its significance, it will be necessary to quote it in its entirety:

He was mistaken. He was destined to see her once again, a few weeks later. It was while he was asleep, in the twilight of a dream. He was walking with Mme. Verdurin, Dr. Cottard, a young man in a fez whom he could not identify, the painter, Odette, Napoleon III and my grandfather, along a path that followed the sea and overhung it sometimes from high above, sometimes from only a few meters, so that they were constantly ascending and redescending. Those of the strollers who went down again were already no longer visible to those who were still going up; the little bit of daylight that remained was failing, and it seemed then that a dark night was going to fall immediately. From time to time the waves dashed against the edge, and Swann could feel on his cheek a freezing spray. Odette told him to wipe it off, but he could not and was embarrassed in front of her because he was in his nightshirt. He hoped that the darkness would make this go unnoticed; however, Mme. Verdurin fixed him with an astonished gaze for a long moment, during which he saw her face deform itself, her nose grow longer, and that she had a large moustache. He turned round to look at Odette; her cheeks were pale, with small red spots, her features drawn and ringed with shadows; but she looked back at him with eyes welling with affection, ready to detach themselves like tears and to fall upon his face, and he felt that he loved her so much that he would have liked to carry her off at once. Suddenly Odette turned her wrist, looked at a tiny watch, and said: "I have to go." She took leave of everyone in the same formal manner, without taking Swann aside, without telling him where she would see him again that evening or the next day. He dared not ask it of her; he would have liked to follow her but was obliged, without turning back towards her, to respond with a smile to a question from Mme. Verdurin; but his heart beat frightfully, he felt that he now hated Odette, he would gladly have gouged her eyes that a moment ago he had loved so much, would have crushed those cheeks devoid of freshness. He continued going up with Mme. Verdurin, that is to say to draw further away with each step from Odette, who was going down in the other direction. At the end of a second it had been many hours since they had parted. The painter remarked to Swann that Napoleon III had slipped away a moment after her. "It was certainly agreed between them that they would meet at the foot of the cliff, but they didn't want to say good-bye together to keep up appearances. She is his mistress." The unknown young man began to cry. Swann tried to console him. "After all, she was right," he said to him in wiping away his tears and removing his fez to make him more at ease. "I've advised her to do it many times. Why be sad? He was obviously the man who could understand her." Thus Swann spoke to himself,

for the young man whom he had not been able to identify at first was
also him; like certain novelists, he had distributed his own personality
between two characters, the one who was dreaming the dream, and
another whom he saw in front of him sporting a fez.

As for Napoleon III, it was to Forcheville that some vague association of ideas, then a certain modification of the baron's usual
physiognomy, and lastly the broad ribbon of the Legion of Honour
across his breast, had made Swann give that name; in reality, and in
everything that the person who appeared in his dream represented
and recalled to him, it was indeed Forcheville. For, from an incomplete and changing set of images, Swann in his sleep drew false
deductions, enjoying at the same time, momentarily, such a creative
power that he was able to reproduce himself by a simple act of
division, like certain lower organisms; with the warmth he felt in his
own palm he modelled the hollow of a strange hand which he thought
he was clasping, and out of feelings and impressions of which he was
not yet conscious he brought about sudden reversals which, by their
logical entailments, led at the point designated in Swann's sleep to
the character required to receive his love or make him wake up. All at
once a black night fell, a tocsin sounded, people ran past him,
escaping from their blazing homes; Swann heard the noise of the
waves which surged and his heart which, with the same violence, beat
anxiously in his breast. All at once the palpitations of his heart
redoubled in speed, he felt a pain, an inexplicable nausea. A peasant,
covered with burns, flung at him as he passed: "Ask Charlus where
Odette went to finish the evening with her friend. He was with her at
other times and she tells him everything. It was they who started the
fire." It was his valet, come to awaken him, saying:

"Sir, it's eight o'clock, and the barber is here; I've told him to come
back in an hour." (1:411–13)

[Il se trompait. Il devait la revoir une fois encore, quelques semaines
plus tard. Ce fut en dormant, dans le crépuscule d'un rêve. Il se
promenait avec Mme. Verdurin, le docteur Cottard, un jeune
homme en fez qu'il ne pouvait identifier, le peintre, Odette,
Napoléon III et mon grand-père, sur un chemin qui suivait la mer et
la surplombait à pic tantôt de très haut, tantôt de quelques mètres
seulement, de sorte qu'on montait et redescendait constamment; ceux
des promeneurs qui redescendaient déjà n'étaient plus visibles à ceux
qui montaient encore, le peu de jour qui restât faiblissait et il semblait
alors qu'une nuit noire allait s'étendre immédiatement. Par moments
les vagues sautaient jusqu'au bord et Swann sentait sur sa joue des
éclaboussures glacées. Odette lui disait de les essuyer, il ne pouvait

pas et en était confus vis-à-vis d'elle, ainsi que d'être en chemise de nuit. Il espérait qu'à cause de l'obscurité on ne s'en rendait pas compte, mais cependant Mme. Verdurin le fixa d'un regard étonné durant un long moment pendant lequel il vit sa figure se déformer, son nez s'allonger et qu'elle avait de grandes moustaches. Il se détourna pour regarder Odette, ses joues étaient pâles, avec des petits points rouges, ses traits tirés, cernés, mais elle le regardait avec des yeux pleins de tendresse prêts à se détacher comme des larmes pour tomber sur lui et il se sentait l'aimer tellement qu'il aurait voulu l'emmener tout de suite. Tout d'un coup Odette tourna son poigner, regarda une petite montre et dit: "Il faut que je m'en aille," elle prenait congé de tout le monde, de la même façon, sans prendre à part Swann, sans lui dire où elle le reverrait le soir ou un autre jour. Il n'osa pas le lui demander, il aurait voulu la suivre et était obligé, sans se retourner vers elle, de répondre en souriant à une question de Mme. Verdurin, mais son cœur battait horriblement, il éprouvait de la haine pour Odette, il aurait voulu crever ses yeux qu'il aimait tant tout à l'heure, écraser ses joues sans fraîcheur. Il continuait à monter avec Mme. Verdurin, c'est-à-dire à s'éloigner à chaque pas d'Odette, qui descendait en sens inverse. Au bout d'une second, il y eut beaucoup d'heures qu'elle était partie. Le peintre fit remarquer à Swann que Napoléon III s'était éclipsé un instant après elle. "C'était certainement entendu entre eux, ajouta-t-il, ils ont du se rejoindre en bas de la côte mais n'ont pas voulu dire adieu ensemble à cause des convenances. Elle est sa maîtresse." Le jeune homme inconnu se mit à pleurer. Swann essaya de le consoler. "Après tout elle a raison," lui dit-il en lui essuyant les yeux et en lui ôtant son fez pour qu'il fût plus à son aise. "Je le lui ai conseillé dix fois. Pourquoi en être triste? C'était bien l'homme qui pouvait la comprendre." Ainsi Swann se parlait-il à lui-même, car le jeune homme qu'il n'avait pu identifier d'abord était aussi lui; comme certains romanciers, il avait distribué sa personnalité à deux personnages, celui qui faisait le rêve, et un qu'il voyait devant lui coiffé d'un fez.

Quant à Napoléon III, c'est à Forcheville que quelque vague association d'idées, puis une certaine modification dans la physiono-mie habituelle du baron, enfin le grand cordon de la Légion d'honneur en sautoir, lui avaient fait donner ce nom; mais en réalité, et pour tout ce que le personnage présent dans le rêve lui représentait et lui rappelait, c'était bien Forcheville. Car, d'images incomplètes et changeantes Swann endormi tirait des déductions fausses, ayant d'ailleurs momentanément un tel pouvoir créateur qu'il se repro-duisait par simple division comme certains organismes inférieurs; avec la chaleur sentie de sa propre paume il modelait le creux d'une main étrangère qu'il croyait serrer et, de sentiments et d'impressions dont il n'avait pas conscience encore, faisait naître comme des péripéties qui, par leur enchaînement logique, amèneraient à point nommé dans le sommeil de Swann le personnage nécessaire pour recevoir son amour ou provoquer son réveil. Une nuit noire se fit tout d'un coup, sauvant des maisons en flammes; Swann entendait le bruit des vagues qui sautaient et son cœur qui, avec la même violence, battait d'anxiété dans sa poitrine. Tout d'un coup ses palpitations de cœur redoublèrent de vitesse, il éprouva une soufrance, une nausée inexplicable; un paysan couvert de brûlures lui jetait en passant: "Venez demander à Charlus où Odette est allée finir la soirée avec son camarade, il a été avec elle autre fois et elle lui dit tout. C'est eux qui ont mis le feu." C'était son valet de chambre qui venait l'éveiller et lui disait:

"Monsieur, il est huit heures et le coiffeur est là, je lui ai dit de repasser dans une heure.] (1:372–4)

The dream's setting is important in several respects. In the *Recherche*, the seashore cannot fail to evoke the name of "Balbec," the locale that will be decisive for Marcel's own erotic and social life, beginning with his first visit there in the next volume. As are many other incidents in "Un amour de Swann," this episode in Swann's life is proleptic for Marcel's to come.[33] More immediately, however, the sea is associated with Odette's recent year-long absence on cruises with the Verdurins and several of "the faithful." The stinging spray from the ocean thus signifies the insult he has sustained from the voyages, just as his helplessness and embarrassment at being out in public clad only in his nightshirt reinforce his and our conviction of the degradation into which his relations with Odette have plunged him. The walk along the shore begins at twilight, but by the end, night is well advanced, since there is some indication that Odette has by then spent the entire evening with a man ("Odette est allée finir la soirée avec son camarade" – a highly ambiguous designation in the context). Again, the reference is clearly to Swann's passion for Odette, which he believes to have waned (like the daylight in the dream). This judgment the dream, a symptom of Swann's ongoing anxiety about Odette's relations with Forcheville, seemingly denies. As the action makes plain, the dream is a more or less transparent allegory of Swann's amorous life at its current impasse. It reveals his continuing desire for Odette, alongside his recognition that he possesses no means for gratifying it because of Odette's aloofness.

Who are the figures represented in the dream? Numerous characters are present, including several members of the Verdurin "clan," the narrator's grandfather, and, somewhat anomalously on first inspection, Napoleon III. The large number of characters can be seen to distribute the dream's action across virtually the whole of Swann's psychic and social life, which has traversed the entire world of the ruling classes of the Second Empire and the Third Republic, as well as the provincial bourgeois milieu into which he was born (here figured principally in Marcel's grandfather, although it is well to recall that the Verdurins themselves originally sprang from this same class fraction). But the principals are four in number and thus lend themselves to schematization in the standard Greimassian model (see diagram 2.1).[34]

Swann's impotence is manifest, for he is powerless to prevent Odette's sneaking off to rendezvous with Napoleon/Forche- ville. This latter is Swann's semantic opposite or contradictory, combining political with sexual success. The doubling of this figure is required by the dual register in which the sign func- tions, since Forcheville alone could only represent an erotic, not a social threat. Similarly, Odette's desirability, her quite palpable physical attractiveness, is negated by the startling transfiguration of Mme. Verdurin into a man, an event that signifies Swann's anxieties about Odette's possible lesbian inclinations (the mistress assuming the role of masculine lover), while looking forward to the later episodes of sexual poly- valence that will become increasingly important to the novel as a whole from *Sodome et Gomorrhe* onwards. Mme. Verdurin's doubling in gender thus parallels the socio-sexual doubling of Napoleon/Forcheville.

As for the combined terms, it requires no particular ingenuity to recognize Charlus's place as the so-called "neutral term" in the dream's semantic schema – or indeed that of the entire narrative as it would be understood by someone as

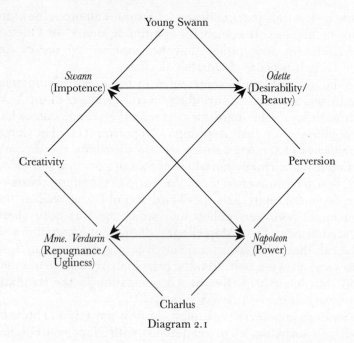

Diagram 2.1

militantly heterosexual (in this he is a rarity in the novel) as Swann. How Charlus can also be a figure of power we shall discover momentarily. That he shares many qualities with Mme. Verdurin – this is the source of their subsequent rivalry – no reader of the *Recherche* is likely to doubt.

Concerning the opposed terms of "creativity" and "perversion," it need only be remarked that here, as throughout the novel, they are composed of precisely the values assigned them by Swann's somatic imagination. Swann and Mme. Verdurin (he explicitly on the narrator's authority: "like certain novelists, he had distributed his own personality between two characters"; "from an incomplete and changing set of images, Swann in his sleep drew false deductions, enjoying at the same time, momentarily, such a creative power that he was able to reproduce himself by a simple act of division, like certain lower organisms") evince the power to produce new images, to alter the shape of reality, in short, to produce works of art. Those who have celebrated art's triumph over society and over life's disappointments in the novel's narration of Marcel's career ought perhaps to consider more carefully the implication that what makes creativity possible is a combination of the repugnant and the impotent. If art is valorized in the *Recherche* – and no one could entirely deny that it is – this is scarcely a fact from which one can draw comfort.

Similarly, while this text generally denounces perversion as such, Marcel's often remarked voyeurism, his odd fascination with the horrors he encounters (ostensibly by chance – first at Monjouvain, later on the stairway above the courtyard in the Hôtel de Guermantes, and ultimately in Jupien's brothel), bespeaks both the curious attractiveness of these scenes to his imagination and the need to maintain his superior position over the objects of his gaze, who are seen without their seeing back. Here, of course, that which is elsewhere designated perverse is figured in the illicit heterosexual union of Odette with Napoleon/Forcheville. Marking heterosexuality in this way is comprehensible in the context of Swann's jealousy, which is predominantly towards men. Only when Marcel replaces Swann as the narrative's focus and Odette is replaced by Albertine, does the novel realize the full implications of these semantic possibilities.

Finally, we come to that most crucial element in the Greimassian schema, the so-called "complex" or "ideal" term, that which represents the resolution of the basic narrative and ideological tensions generated by the text. If we conceive the dream in classical Freudian fashion, it is not difficult to see how the figure of Young Swann (the man in the fez) represents the fulfillment of a wish and thus the management of an otherwise intractable problem in the hapless Swann's waking life. The mature dreamer's capacity to comfort the tearful young man signifies Swann's indifference to Odette's infidelities, a condition he has ostensibly reached when the dream occurs. On this level, then, the dream asserts what Swann wishes to confirm to himself: that he was once (as a less mature man) in a state of inconsolable grief over Odette, but that now he can regard her liaison with Forcheville dispassionately, as even a magnanimous act on his part: "I've advised her to do it many times. Why be sad? He was obviously the man who could understand her."

That this reading of the dream's function as the fulfillment of a wish is insufficient requires no speculation: the dream itself challenges it in its subsequent course. The scene of consolation and resignation that concludes the initial action is followed by another sequence of events, a kind of narrative coda. It not only adds to the materials already presented but re-evaluates the entire structure of jealousy and its abatement that the first action has produced. In this secondary revision of the narrative's contents, a quite different desire operates to resolve the contradictions in Swann's situation. Although no explicit evidence confirms the fact, it seems probable that Napoleon/Forcheville has been destroyed in the fire set by Charlus and Odette. On this construal, the dream fulfills Swann's equally powerful wish to eradicate his rival. He does so via Charlus, who is doubtless able to act as a screen figure for Swann himself because Swann has in the past often employed him to watch over and entertain Odette – as indeed he will continue to do after he marries her. Recall that the man dressed in a white linen suit whom Marcel sees with Odette during the walk by Tansonville turns out to be Charlus, and that Marcel's grandfather assumes Charlus is Odette's lover (1:154–5; 140). Swann thinks no such thing, probably because he knows the truth about Charlus's sexual preferences. Designating Charlus as his more powerful other could, of course, signal Swann's deeper anxiety about his own sexual proclivities, but nothing elsewhere in the novel indicates that such could be the case. To repeat, Swann is, like Marcel in the text, remarkable precisely for his singularly heterosexual desires.[35]

The Charlus narrative would seem, rather, to contradict and to be irreconcilable with the previously articulated wish for resignation and consolation. This co-habitation of two incompatible wishes in a single text (the wish to be resigned versus the wish to eliminate the rival) illustrates perfectly the irreducible antagonism that characterizes Swann's affective state, despite his professed indifference towards Odette. Swann's

inability to resolve these contradictory feelings will produce
the unsatisfactory compromise of his marriage – unsatisfactory
because by marrying Odette, Swann neither destroys his rival
(Odette will marry Forcheville after Swann's death), nor
attains the equipoise projected onto himself as the elder
dreamer. He will continue to be plagued by doubts about
Odette's fidelity in the past, as well as burdened by their
memory when he takes up with another woman who arouses
his jealousy anew just because Odette had once done so (see
1:563–6; 513–16).[36]

To read Swann's dream as an allegorical figuration of his
love for Odette, however complexly that love is presented, does
not exhaust this episode's significance. Without distorting the
Freudian terminology unduly, it is possible to see the erotic
reading as merely the dream's manifest content in relation to
the larger narrative (i.e., the *Recherche* itself) in which it is
embedded. Ultimately, the dream may not be about Swann's
love at all, or, to put the point less provocatively, Swann's love
is not merely to do with Swann. As any number commentators
have observed, and as Proust himself attested, the story of
Swann and Odette was meant to sound the major theme of the
narrator's development early on in the text, forecasting
Marcel's progress up through the various levels of the Faubourg Saint-Germain and his abandonment of society to
pursue his own ill-fated love for Albertine Simonet. It would
thus be perfectly licit to interpret the figural system of Swann's
dream as projecting the general problematic of the entire
Recherche.

That said, it remains to locate the center of this problematic.
The canonical view has held that it resides in the Narrator's
discovery of his vocation to art, that Marcel in effect succeeds
where Swann fails. While the latter never makes significant
progress in his essay on Vermeer, Marcel manages, somewhat
fortuitously to be sure, to realize the secret of artistic creation.
By renouncing once and for all society's temptations and the
lure of the erotic, he is able to compose the text we have been
reading. I'll have something to say about this interpretation of
the *Recherche*'s culminating episode in the final chapter below.

For now I want simply to offer an alternative hypothesis about this text's fundamental locus of value by proposing a second reading of Swann's dream, one that construes it not as an allegory of love, but as a fable about the political structures and history of the Third Republic.

One's suspicion along these lines ought to be aroused quite naturally by the appearance of Napoleon III. In the dream itself, Swann (or is it the Narrator ventriloquizing himself through the dreamer? for present purposes it scarcely matters which) reflects on the odd conflation of his rival Forcheville with the Emperor:

As for Napoleon III, it was to Forcheville that some vague association of ideas, then a certain modification of the baron's usual physiognomy, and lastly the broad ribbon of the Legion of Honour across his breast, had made Swann give that name; in reality and in everything that the person who appeared in his dream represented and recalled to him, it was indeed Forcheville.

[Quant à Napoléon III, c'est à Forcheville que quelque vague association d'idées, puis une certain modification dans la physionomie habituelle du baron, enfin le grand cordon de la Légion d'honneur en sautoir, lui avaient fait donner ce nom; mais en réalité, et pour tout ce que le personnage présent dans le rêve lui représentait et lui rappelait, c'était bien Forcheville.]

This explains why Napoleon III should be associated with Forcheville, but not why the former should have appeared in the dream in the first place. If this figure is Swann's (as we discover in the end, his deadly) rival, then it must be asked: in what sense would Swann feel himself threatened by the deposed Emperor?

Two factors are relevant to solving this puzzle. First is the infamous difficulty of establishing a chronology for the entire novel, and for "Un amour de Swann" in particular. Later volumes seem to be more coherently organized around an actual historical chronology (notably *Le côté de Guermantes*, which can be dated with some precision by reference to the Dreyfus Affair as occurring between 1897 and 1899; and *Le temps retrouvé*, most of which occurs between 1916 and 1925, as references to the war years make reasonably certain). Allusions to historical events in this text suggest that Swann's affair with Odette occurs sometime during the 1880s. But the *Recherche*'s internal chronology (using the dating of *Le côté de Guermantes* as a reliable indicator for calculating Marcel's approximate birthdate, which occurs either just as Swann's affair is beginning or not many years after) demands that this episode take place in 1877–8 at the latest.[37] Why this discrepancy?

If we accept the hypothesis that the *Recherche* narrates the evolution of social structures during the Third Republic, then "Un amour de Swann" is meant generally to represent the long period of political and social instability extending from the Republic's birth in 1871, through perhaps the Boulangist crisis of 1889.[38] The Boulanger episode was the final thrust by the entrenched forces of reaction prior to the Dreyfus Affair's explosion; it ushered in a period of political consolidation among the Opportunist forces that established the firm bases for the conservative republicanism that would dominate French political life until the 1930s.[39] This is to say that the irresolvability of the chronology was probably deliberate on Proust's part. It was an attempt to make Swann's love into an allegorical figure for the chronic social and political instability over the first two decades in the Republic's life.

That this historical reading of "Un amour de Swann" is not simply fanciful can be established by considering a second aspect of Swann's dream, which condenses the historical conditions just referred to into a fable of jealousy, resentment, and either reconciliation (in the dream's first movement) or revenge (in its *dénouement*). The love affair between Swann and Odette is not merely about sex and gender relations. It is at the same time a story of class relations, or more properly, class struggles. Swann's class origins are explicitly and frequently established throughout the novel: he hails from the upper bourgeoisie, specifically from its financial sector (see 1:17; 16), and he is able to leave his daughter Gilberte a considerable legacy (see III:677,701; IV:240,262). But what of Odette? We know little about her early life, save that she was at one time an actress of sorts, and that when Swann is first introduced to her she is a *cocotte* (1:213; 192). We also learn, though on what

authority this information is given remains unclear, that she
had been sold as a young child to a wealthy Englishman (1:399;
361). Scarcely anything else is revealed of her origins, but
much can be inferred from her position as a prostitute.

When Swann commences his relations with Odette, he is
already having an affair with what the English translation calls
"a seamstress" but the French text simply designates "une
petite ouvrière" (1:237; 214). His sexual predilections run
towards lower-class women, as indeed would not have been
unusual for bourgeois in this era. Prostitution in France during
the second half of the nineteenth century underwent some
marked transformations, not least being the wider range of
options open to bourgeois men for satisfying their increasingly
varied erotic tastes. Seamstresses, salesgirls in millinery and
flower shops, bar maids – women in a wide variety of low-
income occupations and public locations came to replace the
more closely regulated *filles de maison* who lived and worked in
the older *maisons closes*.[40]

Atop this occupational hierarchy were the *grandes courtisanes*
or *cocottes* who became prominent during the Second Empire.
These latter enjoyed considerable privilege and a level of
material security, often living alone in comfortable if modest
houses and apartments paid for by their lovers. But all prostitutes, however well off, remained at the mercy of their clients,
only rarely rising above the station to which they had either
been born or into which they had fallen through divorce or
widowhood. T. J. Clark's observation on the social situation of
prostitutes in late nineteenth-century France makes the point
well:

Relations between prostitute and client involved, among other
things, matters of social class. They often meant a transgression of
normal class divisions – a curious exposure of the self to someone
inferior, someone lamentable. That doubtless lent spice to the trans-
action, but only if it were made part of a set of sexual theatricals
which became more cumbersome as the years went on ... the prostitute was obliged to make herself desirable – to run through the
identities in which desire was first encountered by the child. It was a
game in which the woman most often collaborated and to an extent
was trapped; but there were other forces – market forces, essentially –

which threatened to dislodge her from belief in the parts she played. She could be returned quite abruptly to the simple assessment of herself as seller of her own labour power, someone who put physical complaisance on the market and could never be sure what it would fetch. In this sense she belonged to the proletariat as undramatically as Vermeer's loose women.[41]

Swann's erotic attachments, typical for men of his class, are a form of slumming; they are the inverse of his social climbing (which remains entirely free from sexual entanglements). By making Odette a prostitute at this moment, the novel hints broadly at her class position and thus at the social significance of Swann's love affair. His relationship with Odette can be seen as a fantasy of bourgeois desire: the harmony or collaboration between antagonistic classes. Not for nothing is the "little phrase" from Vinteuil's sonata dubbed "the national anthem of their love" (1:238; 215). It will be recalled that the adoption of the *Marseillaise* as the French national anthem and the declaration of Quatorze Juillet as a national holiday were both innovations of the early Third Republic, powerful symbols of the bourgeoisie's program to stamp its image on the nation and lay claim to the patriotic mantle contested by both Bonapartists and royalists.[42]

But the course of true love – or bourgeois politics – never did run smooth. Swann's incapacity to control Odette, his jealousy over her infidelity, can be construed in straightforwardly political and historical terms to indicate the bourgeoisie's tenuous hold over governmental – and to some extent social – power. His rival for Odette's attentions is none other than a representative of the nobility, the Comte de Forcheville, whom Odette introduces into the Verdurin "clan" (1:273; 246). Odette's fickleness is, on this account, a figure for the political volatility of the French masses, i.e., of the nation as such, whose ultimate loyalties towards the royalist aristocracy or the republican bourgeoisie remained in the balance right up to the moment of Boulangism.

Why, then, does Forcheville first appear in the guise of Napoleon III? Two possibilities present themselves; which to adopt will depend upon how one construes the conflagration at

the end of the dream. First, and most obviously, opposition to
the bourgeois republic, particularly during the 1870s, was not
restricted to the legitimist or Orleanist nobility. Though
severely compromised by the defeat at Sedan, Bonapartists
remained a far from negligible force on the political landscape.[43] One gets a glimpse of this intra-class antagonism in
"Un amour de Swann" in the Princesse des Laumes's disparag-
ing remarks concerning the Ienas and their Empire furniture
(1:368–9; 332–3). Swann, however, in the dream's first episode,
counsels accepting the liaison between Odette and Napoleon:
"He was obviously the man who could understand her.
[C'était bien l'homme qui pouvait la comprendre.]" A standard view of the socio-political basis of the imperial state
during the 1850s and 1860s, first advanced by Marx in the
Eighteenth Brumaire, was that the bourgeoisie abdicated its
claims to direct political power and allowed Bonaparte and the
bureaucracy to rule in its place.[44] Bonaparte was repeatedly
reconfirmed in popular plebescites, and class conflict (of the
sort that had pitted workers against bourgeois from 1848
through 1851) was generally at a low ebb under his rule.
Swann's resignation to Odette's infidelity thus signifies the
bourgeoisie's acquiescence in the Bonapartist project, a heark-
ening back to the days of the Second Empire and that regime's
internal stability (not to mention its economic prosperity).

As we have already seen, however, this is not the dream
narrative's final word. The fire at the end destroys, I have
suggested, Swann's immediate rival for Odette's affections. If
this be Napoleon III, then the conflagration might well refer to
the war of 1870, which drove Bonaparte from the throne and
led to the proclamation of the republic. The badly burned
peasant who tells Swann what has happened would represent
the ravages of the war itself, which were disproportionately felt
in the countryside. But this interpretation leaves out an important factor: to wit, that the fire is started by Odette and
Charlus, i.e., by representatives of the popular masses and the
feudal nobility, respectively. No respectable account of the war
with Prussia could ever maintain that it was caused by a class
alliance between these two against the imperial state. On the

contrary, it is generally conceded that Bonaparte himself had blundered into the war, and that the total military collapse over which he presided led to his political downfall. If the fire's instigators are "le peuple" and at least a sector of the aristocracy, then the fire must signify something other than the defeat of 1870.

The immediate occasion for Swann's dream had been a chance encounter on an autobus with Mme. Cottard, who had testified to Odette's loyalty to him. Mme. Cottard herself had recently returned to Paris from a year-long cruise with the Verdurins and against their advice, for "Paris, so M. Verdurin affirmed, was in the throes of revolution ..." (1:406–7) [... M. Verdurin assurait être en révolution ...] (1:368). To what can this rather imprecise and seemingly insignificant remark refer? Again, if this moment in Swann's and Odette's love is pushed back to the early 1870s, it is just possible that the referent of "Paris ... in the throes of revolution" could be the Commune, the only authentically revolutionary moment in French history during the last half of the nineteenth century. But this seems unlikely both chronologically (for the reasons already given) and thematically, if, as seems reasonable, the "revolution" feared by M. Verdurin figures as the fire at the end of Swann's dream. I'll propose instead that the "revolutionary" fervor indicated here can most plausibly be construed as the Boulangist crisis of the late 1880s, which briefly (although in retrospect, probably not seriously) threatened the constitutional republic's existence.[45]

Boulanger's meteoric rise to fame was fueled by a combination of populist nationalism and aristocratic *ressentiment* (not to mention wealth, which bankrolled his national publicity campaign). As one recent historian of the period has put it: "What united Boulanger's supporters was the longing for revenge, glorification of the nation betrayed by the opportunist bourgeoisie. The political parties were divisive; what offered unity was *la patrie*."[46] On this account, Boulangism was a direct repudiation of bourgeois republican rule; it raised the specter of a revanchist coup on the Bonapartist model, as well as the possibility of an alliance between the popular masses and the royalist aristocracy.[47] Swann's extreme anxiety is therefore understandable, since the ideological and political hegemony of his class, only recently and tenuously achieved, has been placed at risk. At the same time, and from the perspective of the Narrator describing Swann's affair many years after the fact (subsequent to the Dreyfus Affair but prior to the First World War, it is reasonable to assume, since this section of the *Recherche* was published in 1913), Boulanger's ignominious flight to Brussels in April 1889, was the *causa efficiens* for the consolidation of conservative bourgeois power. Boulangism's failure put paid to any significant threat to bourgeois rule for nearly a decade. The fire that does away with Napoleon/Forcheville temporarily clears the field of Swann's (i.e., the bourgeoisie's) only consequent rivals. The net result of the Boulanger episode turns out to be a blessing in disguise.

It is of course possible that Napoleon/Forcheville was not destroyed in the fire, and even, as Hicks and Bell assert, that he helped Odette to set it.[48] This seems implausible on the face of it, since the "they" in the final sentence of direct discourse that closes the dream proper would appear to refer to the "he" and "she" of the previous sentence, who can only be Charlus and Odette: "Venez demander à Charlus où Odette est allée finir la soirée avec son camarade, il a été avec elle autrefois et elle lui dit tout" (1:374). Surely the obvious sense here is that "[Odette] tells [Charlus] everything." Hence, the next sentence, "C'est eux qui ont mis le feu," must be construed as "It was [Charlus and Odette] who set the fire."

But if we grant Hicks's and Bell's reading, how would this alter the political allegory of the dream? The alliance of Odette and Charlus would then become one between her and Napoleon/Forcheville, that is, between the working class and a composite sign representing Bonapartism and royalism, an even more apt figure for the political danger of Boulangism, since Boulanger was, in popular iconography, commonly associated with the Napoleonic myth.[49] This leaves the matter of the rival's destruction still in doubt, but it would not be impossible, no specific evidence to the contrary being given, that Napoleon/Forcheville both started and perished in the fire

– an interesting reading politically speaking, since it expresses almost exactly Boulangism's origin and outcome. The threat to parliamentary democracy ultimately rebounded against the forces of reaction who had launched it in the first place.

Once again, at its deepest level, the dream reveals the fulfillment of a wish, although a manifestly contradictory and dangerous one, as the revival of nationalism during the Dreyfus Affair would reveal. But that is part of another story, one that can be left for the exposition of later episodes in Proust's novel. For now, it is sufficient to recognize this ultimate level of fantasy in Swann's dream as signifying the historical project of the French bourgeoisie's progressive sectors to eliminate their principal class antagonist for political (and to a lesser extent social) power: the aristocratic military caste whose capacity to mobilize popular opinion was far from negligible through the late 1880s. The debacle of Boulangism accomplished just that, paving the way for a cross-class alliance between the bourgeoisie and some sectors of the nobility, the dream figure for which is Swann's entrusting (if that's the right word for it) Odette to Charlus. Charlus poses no sexual threat to Swann's relationship, just as those nobles who aligned themselves with the Opportunists had ceased to be contenders for political power. After the elections of 1889, the stage would be set for a long period of bourgeois hegemony in government and class compromise in economic policy symbolized by the Méline Tariff of 1892.

All, however, is not blissful for France's conquering bourgeoisie at this moment. Swann's melancholy, his fecklessness, his entrapment in a passion that gives him no pleasure but that he is powerless to resist – all these features of his subsequent life are already apparent in the episode's final words. Nowhere are the pathologies of the bourgeois social project more nakedly evident than in Swann's culminating judgment on his life's great passion: "'To think that I've wasted years of my life, that I've longed to die, that I've experienced my greatest love, for a woman who didn't appeal to me, who wasn't even my kind!'" (1:415) ["Dire que j'ai gâché des années de ma vie, qu j'ai voulu mourir, qu j'ai eu mon plus grand amour, pour une

femme qui ne me plaisait pas, qui n'était pas mon genre!"]
(1:375) Like the republic she has come to symbolize in Swann's
nightmare, Odette will acquire many attributes of bourgeois
respectability, including, not incidentally, a certain veneer of
culture. However tedious and unglamorous the task, the
republican bourgeoisie recognized that its destiny lay in com-
manding the popular masses' loyalty through education and
the extension of democratic freedoms and rights. Swann discovers that marriage with Odette delivers him from suspicion
about her present conduct, precisely because he no longer
wishes to dominate her directly. (Only in his authentically
erotic involvements is he jealous, because there the issue
remains physical control over the beloved evidenced in her
constant sexual fidelity – in this respect precisely analogous to
Marcel's relations with Albertine.) Similarly, the republican
bourgeoisie learned that the key to holding political power in a
parliamentary democracy lay in securing ideological hegemony. The truth of this lesson, both in history and in the
Recherche, would be confirmed by France's next major social
crisis, the Dreyfus Affair, and by the First World War, which
would provide the ultimate test of the ruling order's ideological
and political strength.[50]

MAPPING SOCIAL CLASS

What can be said in general terms about the class structure in
the *Recherche*? The following enumeration of characters and
class identifications, along with a schematic account of the
novel's chronology, does not claim to be exhaustive. It is,
however, sufficiently representative to indicate the principal
class forces portrayed in the novel and to obtain a preliminary
overview of the narrative's historical trajectory.

Proust's portrait of class distinctions is anything but one-
dimensional. The bourgeoisie constitutes a recognizable entity
in the *Recherche* that is, up to the final volume, clearly demar-
cated from the hereditary nobility and from the working and
serving classes. But like the nobility itself, this class is sharply
and minutely divided into competing fractions. So much is

already clear in the opening pages when Marcel characterizes the world of his youth, the provincial bourgeois milieu of Combray.

The principal representatives of the Combray bourgeoisie are Marcel's family. Their focal point is Aunt Léonie, the widowed invalid whose visible prosperity derives from agricultural rents (1:116, 106). Marcel's father, we observed in the previous chapter, is a state functionary; his mother, it may be inferred from her family's material comfort and the freedom from the necessity to labor, comes from the secure rentier stratum. As a group – Marcel's father seems exceptional in this regard – they are pious and deeply conservative, a fact that is foregrounded in a passage describing the family's attitude towards Swann:

Our utter ignorance of the brilliant social life which Swann led was, of course, due in part to his own reserve and discretion, but also to the fact that middle-class people in those days took what was almost a Hindu view of society, which they held to consist of sharply defined castes, so that everyone at his birth found himself called to that station in life which his parents already occupied, and from which nothing, save the accident of an exceptional career or of a "good" marriage, could extract you and translate you to a superior caste. M. Swann the elder had been a stockbroker; and so "young Swann" found himself immured for life in a caste whose members' fortunes, as in a category of tax-payers, varied between such and such limits of income. One knew the people with whom his father had associated, and so one knew his own associates, the people with whom he was "in a position to mix" ... had it been absolutely essential to apply to Swann a social coefficient peculiar to himself, as distinct from all the other sons of other stockbrokers in his father's position, his coefficient would have been rather lower than theirs, because, being very simple in his habits, and having always had a craze for "antiques" and pictures, he now lived and amassed his collections in an old house which my grandmother longed to visit but which was situated on the Quai d'Orléans, a neighborhood in which my great-aunt thought it most degrading to be quartered. (1:16–17)

[L'ignorance où nous étions de cette brillante vie mondaine que menait Swann tenait évidemment en partie à la réserve et à la discrétion de son caractère, mais aussi à ce que les bourgeois d'alors se faisaient de la société une idée un peu hindoue et la considéraient

comme composée de castes fermées où chacun, dès sa naissance, se
trouvait placé dans le rang qu'occupaient ses parents, et d'où rien, à
moins des hasards d'une carrière exceptionnelle ou d'un mariage
inespéré, ne pouvait vous tirer pour vous faire pénétrer dans une caste
supérieure. M. Swann, le père, était agent de change; le "fils Swann"
se trouvait faire partie pour toute sa vie d'une caste où les fortunes,
comme dans une catégorie de contribuables, variaient entre tel et tel
revenu. On savait quelles avaient été les fréquentations de son père,
on savait donc quelles étaient les siennes, avec quelles personnes il
était "en situation" de frayer ... si l'on avait voulu à toute force
appliquer à Swann un coefficient social qui lui fût personnel, entre les
autres fils d'agents de situation égale à celle de ses parents, ce
coefficient eût été pour lui un peu inférieur parce que, très simple de
façon et ayant toujours eu une "toquade" d'objets anciens et de
peinture, il demeurait maintenant dans un vieil hôtel où il entassait
ses collections et que ma grand-mère rêvait de visiter, mais qui était
situé quai d'Orléans, quartier que ma grand-tante trouvait infamant
d'habiter.] (1:16)

The reference to caste – however ethnographically imprecise –
reveals a fundamental feature about this provincial bourgeois
world, one that is not incidental to Marcel's own recollection of
it. In the eyes of its ruling elites (and, if Françoise is any
indication, its servants as well) this society's structure is utterly
static. The image of an unchanging social hierarachy would of
course have been much more powerful in the country than in
the city, but the historical moment of "Combray" is an equally
important determinant. We know that these scenes must come
before the Dreyfus Affair and after the bourgeoisie's accession
to undisputed parliamentary dominance, i.e., during a period
of relative social quiescence and stability. Everything about
Combray confirms the impression that it is a class-divided
world exhibiting no outward signs of class conflict. That it lies
definitively in the past is not merely a fact of the Narrator's
consciousness; it is equally a social fact produced by the subsequent course of French history shaped by, among other
things, the changing nature of the bourgeois social project.

This project is most clearly delineated in "Combray"
through three characters outside Marcel's family circle:
Swann, Legrandin, and Bloch. Swann's class background and

career are familiar enough: the only son of an immensely wealthy stockbroker, by the time the novel opens he has become a dilettante and socialite who has made, in the eyes of both his aristocratic friends and Marcel's family, an extremely unfortunate marriage. Bloch is a different matter. Of Jewish extraction (as is Swann, of course), he first appears in the guise of a pretentious aesthete. His subsequent career will reveal his social insecurities, which derive principally, it seems clear, from his ethnic background. That Bloch has reason to be sensitive is driven home by the cruel treatment he receives from Marcel's grandfather, who indulges his antisemitism without compunction – much to Marcel's chagrin. Of the three, the most interesting is Legrandin, an engineer and a socially ambitious snob. When we first encounter him, he professes to be a radical republican, consistently making "violent attacks upon the nobility, going so far as to blame the Revolution for not having guillotined them all" (1:73) [des attaques aussi violentes contre les nobles, allant jusqu'à reprocher à la Révolution de ne les avoir pas tous guillotinés] (1:67). Later on, as is well known, he will illictly appropriate the *particule* and style himself "Legrandin de Méséglise." In each of these cases, Combray's "caste" structure is implicitly undermined. The apparently secure and changeless provincial bourgeois world already contains elements that will lead to its supercession.

Presiding over this provincial bourgeois enclave are the Guermantes, who, to be sure, are barely in evidence in the "Combray" section itself, save in the famous "way" of Marcel's family's walks and in the local chapel's monuments to the Guermantes's noble past. The Duchess does appear for a relative's wedding, but the immense social power for which she and her family stand is nowhere apparent here. Marcel's connecting her to Geneviève de Brabant, a figure from the Merovingian epoch, indicates quite clearly the social relations that obtain in this region at this period: the feudal nobility are for the provincial bourgeoisie relics of an ancient past whose position is respected but whose lives and activities scarcely impinge on their own. Combray is, in this sense, a post-revolutionary but essentially pre-republican world, where the penetration of capitalist social relations has not yet altered the basic hierarchy of distinction and rank. Nowhere is this fact more evident than in the position Swann occupies at Combray in comparison to that which he has acquired in Paris.

The novel's diegesis makes this very point. After "Combray" comes "Un amour de Swann," which presents a bourgeois milieu of an altogether different stamp. The dominant social site in the latter episode is the Verdurin salon, a gathering point for well-to-do bohemian bourgeois (later on for Dreyfusards). Mme. Verdurin presides over a socially heterogeneous group of rentiers (the Verdurins themselves, Swann), professionals (Cottard, later Brichot), artists (Elstir, then known as "Biche," the Polish sculptor "Ski," and the nameless pianist), a courtesan with social aspirations (Odette), and at least one titled aristocrat (the Comte de Forcheville).

Ressentiment dominates the Verdurin world, symbolized by the mistress's continual references to the Faubourg Saint-Germain as the domain of "bores." While Proust obviously intended to satirize their pretensions and foibles, he has also given an illuminating portrait of class solidarity among the upwardly mobile urban bourgeoisie. So much is apparent in this section's opening sentences:

To admit you to the "little nucleus," the "little group," the "little clan," at the Verdurins', one condition sufficed, but that one was indispensable: you must give tacit adherence to a Creed one of whose articles was that the young pianist whom Mme. Verdurin had taken under her patronage that year and of whom she said "Really, it oughtn't to be allowed to play Wagner as well as that!" licked both Plante and Rubinstein hollow, and that Dr. Cottard was a more brilliant diagnostician than Potain. Each "new recruit" whom the Verdurins failed to persuade that the evenings spent by other people, in other houses than theirs, were dull as ditch-water, saw himself banished forthwith. Women being in this respect more rebellious than men, more reluctant to lay aside all worldly curiosity and the desire to find out for themselves whether other salons might not sometimes be as entertaining, and the Verdurins feeling, moreover, that this critical spirit and this demon of frivolity might, by their contagion, prove fatal to the orthodoxy of the little church, they had been obliged to expel, one after another, all those of the "faithful" who were of the female sex. (1:205)

[Pour fair partie du "petit noyau," de "petit groupe," du "petit clan" des Verdurin, une condition était suffisante mais elle était nécessaire: il fallait adhérer tacitement à un Credo dont un des articles était que le jeune pianiste, protégé par Mme. Verdurin cette année-là et dont elle disait: "Ça ne devrait pas être permis de savoir jouer Wagner comme ça!," "enfonçait" à la fois Planté et Rubinstein et que le docteur Cottard avait plus de diagnostic que Potain. Toute "nouvelle recrue" à qui les Verdurin ne pouvaient pas persuader que les soirées des gens qui n'allaient pas chez eux étaient ennuyeuses comme la pluie, se voyait immédiatement exclue. Les femmes étant à cet égard plus rebelles que less hommes à déposer toute curiosité mondaine et l'envie de se renseigner par soi-même sur l'agrément des autres salons, et les Verdurin sentant d'autre part que cet esprit d'examen et ce démon de frivolité pouvait par contagion devenir fatal à l'orthodoxie de la petite église, ils avaient été amenés à rejeter successivement tous les "fidèles" de sexe féminin.] (1:185)

As is made clear in subsequent paragraphs, the pretense of absolute equality among all "the faithful" is a cornerstone of the Verdurin ideology. Unlike the anti-republican world of Combray, the Verdurin salon is unified by its progressive, vehemently anti-aristocratic self-image. The threat posed by Swann is therefore patent: already occupying a higher rung on the social ladder because of his access to the Faubourg Saint-Germain's most exclusive drawing rooms, he cannot be relied upon to honor the code of solidarity binding together the other members of "the little clan." Swann does not share in the sense of social inferiority that drives the Verdurins and their minions on, for he has long since established an identity in the very world that the Verdurins simultaneously denigrate and desire. The entire episode reveals a further differentiation within the ranks of the bourgeoisie itself, one that pits its aristocratic-identified sectors against its putatively more radical republican wing.

Swann's own peregrinations expose the other side of social stratification. His access to the *gratin* is made plain throughout. He once attends a reception at Mme. de Sainte-Euverte's where he meets, after a long absence from this world, his great friend, the Princesse des Laumes (soon to be Duchesse de Guermantes). The aristocratic milieu to which he has ascended is thus figured not only in the bourgeois fantasies about it propagated by the Verdurins; it appears *in propria persona* for the first time in the novel. Moreover, the text indicates what will become increasingly apparent as time passes: that the nobility and the bourgeoisie, however much they are contending for social power, share certain common cultural material. This fact is represented most vividly by Vinteuil's sonata, the signifier of Swann's and Odette's love, which is played at Mme. de Sainte-Euverte's reception. Swann's circulation across this otherwise impermeable class barrier is ratified by the social promiscuity of aesthetic production. (Later on, Marcel will view Elstir's paintings in the Guermantes's Paris residence). Money capital will only become a bourgeois entrance ticket into the Faubourg Saint-Germain late in the novel. Cultural capital allows a select bourgeois fraction to enter this forbidden realm from the first.

While it is not immediately an issue in "Un amour de Swann," with hindsight one can discern the social stakes in Odette's presence at the Verdurins'. A *demi-mondaine*, after her marriage to Swann she will begin to assemble her own salon, drawing upon lessons learned at Mme. Verdurin's feet. Bergotte, a marginal presence in *Du côté de chez Swann*, will become a fixture in Odette's drawing room. She herself will withdraw from the Verdurin milieu, but for the bulk of the novel she will continue to be denied access to that world where her husband can freely move. Although she is the estranged wife of an English nobleman (she is Mme. de Crécy when we first encounter her), in this volume she remains confined to the more or less vulgar environs dictated by her position as a kept woman. Her ridiculous tastes – manifest in the *chinoiserie* with which she surrounds herself at home – reveal her true class origins and indicate the Verdurin salon's comparatively indiscriminate composition. In the volume's final movement, "Nom de pays: le nom," she appears on display in the Bois de Boulogne, an object of Marcel's admiration and desire and the subject of scurrilous gossip among fashionable noblemen (1:455; 413). We might say that Odette is the quintessence of what Gambetta called the *nouvelles couches sociales*, and that her career demonstrates the fluidity of the Third Republic's class boundaries early in its history. Despite the *gratin*'s utter disdain, and contrary to Combray's convictions about the social hierarchy's fixity, *Du côté de chez Swann* argues that French upper-class society's apparent stability is, already in the 1870s and 1880s, beginning to disintegrate. What has been dubbed "the stalemate society" politically was far from being such on the level of social rank.

Social stratification and mobility in the *Recherche* issue not only from the accession of some few bourgeois to aristocratic society – although this is undoubtedly the preponderant tendency. The Faubourg Saint-Germain exhibits as much internal differentiation and rises and falls in fashion as other social regions. Earlier, I remarked on the split between the ancient titled nobility and the Bonapartist *titrés*, a tension that will recur between Saint-Loup and the Prince de Borodino in the Doncières section of *A l'ombre des jeunes filles en fleurs*. In *Le côté de Guermantes*, the Guermantes clan will prove to be divided between its Courvoisier and Guermantes branches, each vying with the other for the pinnacle of prestige and exclusiveness.

Perhaps the surest indication of how the Faubourg Saint-Germain itself is highly stratified appears in the careers of Mme. de Villeparisis and Mme. de Sainte-Euverte. The former was Marcel's grandmother's schoolmate; among his family her hereditary social position is completely unknown. During the first visit to Balbec, even the hotel staff think her no more than a frumpy older woman of no particular distinction. Yet, as Marcel learns, she was born into the Faubourg's very highest reaches, and it is through her that he gains access, first to its lower rungs and ultimately to its current inner sancta. In "Un amour de Swann," Mme. de Sainte-Euverte's drawing room is comparatively exclusive, as indicated by Oriane's and Swann's presence there. But when Marcel attends the reception at the Prince and Princesse de Guermantes's early in *Sodome et Gomorrhe*, it is clear that Mme. de Sainte-Euverte has fallen from favor, since she has to scramble around to obtain promises to attend her own *fête* the following day. To no avail in the end: the promises she extracts are all broken, and her party is a flop. Here, too, social conflict is palpable, albeit within the restricted confines of the urban nobility.

It should be reasonably clear by this point that the *Recherche* enacts a series of jockeyings for social power symbolizing the class struggles in the early Third Republic. These struggles are almost exclusively concerned with the two upper classes, the bourgeoisie and titled nobility. What of the lower classes? One has, in fact, a rich array of characters to choose from, but I shall concentrate on only three: Françoise, Morel, and Jupien. I have selected them because they encompass the three principal tendencies among the non-elite orders historically and in Proust's imaginative social topography.

Françoise is born of peasant stock, and she continues to signify this class throughout the novel. Marcel remarks upon her language (a Breton *patois*), as well as upon her powerful jealousy and her tendency towards brutality. More telling, however, is her deference. Capable of bad temper and extreme moral disapproval (as in her treatment of Albertine when the latter is confined to Marcel's Paris residence), she nonetheless remains utterly faithful to Marcel and his family after Aunt Léonie's death. As was generally true of the French peasantry throughout the nineteenth century, she accepts her social position without a hint of political rebellion. Congruent with the world of Combray where we first encounter her, she symbolizes the pre-republican past that bequeathed a significant legacy of social cohesiveness and political quiescence in the countryside to the republic's bourgeois elites.[51]

Morel is an altogether different case. He comes on stage in Balbec, where he is pursued by Charlus and recognized by Marcel as the son of his Uncle Adolphe's faithful manservant. Morel's musical talent has enabled him to rise from humble origins; he will subsequently employ it, in tandem with the prospect of sexual favors, to obtain Charlus's patronage. In friendship and in love (as later in duty to country), Morel will prove utterly faithless, concerned solely with his own career and social standing. Devoid of loyalty, he represents the deracinated serving classes who were to become one fraction of the *nouvelles couches sociales* under the Third Republic.

The core of this increasingly numerous social stratum is even better illustrated by Jupien. When we first encounter him, he is a shopkeeper in the Hôtel de Guermantes, living off his niece's labors. After the infamous *rencontre* with Charlus witnessed by Marcel, Jupien becomes the former's pimp and, in *Le temps retrouvé*, his guardian. Unlike Morel, he exhibits certain loyalties – at least towards Charlus – but this fact cannot obscure Jupien's calculating and essentially craven personality. His labors on Charlus's behalf are scarcely disinterested, as he schemes to obtain a provider for his niece, and is rewarded with the proprietorship of a male brothel during the First World War. *Petit bourgeois* in origin, he climbs slowly up the economic ladder by catering to the decadent tastes of a wealthy aristocrat. He thus aptly figures a social propensity observed in a variety of other characters, e.g., the hotel manager in Balbec or Aimé: all are parasitic on the upper classes, compelled by their precarious economic position to act the part of servants while lacking the traditional security that an older class of retainers like Françoise enjoyed. Plainly, these new service workers constitute the vestiges of the servant class in the epoch of capitalist social relations.

THE DISCREET CHARM OF THE BOURGEOISIE

It is commonly held that the *Recherche* only intermittently concerns itself with society, by which is meant, in the novel's own terms, the Faubourg Saint-Germain and those who seek to enter it. This impression is enforced by the Narrator's frequent references to *le monde* as a site distinct from the world of his youth, a place outside his family circle where different laws operate. To show that this view of the novel is neither licit nor a discrimination that the text itself rigorously observes, we may consider the structure of *A l'ombre des jeunes filles en fleurs*.

The title indicates what will be the volume's principal thematic focus: eros, in particular Marcel's awakening to sexual desire, which proceeds from his masturbatory episode with Gilberte in a park on the Champs Elysées, to his and Bloch's visit to a brothel, to his desire for the little band of girls at Balbec, and finally to his attempt to kiss Albertine with which the volume closes. Over this ground bass unifying the volume's plot, other themes are sounded. For example, while the first half is concerned primarily with Marcel's love for Gilberte, diegetically this episode begins with the dinner at Marcel's parents' home attended by M. de Norpois, where politics, art, and social distinction (or lack of it, since the topic is introduced via reflections on Swann's marriage to Odette) dominate the conversation. Indeed, the key issue at this dinner involves Marcel's choice of a career. He has rejected the diplomatic service, favored by his parents, for literature. One reason for Marcel's unwillingness to become a diplomat, we learn, is that to do so would separate him from Gilberte. As always in this novel, it is difficult to disaggregate one motif from another. Nevertheless, it may be possible to see through the foregrounded erotic matter to get at the social significance by rehearsing the trajectory of this volume's plot.

The first half bears the title, "Autour de Mme. Swann." Who or what is gathered around Odette? Why does the first half of the volume concern her and her immediate environment? Diegetically, this section continues the story told in "Un amour de Swann," and "Nom de pays: le nom." In the latter Marcel had admired Odette during her public appearances in the Bois. In addition, the first half of this narrative bloc tells of Marcel's love for Gilberte, which had emerged, however tentatively, at the end of *Du côté de chez Swann*. Marcel's visits to Odette are principally motivated by his desire for her daughter. Thematically, Marcel's itinerary replicates Swann's, not least in the former's pursuit of a young girl into what is, by the standards of Marcel's own family, a socially inferior milieu. At the Swann home, Marcel first encounters Bergotte, who figurally stands for the world of art that will play a decisive role in his subsequent life. Art is also represented here, as elsewhere in the text, by Vinteuil's music, which Odette performs. (I'll return to this passage below.) But most of all, "Autour de Mme. Swann" expands the minute exploration of bourgeois society that was briefly set forward in "Combray" and more elaborately articulated in "Un amour de Swann."

In *A l'ombre des jeunes filles en fleurs*, we encounter a fuller array of bourgeois characters who present this class's internal stratification and its relationship to the nobility in a more nuanced manner. Complex ties of patronage and affiliation bind this society together. For example, Norpois, a marquis and a diplomat, represents that fraction of the old aristocracy who made up a semi-permanent administrative class serving the state regardless of its political orientation (see 1:468–9; 426–7). His otherwise inexplicable presence in the Narrator's home is accounted for by the fact that Marcel's father works in the Foreign Ministry – and, as we learn, because he wishes Norpois to support his candidature to the Academy. From the very first, then, social ambition provides the rationale for characters' actions. The Narrator comes by his own social climbing honestly.

The Swann household seemingly stands outside the more nitty-gritty business of bourgeois politics – not least because Swann himself remains resolutely apolitical during this period – but its republican character is explicitly noted (1:556; 507). Swann is related to the highest reaches of the bourgeoisie, which, in the persons of the Rothschilds, had been closely allied with the French aristocracy since the July Monarchy (1:557–8; 508–9). Swann's ties to the nobility are not much in evidence here, although he does familiarly greet the Princesse Mathilde while visiting the zoo. It may perhaps be taken as a sign of his declining position in the fashionable world that it is she, a relic of Bonapartism, whom he now encounters rather than the Guermantes and their circle. Not that Swann is no longer admitted into the *gratin* – he does appear at the Guermantes reception in *Sodome et Gomorrhe* – but his marriage has adversely affected his social standing. His reputation will be further tarnished during the Dreyfus Affair, as the social tensions between bourgeois and noble burst into the open under pressure from this ideological and political flood. In effect, Swann has chosen the path of the republican bourgeoisie, for that is where his wife can pursue her own social ambition – and so she does, patently attempting to rival Mme. Verdurin and surrounding herself with people like the Cottards and the Bontemps (1:645–7; 589–91). The point of this episode is to depict the fluid, mobile Parisian bourgeoisie, in contrast to Combray's older, essentially unchanging middle classes.

Marcel's initiation into "society" begins with his own class, but among them he encounters a fraction distinct from that into which he had been born. Just as *Le côté de Guermantes* will reveal the fissures within the Faubourg Saint-Germain, "Autour de Mme. Swann" discloses the intra-class struggles among competing sectors of professional and rentier bourgeois.

At what period does this action occur? If we follow the novel's internal chronology, Marcel's visits to the Swann household must be set in the early to mid-1890s. Specific references to historical events confirm this impression. For example, Aimé's allusion to Dreyfus (1:864; 11:164) dates the first trip to Balbec in "Noms de pays: le pays" after 1894, since Dreyfus was arrested in October and convicted on December 22 of that year. Marcel visits Balbec at least two years after his love for Gilberte (see 1:691; II:3), so that "Autour de Mme. Swann" cannot take place before 1893 (when Marcel is in his mid-teens), or after 1896–7, because Aimé's reference would be nonsensical after the publication of *J'accuse* in January 1898. The point to be emphasized is that this volume evokes the tag end of a comparatively stable period politically and ideologically, a time when the republic was governed by a center–right coalition that had cancelled any significant state power for the nobility. If, as I have maintained, *Swann's Way* is about the class struggles during the early Third Republic (from 1871 through 1889), *A l'ombre des jeunes filles en fleurs* concerns the period of somewhat less than a decade (1889–98) when the bourgeoisie consolidated its political and social hegemony over the nobility while remaining politically at odds with itself, a condition indicated by the frequent cabinet changes it witnessed. How, then, does the Balbec episode itself fit into this picture? What is its narrative function? What is it meant to represent?

On the most immediate level, Balbec is a resort, primarily although not exclusively, for the bourgeoisie (see 1:726; 11:35–6). While there, Marcel meets the following characters who present a reasonable cross-section of the upper classes: the little band of girls dominated by Albertine Simonet, offspring of the professional and commercial bourgeoisie; M. and Mlle.

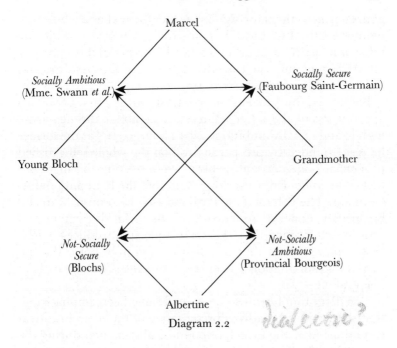

Diagram 2.2 *dialectic?*

de Stermaria, along with M. de Cambremer, unfashionable members of the titled nobility (the latter allied by marriage to Legrandin); Mme. de Villeparisis and her relatives, including Saint-Loup, the Princesse de Luxembourg, and Charlus, all inhabitants of the Faubourg Saint-Germain; and the Bloch family, bourgeois *arrivistes*. In addition to the hotel patrons, Marcel notices and minutely describes the local servile classes represented by the hotel staff. Exemplified in the lift-boy's speech patterns, these newer servants are, according to their own self-image, workers, a "modern proletariat" (1;857; II:157). With his customary incisiveness, Proust puts his finger on a general social process by poking fun at the lift-boy's linguistic pretensions: during the Third Republic, the country-side witnessed a gradual depopulation through peasants and others migrating to the towns, typically to become servants, domestics, or if female, prostitutes.

Marcel also makes the acquaintance of another character

with enormous thematic significance to the text as a whole: the painter Elstir. But Elstir is pointedly positioned outside the resort milieu, living apart and scarcely mixing in this society at all. As is generally the case throughout the *Recherche*, art and society constitute antitheses in this volume.

Balbec is thus meant to contrast with Mme. Swann's apartments: in the latter Marcel learns about the upwardly mobile and socially ambitious urban bourgeoisie; at the former he is surrounded by prosperous and on the whole self-satisfied provincial bourgeois and gentry, while making the first contacts that will one day introduce him into the Faubourg Saint-Germain. The volume functions narratively to push Marcel a bit further along his itinerary towards social distinction and artistic achievement. At the same time it introduces a new erotic entanglement that will distract him from both. We can map the social relations in *A l'ombre des jeunes filles en fleurs* as in diagram 2.2.

The diagram illustrates the point I have been emphasizing: that the novel is broadly representative of the socio-historical conditions (and the principal political alignments) during the mid-1890s. At this period, only the *haute bourgeoisie* stood any serious chance of being admitted into the highest circles of social and political power. Prior to 1898, politics in the Third Republic was almost exclusively the province of the upper elites; increasingly, accommodation between the nobility and the bourgeoisie was the order of the day. The Dreyfus Affair would alter this situation permanently.

Discussion of this latter episode is reserved for the following chapter, which treats it under the rubric of ideology. Such was its principal distinguishing feature in the period. Its outcome was determined less by economic or political than by ideological considerations.

HISTORICISM AND ART

Canonically, Balbec signifies "art," most immediately in the person of Elstir, but equally in the Romanesque cathedral there that much earlier Swann has urged Marcel to visit. But the matter of art circulates throughout the *Recherche*, punctuating a variety of situations and providing the occasion for the Narrator's reflections on a range of aesthetic theories and taste cultures, for example, the principles enunciated by Mme. de Villeparisis (I:762; II:69–70). Characteristically, the Narrator utilizes the aesthetic judgments and dicta of others (in the case of Mme. de Villeparisis a certain classicism that is not entirely alien to Marcel's – or Proust's own – prejudices) to explore more deeply the evolution of a concept of art that will only crystallize at the novel's end. Doubtless it would be profitable to examine closely Marcel's youthful interpretation of Elstir's paintings (I:892–9; II:190–6). Instead I wish to consider an earlier passage dealing with Vinteuil's sonata, since it is, in my opinion, more consonant with the aesthetic theory that lies at the heart of the *Recherche*. To deal with Vinteuil's music as illustrative of the novel's aesthetic can hardly be thought eccentric. Among the *Recherche*'s several signifiers for "art," Vinteuil's corpus is second to none in importance.

The passage (I:570–3; 520–3) is deceptively simple and might be summarized thus. One day Mme. Swann played for Marcel that part of Vinteuil's sonata containing the "petite phrase" that had been "the national anthem" of Swann's and her love. At first, Marcel does not hear or understand (*entendre*) anything, but when the piece is played for him two or three more times, he realizes that he knows it (*connaître*) perfectly. Marcel attributes his initial ignorance more to lack of memory than to any failure in comprehension, i.e., the complex material impressions left no conscious trace on his mind. His subsequent realization that he in fact knows the piece perfectly well proves he had understood it all along, that its materiality had indeed been retained without his being aware of it. Marcel gives two analogies for what had transpired: first, a student who goes to sleep believing he does not know a lesson only to awake and recite it by heart; second, the sudden recollection of a name one has sought in vain to recall. So recounted, the passage appears to be a textbook illustration of the theory of involuntary memory that motivates the madeleine episode and seems later on to govern the final movement in *Le temps retrouvé*.

As such, the passage would endorse a model of reading, understanding, and remembering that is, to recall Paul de Man's
terminology (taken over from Gérard Genette), metaphoric.
The model of understanding here is that of grasping in a single
intuition a text's entire complex structure; it reproduces an
absolutely classical concept of the aesthetic, which Proust's
novel has often been taken to endorse. On this view, the
Recherche both announces and enacts a poetics of totalization.
This is not, however, the passage's final word.

Having proposed a metaphoric theory, the Narrator
immediately denies this model of totalizing understanding:
"Since I was only able to enjoy all that this sonata brought me
in successive times, I never entirely possessed it: it resembled
life. But less deceptive than life, these great masterpieces do not
begin by giving us the best they have" (1:571; 521). Each new
hearing alters the Narrator's grasp or comprehension of the
piece; earlier intuitions are replaced by subsequent ones. The
passage thus asserts an irreducibly temporal model of understanding that blocks any attempt to give a complete account of
its object. At this point, we would seem to be following the de
Manian account of the *Recherche*, with the novel's meaning
perpetually "in flight."[52] But the passage advances one step
further.

The temporal dimension in any understanding applies
equally to the history of the reception of great works, which are
only comprehended after many years, even centuries, have
passed. How does this occur? Certainly not by any prediction
or forethought on the author's part, since he cannot forecast his
work's future, any more than a horoscope will provide a
reliable guide for living one's life (1:573; 523). To launch a
work into the "full and distant future" (1:572; 522), the necessary condition for any work to be or become great, is just to
give up on the possibility of assessing its outcome or impact; it is
to deny that the work's effects can be foreseen or controlled.
The work itself must be detached from the author's intentions.
Perhaps it was this very passage Benjamin had in mind when
he maintained that only in the future would the *Recherche* be
truly understood. In any event, a great deal hangs on the

theory of art proposed here, not least because this aesthetic
theory is, like Hegel's, a theory of historical understanding. If,
as the final volume will make clear, the *Recherche*'s theory of art
applies reflexively to its own plot (focused on the story of
Marcel's life), this novel, like all art works, can only reach its
true destiny in an unforeseeable future; neither the work of art
nor history itself is a predicable subject. The limits of our
understanding are circumscribed by our capacity to know how
a particular story comes out, and this is per definition available
only to those who are no longer inside the story itself. Such an
understanding would, if only provisionally, be achieved by
Proust after the First World War, when the class struggle
between bourgeois and aristocrat had reached its definitive
terminus. Poetically speaking, the *Recherche* could never have
been completed sooner, since the historical processes it narrates
only reached fruition at that moment. If the Narrator's discovery of his vocation to write a novel about his own life was a
contingent event that might never have occurred, it is nonetheless presented as a necessary consequence of all that preceded it
in his life, as the fulfillment of an intention that had lain
dormant within the structures of his unconcious. Similarly,
from the perspective of the post-war period, the decline and
ultimate demise of the French nobility, its replacement by the
bourgeoisie as the nation's dominant class, will appear to have
been inevitable.

Before endorsing this historicist schema, however, we should
observe how Proust conceives such a concept of historical
understanding:

Doubtless it is easy to imagine, in an illusion analogous to that which
renders everything on the horizon uniform, that all the revolutions
which have occurred up to this point in painting or in music
respected at least certain rules, and that what is immediately before
us, impressionism, the search for dissonance, the exclusive employment of the Chinese scale, cubism, futurism, differ outrageously from
that which came before. One considers what came before without
taking into account the fact that a long assimilation has converted it
for us into a substance, varied no doubt, but completely homo-
geneous, where Hugo adjoins Molière. (1:573)

[Sans doute, il est aisé de s'imaginer dans une illusion analogue à celle qui uniformise toutes choses à l'horizon, que toutes les révolutions qui ont eu lieu jusqu'ici dans la peinture ou la musique respectaient tout de même certaines règles et que ce qui est immédiatement devant nous, impressionnisme, recherche de la dissonance, emploi exclusif de la gamme chinoise, cubisme, futurisme, diffère outrageusement de ce qui a précédé. C'est que ce qui a précédé on le considère sans tenir compte qu'une longue assimilation l'a converti pour nous en une matière variée sans doute, mais somme toute homogène, où Hugo voisine avec Molière.] (I:522–3)

The irreducible singularity of aesthetic achievement, that which distinguishes one work of art from another, is effaced in conventional histories of art. A work like the *Recherche* that ostensibly imposes a retrospective understanding on the events it has narrated is no less subject to the cautionary statement asserted here. We shall have to bear this point in mind when considering the theory of art proposed in *Le temps retrouvé*. Nothing would be less Proustian than to impute to this text a totalizing, teleological concept of art and history.

LE SEUIL DU FAUBOURG

After failing to seduce Albertine into carnal relations – in this novel, one might say, a kiss is not still a kiss – Marcel returns to Paris, where *Le côté de Guermantes* opens. His grandmother's illness has compelled his family's removal to a new dwelling in a more salubrious quarter. Their apartments occupy one wing of the Hôtel de Guermantes. In this milieu, Marcel's love for Albertine is displaced by his passionate pursuit of Oriane de Guermantes. The text denominates this latter "love," but it would be wrong to understand it as erotic in the customary sense of the term. Marcel's desire for the Duchess is almost purely social, as becomes clear when he pays his long-postponed visit to Saint-Loup at Doncières to enlist the latter's assistance in securing an invitation to the Duchess's salon. He will succeed, of course, but not through Saint-Loup's good offices. Rather, his unexpected meeting with the Duchess at Mme. de Villeparisis's *matinée* will propel him into the Faubourg's most exclusive regions. The first part of *Le côté de Guermantes* then closes with Marcel's grandmother's death.

It is impossible not to connect the narrative's framing episodes in this section – the grandmother's failing health culminating in her death – with Marcel's social ascent. His family moves close to the Guermantes because of her physical decline, and it would appear that the symbolic price paid for Marcel's social career is his grandmother's demise.[53] The reading is commensurate with the symbolic economy of the novel as a whole. Marcel's grandmother has consistently been the caretaker of his ambition to become a writer, and it is just this latter that is, temporarily to be sure, sacrificed to his social career. As is the case throughout the *Recherche*, the first part of *Le côté de Guermantes* narrates the opposition between art and society, nowhere more clearly than in the semic system governing the action at Mme. de Villeparisis's *matinée*, which can be mapped as in diagram 2.3.

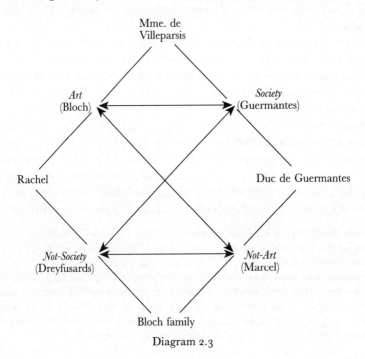

Diagram 2.3

That the Duc de Guermantes is a rich philistine, the diametric opposite of the impoverished artist (and sometime prostitute) Rachel, is easily recognized. Bloch's standing in for art here is also obvious enough, as are the contradictory values figured by Dreyfusism and the Guermantes family. The Bloch family – the son excepted – are both philistines (a source of constant embarrassment to young Bloch, whose artistic career is at this point far from assured) and social outcasts (by virtue of their Jewishness, something young Bloch himself has hitherto tried hard to conceal). Somewhat surprising, however, is Marcel's essentially negative position. Not only is he here the semantic opposite to the art represented by Bloch (since he has apparently opted for the life of a socialite), but he is also engaged in dubious fellow-travelling with the forces of anti-Dreyfusism. At the Guermantes reception in *Sodome et Gomorrhe*, Swann will assume that Marcel is a Dreyfusard, but the Narrator never discloses his opinions in the matter – doubtless a sign of Proust's ambivalence towards his own previous involvement in the Affair.[54]

The diagram further illustrates what may seem surprising at this point but will be beyond doubt at the novel's end: to wit, that society and art are not absolutely antithetical, that the two can be reconciled, albeit at a cost. Mme. de Villeparisis, who occupies herself during the reception by painting still-lifes, no longer moves in the Faubourg's upper echelons. Her art – and her cultivation of the rising young playwright Bloch – is a means to recapture her lost social position. One is led to suspect that already at this moment social barriers are not so impregnable, that society has become more fluid than the Guermantes would believe or wish. Charlus indicates as much to Marcel:

"All this Dreyfus business," continued the Baron still holding onto my arm, "has only one drawback: that is that it destroys society (I don't mean good society; it's been some time since society any longer merited that laudatory epithet) by the influx of Sir and Lady Cur or Curette or Curness, finally by unknown people whom I find even in my cousins' homes because they belong to the Patriotic or the Anti-Jewish League, or I don't know what, as if a political opinion gave one the right to a social qualification." (ii:300)

["Toute cette affaire Dreyfus, reprit le baron qui tenait toujours mon bras, n'a qu'un inconvénient: c'est qu'elle détruit la société (je ne dis pas la bonne société, il y a longtemps que la société ne mérite plus cette épithète louangeuse) par l'afflux de messieurs et de dames du Chameau, de la Chamellerie, de la Chamellière, enfin des gens inconnus que je trouve même chez mes cousines parce qu'ils font partie de la ligue de la Patrie française, antijuive, je ne sais quoi, comme si une opinion politique donnait droit à une qualification sociale."] (II:586)

Mention of the Dreyfus Affair takes us to the core social problem in *Le côté de Guermantes*, which involves the extent to which this historical episode would dissolve, almost at a stroke, many of the most sacrosanct social hierarchies. But once again, I must defer discussion of this historical watershed until the next chapter.

What is most significant in the present context is that Charlus's diatribe must apply in large degree to Marcel himself, who is well on his way to entering the very homes Charlus mentions – and, most injurious to the Baron's pride, without his aid. The bulk of this volume is taken up by Marcel's sojourns in high society. *Le côté de Guermantes* will culminate, famously, in Marcel's virtual social equality with the dying Swann, whose place and function the younger man has more or less unceremoniously usurped. It has been too little remarked how the symbolic economy that pits art against society in Marcel's (and the novel's) system of values correlates with the socio-political situation of the period during which it is set. To recapitulate, Marcel's entry into the *gratin*, emblematically achieved when he dines with the Duc and Duchesse de Guermantes, follows his grandmother's death. While this latter event is notoriously difficult to locate precisely in relation to the diegesis,[55] it certainly occurs after the first explosions of the Dreyfus Affair but prior to the Rennes trial. Her death thus punctuates the narrative in a highly charged socio-symbolic manner. The principal representative, I have maintained, of a previous epoch and of a distinctive class fraction (the provincial bourgeoisie), with her passes away the comfortable, unambitious, secure world that the novel denominates

"Combray" and to which is attributed "almost a Hindu view of society." Henceforward, the class struggles in the Third Republic will be conducted in the open, as politics and social power are fought over at the level of competing ideologies of the nation.

CHAPTER 3

Ideology

> If in all ideology men and their relations appear upside-
> down as in a *camera obscura*, this phenomenon arises just as
> much from their historical life-process as the inversion of
> objects on the retina does from their physical life-process.
> (Marx and Engels, *The German Ideology*)

In his first, failed attempt to write a novel, *Jean Santeuil*, Proust
situated the Dreyfus Affair at the very center of his narrative.
While the *Recherche* often alludes to this historical episode, it is
no longer decisive to the text's action, nor is it given any
focused treatment. Rather, the matter of the Affair is dispersed
across three volumes, from the Doncières section in *A l'ombre des
jeunes filles en fleurs*, through *Le côté de Guermantes* (where it is used
to distinguish among competing salons and to show how politics has infiltrated upper-class society), down to the famous
reception at the Prince and Princesse de Guermantes's, where
Swann makes his last appearance in the novel. It is worthwhile
reflecting upon why the most celebrated political and ideological event of the early Third Republic has been all but
displaced from Proust's narrative of class struggle. Before doing
so, however, it will be necessary to look briefly and sche-
matically at the historical record and consider the reasons why
the military took the line of attempting to prevent any intrusion by the civil authorities.

Canonically, the Affair has been cited as an egregious
instance of French antisemitism. I shall be arguing that it is
impossible to comprehend this latter without reference to
nationalism and the class struggle over the meaning of *la patrie*.

The central figures representing this struggle in the novel are
Robert de Saint-Loup and Charles Swann.

What socio-political position did the French army assume in
the quarter-century leading up to the First World War? A
rough consensus exists among military, and other, historians
that the period between 1871 and 1890 constituted the French
army's "Golden Age." The humiliation of 1870 led the
republic's leaders, left and right alike, to rebuild the nation's
armed forces into an efficient, modern fighting force. Universal
military service was established (though the term of obligation
would vary over time between two and five years), and educational attainments among the officer corps rose.[1] More
important, the nation as a whole, which had been divided in its
opinions (the working class had scarcely forgotten the military's role in the June Days of 1848 or its support for the
Bonapartist coup in 1851), was integrated into the army. This
latter was no longer seen as the republic's enemy but as its
support – perhaps the only reliable one. Douglas Porch sums
up the general feeling during this period:

Far from entrenching the old army, national service, regional recruitment and military reform, combined with successful republican
attempts to stimulate patriotic sentiments in the country, drew a once
outcast army into the pale of French society. With universal service,
as with schools, roads and railways, republicans looked to pour the
foundations of a strong nation. Three years with the regiment forged
a greater sense of national unity, melting rich and poor, Bretons and
Basques, Provençals and Parisians into one community ... The army
was no longer the occupying force imposed by Parisians and prefects,
but a joint stock company in which all Frenchmen held shares.
Rather than create a gulf between the nation and the army, the
Third Republic's conscription laws joined the two in a bond broken
only by the Dreyfus affair. (Porch, *March*, p. 32)[2]

Actually, the tide began to turn somewhat earlier, and this
was due in no small measure to Boulangism. Although there is
no evidence that the army colluded with Boulanger – just the

opposite – the General's popularity produced considerable nervousness among republican politicians. Boulanger had been the war minister in Freycinet's government, but he was shuffled off to Clermont-Ferrand when his publicly declared revanchism raised alarms in Berlin. His subsequent plebiscitary popularity had created suspicions about the reliability of military men, above all about their ultimate subservience to the parliamentary state. The reasons for these worries were complex.

Opinion differs concerning the composition and the political inclinations of the officer corps prior to the Dreyfus Affair.[3] But it is generally agreed that however much the army remained officially and in practice above politics, its officers, particularly those higher up in the chain of command, were mostly conservative, leaning towards royalist, Bonapartist, and above all Roman Catholic opinion.[4] One stage on which republican politics and military imperatives consistently clashed was the war ministry. Charles de Freycinet's accession to the rue Saint-Dominique in 1888 created a serious dilemma: how could a civilian responsibly run the army? Freycinet's reply was to strengthen the military's hold on power by giving a more central role to the Conseil Supérieure de la Guerre (created in 1872, but effectively moribund since 1874), and by establishing a new post, the chief of the army general staff (Porch, *March*, pp. 52–3). The army was understandably pleased, but the day of reckoning was merely postponed. Republican politicians like Clemenceau would rail against the "warren of Jesuits" in the high command through the early years of the First World War, and tensions between civilian power and military influence would remain up to the Versailles negotiations and beyond.[5] The flashpoint for these struggles, the moment when civil and military authority would collide head-on, came with the Dreyfus Affair, although it is clear in retrospect that prior to 1902, no republican government had any interest in directly challenging or embarrassing the army. To understand why this was so, it is necessary to consider the major ideological movements that were mobilized during the Affair but that had sprung up somewhat earlier.

Madeleine Rebérioux observes that at the Affair's height, while the traditional right-wing elites were more or less unified (but even here there were exceptions: she notes the secret Dreyfusard sympathies of the Prince and Princesse de Guermantes in the *Recherche*), the organized political forces on the left remained divided.[6] Only as matters were drawing to a close in 1899, did the Affair begin to assume a coherent political form (Rebérioux, "Radical Republic," pp. 197–8). At the outset, it will be recalled, even Jaurès had called for Dreyfus's execution (forgetting that treason was a capital offense only in wartime). The republican left had been slow to leap to Dreyfus's defense, and it remained fractured until the revisionist cause was well-advanced. Why should this have been the case?

Douglas Porch puts his finger on the salient contradiction between the effects the Affair would engender (including its lasting notoriety in the popular imagination) and the socio-political realities that held the government in check for some five years:

The affair did not originate in the social and religious attitudes of the officer corps, the resistance of old France to the modernization and "republicanization" of the army. On the contrary, many of the officers involved in the Dreyfus cover-up were known for their republican sympathies. The Dreyfus affair was rather sparked by an institution founded and nurtured by republican reformers and regarded as distinctly middle class in its composition and outlook – the general staff. (Porch, *March*, pp. 56–7)

No one with political instincts in 1894 wished to be associated with a movement that sought to discredit the army, hence the nation. As even *J'accuse* attests, the fundamental Dreyfusard position was moral: Dreyfus was innocent, a victim of justice miscarried. Jean-Denis Bredin, whose book *The Affair* is the definitive study to date, consistently argues that the emergence of a *cause célèbre* was for the most part fortuitous, less the result of political coherence and calculation by the Dreyfusards than blind luck and a series of blunders by those who conspired to hide the truth. In a different political conjuncture, things might have gone differently. Porch persuasively maintains that the government during the 1890s had no interest in persecuting the army or in upsetting the newly recruited Catholic *ralliés* (Porch, *March*, p. 61).

But the question remains why the left, Socialists and Radicals alike, were so slow to respond. Porch avers that they ultimately took up the cause in order to gain political advantage (Porch, *March*, p. 61). Yet they were just as marginalized in 1894 as in 1898 (having been driven from power in the elections of 1893), so one wonders why they hesitated at first. The key issue was almost certainly ideological. In the first place, neither Radicals nor Socialists (with the possible exception of the Guesdists) were hostile at this period to the patriotic nationalist consensus. Boulanger (who had been promoted early on by Clemenceau) made it plain that patriotism remained a powerful card with the popular masses, including the Parisian working class who supported him heavily. Moreover, as Stephen Wilson points out in his massive study of antisemitism at the time of the Affair, the appeal of this vicious prejudice among the rural and urban *petite bourgeoisie* (supporters of the Radicals) and the urban working class (the Socialist base) was quite widespread.[7] In short, the political forces that ultimately triumphed were initially in no position to contest the verdict lest they risk losing significant portions of their mass base. One might even hazard the opinion that only because the right overplayed its hand, and as evidence of the army's malfeasance mounted, were Socialists and Radicals given the opportunity to take up the patriotic mantle. Only then could they claim to be defending the republic against its clerical and royalist enemies. Only then could parliamentary power be reasserted over a military that had gotten out of control and was acting counter to the national interest as expressed by the elected government (Bredin, *Affair*, pp. 534–41).

The long-term effects of the Dreyfus Affair are perhaps difficult to gauge with precision, but its short-term results seem clear enough in retrospect. To the extent that anti-Dreyfusism rode a wave of clerical and generally Roman Catholic antisemitism, the anti-clerical backlash of the Combes Laws was one immediate outcome. Similarly, the army's "Golden Age" came to an abrupt end, as the civil authorities recovered their dominance (Porch, *March*, pp. 72, 246). On the other side, the anti-Dreyfusard right established a coherent (albeit minority) position, with the republic as its principle *bête noire*. The launching of Action Française's daily newspaper in 1908 symbolized the maturation of a movement that had stood on the political fringe a decade earlier.[8] As for the far left, it emerged from its early disorientation to become solidly opposed to antisemitism (Bredin, *Affair*, p. 530). During the decade before 1914, anti-militarism would become one of the left's main pillars. They were encouraged no doubt by the increasing tendency of republican governments to utilize troops to break up strikes (de la Gorce, *French Army*, pp. 58–9; Porch, *March*, 130–1, 187–9, 203–4). Jaurès's *L'Armée nouvelle* (1911), which called for a non-professional army, conscripted for a limited initial term and geared completely towards defending the nation, was the canonical statement of Socialism's anti-militarist posture, abandoned only when the German Social Democratic Party voted war credits in 1914 and paved the way for their French comrades to join the *union sacrée*.[9]

In sum, while it appeared that the left-wing Dreyfusard forces triumphed definitively over reaction, Bredin is surely correct to emphasize that the real victor was nationalism itself. Radicals, Socialists, royalists, workers, soldiers, farmers – all laid claim to *la patrie*. Never seriously challenged by the left, nationalism became the unifying ideology that brought France into conflict with Germany increasingly often from 1906 onwards, making the bloodbath of 1914–18 effectively unavoidable. Its legacy would survive even that cataclysm, as the post-war government was dominated by the Bloc National. (The first Chamber elected after the armistice has gone down in history as the "bleu horizon" because of the numerous war veterans elected to it.) Not for nothing was the term "chauvinism" coined from a Frenchman's name. For anyone who watched the paroxysm of the Quatorze Juillet celebrating the Revolution's 200th anniversary in 1989, its continuing hold over the nation's dominant self-image was perfectly evident.[10]

VARIEGATED NATIONALISMS

How does nationalism appear in the *Recherche*? I have already indicated that this ideologeme, insofar as it can be equated with the matter of the Dreyfus Affair, is dispersed over several volumes. We first encounter it in the Doncières section of *A l'ombre des jeunes filles en fleurs*, which is related diegetically to the *matinée chez* Mme. de Villeparisis. Doncières represents a parallel social institution to the salon: the army. This episode is dominated by the *intra*-class rivalry between two fractions within the nobility: the Bonapartists represented by the Prince de Borodino; and the Legitimists represented by Saint-Loup. By contrast, Mme. de Villeparisis's salon is a site of *inter*-class collaboration between the bourgeoisie (Marcel, Bloch, Legrandin) and the titled nobility (Mme. de Villeparisis herself, Charlus, Oriane de Guermantes, Saint-Loup, and the latter's mother, Mme. de Marsantes). While the Dreyfus Affair appears in and largely defines attitudes throughout both, its effect upon each is utterly different.

At Doncières, Saint-Loup's rabid Dreyfusism (imbibed, it is said, from his Jewish mistress Rachel) is muffled, lest he offend his fellow officers, who are all loyal to the army and therefore violently anti-Dreyfusard. In the salon, as Charlus's little speech cited in the previous chapter illustrates, the Affair discloses deep rifts in upper-class society's political and ideological structure. The socialite world, *le monde*, and the army constitute distinct ideological spaces, even though the same ideological material circulates in both. Proust's presentation is historically perspicacious, for the social dislocation that resulted from the Affair never split the army (see Bredin, *Affair*, pp. 235–6). Moreover, the novel reveals what was perhaps the key ideological puzzle for Proust himself, one that would continue to haunt his writing through the war episode in *Le temps retrouvé*.

An early Dreyfusard who attended the *procès* Zola, Proust would nonetheless never shed the fervent patriotism that had led him to do his military service (from which he could easily have been exempted for health reasons) and would later cause him to affirm the patriotic values exhibited by Saint-Loup during the war. The crucial distinction here is between loyalty to the culture, mores, and territorial integrity of a national linguistic community, and the racist jingoism of a Drumont, a Barrès, or a Maurras.[11] Although the issue is only definitively resolved in the final volume, it is already fully posed early in *Sodome et Gomorrhe*, in the scene where Swann reports his conversation with the Prince de Guermantes to Marcel.

The Prince is a snob, an antisemite, and a fervent supporter of the army.[12] Swann is of course a Dreyfusard and a Jew. In the nobility's eyes, he is a Dreyfusard just because he is Jewish. It is impossible for the Faubourg to recognize Dreyfusism as anything other than a racial aberration. Swann and Bloch are both Jews and thus naturally inclined towards Dreyfusism; Saint-Loup is a Dreyfusard because his mistress is Jewish. (In the latter case, the Faubourg apparently judges correctly, since Saint-Loup has by this point abandoned his earlier Dreyfusism just as he has given up Rachel; see II:724; III:97.) The aim of the episode is, however, to demonstrate the complexities of feeling and commitment among these characters, above all to reveal that both the Prince and Princesse de Guermantes secretly believe in Dreyfus's innocence, and that Swann, though a Dreyfusard, is not unpatriotic (see II:737–9; III:109–11). Nonetheless, the ideological values put into motion and initially represented by one or more characters can be modelled in standard Greimassian fashion (see diagram 3.1).

Most surprising in this schema are the so-called neutral and complex terms. It is well known that Theodore Herzl, chief theoretician of twentieth-century Zionism, was profoundly influenced by the spectacle of Dreyfus's humiliation (see Bredin, *Affair*, p. 529). But why would Zionism figure as the neutral term, the semantic nadir of all the ideologemes mobilized here? To understand Zionism's place here, one must take into account the values exemplified by Swann and the Narrator. Swann's patriotism affirms his identity as a Frenchman; he embodies just those values that the Duc de Guermantes believes it is possible to combine but that, in the Duke's view,

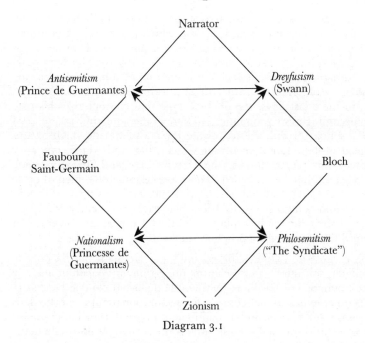

Diagram 3.1

Dreyfusism negates (see II:703; III:77). As I have been arguing, patriotism is distinct from – indeed it is opposed to – the right-wing nationalism of the anti-Dreyfusards. This essentially Dreyfusard view coincides with what is known of Proust's own convictions. It is nonetheless somewhat curious that the Narrator embodies the intersection of antisemitism with Dreyfusism. Swann certainly assumes the latter (see II:723; III:96), even though the Narrator never makes his political position plain. That the Narrator may harbor antisemitic prejudices has been asserted by some recent critics of the novel,[13] and there is warrant in this very scene for such a charge.

The Narrator draws attention to the difference between Swann's "Jewish gaiety" and his more normal "pleasantries of a man of the world," finding the former "less refined" (II:723; III:96). Somewhat earlier, in an astonishing passage, the Narrator participates in the kind of soft-core antisemitism that was and is a constitutive feature of French upper-class thinking:

Whether because of the absence of those cheeks, no longer there to modify it, or because arteriosclerosis, which is also a form of intoxication, had reddened it as would drunkenness, or deformed it as would morphine, Swann's punchinello nose, absorbed for long years into an agreeable face, seemed now enormous, tumid, crimson, the nose of an old Hebrew rather than of a dilettante Valois. Perhaps, too, in these last days, the physical type that characterizes his race was becoming more pronounced in him, at the same time as a sense of moral solidarity with the rest of the Jews, a solidarity which Swann seemed to have forgotten throughout his life, and which, one after another, his mortal illness, the Dreyfus case and the antisemitic propaganda had reawakened. There are certain Jews, men of great refinement and social delicacy, in whom nevertheless there remain in reserve and behind the scene – finally to make their entry at a given hour of their life, as in a play – a cad and a prophet. Swann had arrived at the age of the prophet. (ii:715–6)

[Soit à cause de l'absence de ces joues qui n'étaient plus là pour le diminuer, soit que l'artériosclérose, qui est une intoxication aussi, le rougît comme eût fait l'ivrognerie ou le déformât comme eut fait la morphine, le nez de polichinelle de Swann, longtemps résorbé dans un visage agréable, semblait maintenant énorme, tuméfié, cramoisi, plutôt celui d'un vieil Hébreu que d'un curieux Valois. D'ailleurs peut-être chez lui en ces derniers jours la race faisait-elle reparaître plus accusé le type physique qui la caractérise, en même temps que le sentiment d'une solidarité morale avec les autres Juifs, solidarité que Swann semblait avoir oubliée toute sa vie, et que greffées les unes sur les autres, la maladie mortelle, l'affaire Dreyfus, la propagande antisémite avaient réveillée. Il y a certains Israélites, très fins pourtant et mondains délicats, chez lesquels restent en réserve et dans la coulisse, afin de faire leur entrée à une heure donnée de leur vie, comme dans un pièce, un mufle et un prophète. Swann était arrivé à l'âge du prophète.] (iii:89)

The passage continues, as the Narrataor remarks upon his own changed relationship to Swann, his lack of awe or nervousness in the latter's presence. His new-found ease is a sign of what this episode is in part meant to suggest: that Marcel has now replaced Swann as the favorite cultured bourgeois in the Faubourg's most exclusive salons.

At stake here is a problem Proust himself must have felt acutely. The price of admission into the *gratin* for Jews was that they renounce their Jewishness.[14] The Narrator's reticence about his political opinions can be taken to indicate his awareness of this fact. And yet it would be wrong to assert Proust's or the Narrator's simple identification with right-wing nationalism, or even with a certain sympathy for its prejudices. Both the Prince and the Duc de Guermantes become Dreyfusards (see II:767; III:138), although the former only covertly. The point here is to uncouple antisemitism from nationalism, to show how aristocratic prejudices can be combined with progressive political views, how the standard story of the Dreyfus Affair, which held that the Dreyfusards were secular, bourgeois, and anti-militarist, the anti-Dreyfusards Roman Catholic, aristocratic, and pro-army, fails to capture the complex determinations of politics and social life during this period. Political positions, while they are never completely autonomous of social determinations, do not always (or very often) simply reflect them either.

Nothing in the novel demonstrates this truth more explicitly than Mme. Verdurin and Odette, whose careers at this period are chronicled some pages after Marcel leaves the reception to rendezvous with Albertine. On the eve of his second trip to Balbec, the Narrator pronounces on society and history:

To a certain extent social manifestations (very much inferior to artistic movements, political crises, the evolution that leads public taste towards the theater of ideas, then towards impressionist painting, then towards complex and German music, then towards Russian and simple music, or towards social ideas, ideas of justice, religious reaction, patriotic bursts) are nevertheless their distant, cracked, uncertain, cloudy, changing reflection. Such that even the salons cannot be depicted in a static immobility which has been convenient until now for the study of characters; the latter themselves must also be as if dragged along in a quasi-historical movement. (II:769)

[Dans une certaine mésure les manifestations mondaines (fort inférieures aux mouvements artistiques, aux crises politiques, à l'évolution qui porte le goût public vers le théatre d'idées, puis vers la peinture impressioniste, puis vers la musique allemande et complexe, puis vers la musique russe et simple, ou vers les idées sociales, les idées de justice, la réaction religieuse, le sursaut patriotique) en sont cependant le reflet lointain, brisé, incertain, troublé, changeant. De sorte que même les salons ne peuvent être dépeints dans une immobilité statique qui a pu convenir jusqu'ici à l'étude des caractères, lesquels devront eux aussi être comme entraînés dans un mouvement quasi historique.] (III:139–40)

The passage directly asserts society's historicity. The succeeding pages illustrate this fact through the examples of Odette's and Mme. Verdurin's fortunes during the Dreyfus Affair. The former hosts a nationalist salon and is thereby carried into circles hitherto closed to her. The pinnacle of her success is attained when she appears at the theater in the company of Mme. de Marsantes (her daughter's future mother-in-law, as it happens) and the Comtesse Molé (II:773; III:143). By contrast, Mme. Verdurin remains more or less stuck at her present level, since the aristocracy cannot conceive that anything like a salon could be associated with Dreyfusism (see II:771; III:141). At the same time, the next episode in Balbec will witness the Baron de Charlus's descent into the Verdurin world (albeit not for political reasons, as we shall see), revealing an inexorable tendency that culminates in Mme. Verdurin's ultimate accession to the Faubourg in the final volume. The intricate interweaving of politics, ideology, and social position illustrates what I have been hinting at throughout: in the *Recherche* society is a complex, overdetermined structure; its history is in the last instance the history of class struggles. *Sodome et Gomorrhe* complicates the matter even further, revealing yet another dimension of social existence, one that has not to this point featured prominently in my exposition. If social rank is negotiated in class terms, it is also inflected by a factor that knows no class boundaries: namely, sexuality.

THE MEN OF SODOM

Marcel's long trek into and through the Faubourg Saint-Germain is twice interrupted: first by his grief over his grandmother's death; then by his pursuit and capture of Albertine. The reception at the Prince and Princesse de Guermantes's can be reasonably judged to take place during the summer of 1899, so it is fair to conclude that Marcel's exit from the Guermantes world coincides with the post-Dreyfus era in French history.

During the long period 1899–1916 (at the end of which Marcel returns to Paris from the sanitorium), we know some of what Marcel does, and we learn about the transformation he has undergone; but it is quite difficult to situate these events in relation to the actual history that has never been far from the novel's explicit concerns. Unlike previous historical moments, and unlike the First World War, the *belle époque* receives no detailed treatment in the *Recherche*. Concerning that era's punctual historical and political developments it is uncharacteristically silent. I shall return to this textual reticence in the final chapter below, but here I shall concentrate on what the novel does speak about, openly and at considerable length: the hitherto hidden sexual preferences of various social strata, mixed up with (and considerably complicated by) the Narrator's jealous passion for Albertine.

Sodome et Gomorrhe opens with the scene Marcel observes at the end of the previous volume but postpones so that *Le côté de Guermantes* can end with the thematically more coherent episode of the Duchess's red shoes (II:618–9; 883–4). This latter acts as a useful bridge to the Charlus-Jupien encounter and all that it will introduce into the novel's ideological structure, since the problem of whether to wear red or black shoes with a red dress epitomizes what the next several volumes will enact on several levels. The shoes incident introduces a moment of semiotic confusion (is red or black a sign of good taste?), as well as of social indeterminacy (who is the better judge in such matters, the Duke or Swann?).[15] In addition, the Duchess is torn between her loyalty to Swann, who has just announced that he is mortally ill, with perhaps three or four months at most to live, and her social duties to her husband and the other members of her social set. While the problems are all resolved in favor of the existing system of values (red shoes with a red dress, as the Duke insists; duty to one's class put above compassion for an old friend), this confirmation of the Guermantes worldview will not survive the very next scene, which tells of the encounter between Charlus and Jupien. If the Dreyfus Affair opens an irreparable breach in the Faubourg's fortifications against intruders, Charlus's career henceforward will

illustrate that the nobility are descending from their lofty perch
for other than purely political reasons as well.

Marcel's fortuitously witnessing the sexual liaison between
Jupien and Charlus participates in the same structure of semantic indeterminacy that operates in the episode of the
Duchess's red shoes. Here, however, the semiotic confusion has
less to do with judgments of taste or class relations (although
these latter are not irrelevant, as Jupien's subsequent exploitation of the Charlus connection will demonstrate), than with
this society's system of gender and sexual preference. The issue
arises first in relation to Charlus's ambiguous sexual identity:

... I found in [Charlus's] face seen thus in repose and as it were in its
natural state something so affectionate, so defenceless, that I could
not help thinking how angry M. de Charlus would have been could
he have known he was being watched; for what was suggested to me
by the sight of this man who was so enamoured of, who so prided
himself upon, his virility, to whom all other men seemed odiously
effeminate, what he suddenly suggested to me, to such an extent had
he momentarily assumed the features, the expression, the smile
thereof, was a woman. (II:626)

[je trouvai à sa figure vue ainsi au repos et comme au naturel quelque
chose de si affectueux, de si désarmé, que je ne pus m'empêcher de
penser combien M. de Charlus eût été fâché s'il avait pu se savoir
regardé; car ce à quoi me faisait penser cet homme qui était si épris,
qui se piquait si fort de virilité, à qui tout le monde semblait
odieusement efféminé, ce à quoi il me faisait penser tout d'un coup,
tant il en avait passagèrement les traits, l'expression, le sourire, c'était
à une femme.] (III:6)

As with so many other characters and events in the text,
Marcel is here trying to decipher certain mysteries that have
hitherto puzzled him. The new information, supplemented by
what transpires in Jupien's shuttered shop, leads Marcel to a
fresh understanding of M. de Charlus's character, which is
then overlaid on prior events and judgments to produce a
wholly different concept of the person and his existence:

In M. de Charlus another being had been skillfully coupled that
differentiated him from other men, as the horse [is] in the centaur;
this other being had been made into a single body with the Baron,

[and yet] I had never perceived it. Now, the abstraction having been materialized, the being finally comprehended had immediately lost its power to remain invisible, and the transformation of M. de Charlus into a new person was so complete that not only the contrasts of his face, of his voice, but retrospectively the very ups and downs of his relationship with me, all that had appeared hitherto incoherent in my mind, became intelligible, showed themselves clearly, like a sentence that makes no sense as long as it remains decomposed into letters arranged by chance, [but] expresses, if the characters are found rearranged in the necessary order, a thought that one could not thereafter forget.

Furthermore, I now understood why earlier, when I had seen him leaving Mme de Villeparisis', I had been able to discover in M. de Charlus the air of a woman: he was one! He belonged to the race of those beings, less contradictory than those who do not have that air [of being a woman], whose ideal is virile precisely because their temperament is feminine ... (II:637)

[En M. de Charlus un autre être avait beau s'accoupler, qui le différenciait des autres hommes, comme dans le centaure le cheval, cet être avait beau faire corps avec le baron, je ne l'avais jamais aperçu. Maintenant l'abstrait s'était matérialisé, l'être enfin compris avait aussitôt perdu son pouvoir de rester invisible et la transmutation de M. de Charlus en une personne nouvelle était si complète que non seulement les contrastes de son visage, de sa voix, mais rétrospectivement les hauts et les bas eux-mêmes de ses relations avec moi, tout ce qui avait paru jusque-là incohérent à mon esprit, devenait intelligible, se montrait évident comme une phrase, n'offrant aucun sens tant qu'elle reste décomposée en lettres disposées au hasard, exprime, si les caractères se trouvent replacés dans l'ordre qu'il faut, une pensée qu'on ne pourra plus oublier.

De plus je comprenais maintenant pourquoi tout à l'heure, quand je l'avais vu sortir de chez Mme de Villeparisis, j'avais pu trouver que M. de Charlus avait l'air d'une femme: c'en était une! Il appartenait à la race de ces êtres moins contradictoires qu'ils n'en ont l'air, dont l'idéal est viril, justement parce que leur tempérament est féminin ...] (III:16)

The passage seems definitively to resolve the matter of Charlus's gender. Yet the very figure that represents what he is, the centaur, suggests more interesting and complex possibilities: to wit, that Charlus is neither simply male nor female, but both at once. This reading is confirmed some pages later in the long discussion of "inverts," whose origins go all the way back to the epoch of the human species's original hermaphroditism (see II:653; III:31).

Two sets of metaphors dominate the Narrator's account of male homosexuality: the biological (plants, insects, animals, disease); and the political or social (preeminently Zionism). These two sets propose distinct theories or concepts of homo-eroticism – and, by extension, other aspects of social life such as Jewishness. Both are deterministic, but the former is more so. Inversion, on the biological model, cannot be altered in its fundamental structure, although the appearance it presents can change:

No doubt the life of certain inverts appears sometimes to change; their vice (as it is called) no longer appears in their habits; but nothing is lost: a missing jewel is found again ... As is the case for the sick, in whom an attack of urticaria makes their chronic ailments disappear for a time, the pure love for a young relation in the invert seems for the moment to have replaced, by metastasis, the habits that one day or the other will take the place again of the vicarious and conquered illness. (II:648–9)

[Sans doute la vie de certains invertis paraît quelquefois changer, leur vice (comme on dit) n'apparaît plus dans leurs habitudes; mais rien ne se perd: un bijou caché se retrouve ... Comme il en est pour ces malades chez qui une crise d'urticaire fait disparaître pour un temps leurs indispositions habituelles, l'amour pur à l'égard d'un jeune parent semble, chez l'inverti, avoir momentanément remplacé, par métastase, des habitudes qui reprendront un jour ou l'autre la place du mal vicariant et guéri.] (III:26–7)

One suffers from inversion as one suffers from cancer or uremia; its course may meander, but it is not possible to escape its inexorable hold over one's psyche.[16]

Earlier on, however, inversion is compared to several social ideologies (see II:642–3; III:21–2), and the long passage on homosexuality ends on this same note. Of the "descendants of the Sodomites" the novel says:

Certainly they form in every country an oriental colony, cultivated, musical, malicious, that has charming qualities and insupportable defects. We shall encounter them in a more profound manner in the

course of the pages that follow, but we have wished to warn provisionally against the lamentable error that consists (just as people
have encouraged a Zionist movement) in creating a Sodomist movement and rebuilding Sodom. Now, scarcely have they arrived, than
the Sodomites would leave the city in order not to appear to be part
of it, taking a wife, keeping mistresses in other cities where they,
moreover, would find agreeable distractions. They would only go to
Sodom on days of supreme necessity, when their city was empty, at
those times when hunger drives the wolf from the woods; that is to
say, everything would continue on the whole as it does in London, in
Berlin, in Rome, in Petrograd, or in Paris. (II:656–6)

[Certes ils forment dans tous les pays une colonie orientale, cultivée,
musicienne, médisante, qui a des qualité[s] charmantes et d'in-
supportables défauts. On les verra d'une façon plus approfondie au
cours des pages qui suivront; mais on a voulu provisoirement prévenir
l'erreur funeste qui consisterait, de même qu'on a encouragé un
mouvement sioniste, à créer un mouvement sodomiste et à rebâtir
Sodome. Or, à peine arrivés, les sodomistes quitteraient la ville pour
ne pas avoir l'air d'en être, prendraient femme, entretiendraient des
maîtresses dans d'autres cités où ils trouveraient d'ailleurs toutes les
distractions convenables. Ils n'iraient à Sodome que les jours de
suprême nécessité, quand leur ville serait vide, par ces temps où la
faim fait sortir le loup du bois, c'est-à-dire que tout se passerait en
somme comme à Londres, à Berlin, à Rome, à Pétrograd ou à Paris.]
(III:33)

The Narrator inveighs against any form of separatism, arguing
that the only possible course, for homosexuals and for Jews, is
assimilation. Why? Because it is in the very nature of homosexuality (and by implication Jewishness) to depend upon
dissimulation and deceit, that is, to appear like other, heterosexual or non-Jewish, members of the community.[17] Doubtless,
it was passages such as this one that led Gide to vilify Proust in
his *Journals*, and to remark, apropos of what he understood to
be Oscar Wilde's theory of the mask: "This artistic hypocrisy
was imposed on him by respect, which was very keen in him,
for the proprieties; and by the need of self-protection. Likewise,
moreover, for Proust, that great master of dissimulation."[18]
Charges of Proust's antisemitism take a similar line.

Before concluding too swiftly that Proust was homophobic
and antisemitic (or at the very least a self-hating Jew), one

should consider how this episode functions diegetically and thematically in the *Recherche* as a whole. As a guide, it may be well to recall Sartre's famous aside on Charlus in *What Is Literature?*: "Proust never discovered the homosexuality of Charlus, since he had decided upon it even before starting the book."[19] Sartre's point, I take it, is that homosexuality is a constitutive element in the novel's structure, a judgment confirmed by the social significance of the Charlus–Jupien relation from this point onwards. The opening scene in *Sodome et Gomorrhe* marks the beginning of Charlus's fall from the social pinnacle he has hitherto occupied, a fact revealed to Marcel later on when he discovers that Charlus's ability to enforce obedience within the *gratin* has begun to wane. One sign of this development is Marcel's own presence at the Guermantes reception to follow. Charlus has insisted that Marcel could never enter those precincts without his assistance (a favor Charlus never grants), and yet Marcel is invited anyway.

 Charlus's sexual proclivities impel him to enlist the services of a *petit bourgeois* procurer (Jupien) and to begin moving in a much lower social sphere (that of the Verdurins). The clear implication is that homosexuality is taboo in the Faubourg Saint-Germain (Mme. de Villeparisis seems aware of Charlus's actual tastes but conceals the fact), as heterosexual infidelity is not. Homosexuality here and throughout the remainder of the *Recherche* is a sign of aristocratic decadence; it constitutes a threat to the nobility's class solidarity and indicates that its hold over social power is loosening. Just as the Faubourg's social exclusivity has been fissured by the Dreyfus Affair, so Charlus's homosexual promiscuity will cause a further breach in society's invisible barriers against unrestricted circulation. And just as the political and ideological identifications of aristocrats and bourgeois will prove complicated and somewhat unpredictable at the Prince and Princesse de Guermantes's reception, so the sexual preferences and gender identities of various characters are revealed to be virtually indeterminate by novel's end. Such will be the burden of the entire Albertine episode that extends from the second part of *Sodome et Gomorrhe* through *Albertine disparue*.

The social dimensions of the Marcel–Albertine liaison are of great interest, and I shall consider them below. For now, though, I wish to focus upon its specifically erotic component. Introduced under the sign of heterosexual desire, this relationship would appear to be diametrically opposed to that between Charlus and Jupien. Following the Greimassian schema for mapping sexual relations in a system of contrary and contradictory values, we can project a preliminary model of the novel's erotic system in diagram 3.2.[20]

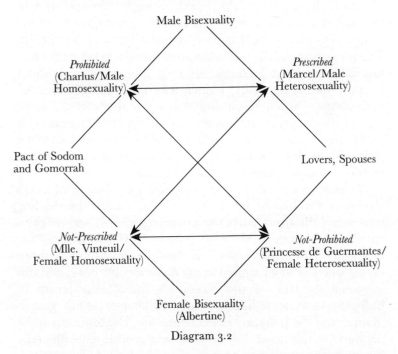

Diagram 3.2

This system of sexual values operates with some consistency throughout *Sodome et Gomorrhe*, as Marcel is gradually introduced into the Gomorrhan world, which had hitherto been a closed book to him (save for the brief view of Mlle. Vinteuil and her lover in "Combray," a scene that was put, somewhat

oddly, under the sign of "sadism"). That Albertine may be
bisexual and that she grew up in Mlle. Vinteuil's care determine Marcel to marry Albertine, inaugurating the rather
different action of *La prisonnière*, which I shall consider more
fully below. Until he begins to suspect Albertine of lesbian
tastes (this fear emerges gradually during his second visit to
Balbec), Marcel is comparatively tolerant of female homosexuality, exhibiting none of the disgust others heap on, for
example, Bloch's sister and her actress friend. Moreover, it is
precisely Albertine's potential *bi*sexuality that is most threatening to him, as we shall see.

Finally, it may seem odd that the complex or ideal term in
this diagram would be male bisexuality. Indeed, there is little
evidence to this point that such a sexual type can even exist.
The great virtue of the Greimassian rectangle, in my opinion, is
just this capacity to predict what a narrative must say without
its quite stating it openly. I shall defer this question until the
final chapter when discussing the war episode in *Le temps
retrouvé*, for the preeminent representative of male bisexuality is
undoubtedly Saint-Loup. His fate and Marcel's understanding
of it will be decisive for the novel's resolution of the sexual
relations it anatomizes across many volumes.[21]

We need to turn now to the complex narrative of Marcel's
second visit to Balbec, where he observes so many disorienting
scenes and discovers what the novel ingeniously terms (principally in relation to his dead grandmother's memory) "the
intermittencies of the heart." It should probably go without
saying that nothing happens in the *Recherche* only once, and this
is manifestly true of the Narrator's initial experiences in
Balbec, where he is haunted by recollections of his grandmother and the pain he caused her in life. Deaths occur quite
regularly in this novel, but none is more crucial to its thematic
structure and aesthetic coherence, as Leo Bersani has argued,
than that of Marcel's grandmother.[22]

Marcel returns to Balbec for specifically erotic reasons: first,
to attempt a seduction of Mme. Putbus's chambermaid, whom
he hopes to encounter at the Verdurins' rented summer residence, La Raspelière (II:779; III:149); and, second, to meet

women generally (II:782; III:152). But his intentions are
thwarted immediately upon arrival when the memory of his
dead grandmother overwhelms him and drives him into soli-
tude. When Albertine arrives unexpectedly, Marcel declines to
see her – or indeed anyone (II:791; III:160). As he remarks:
"grief had destroyed in me the possibility of desire as completely as a high fever takes away one's appetite" (II:795). [le
chagrin avait aboli en moi la possibilité du désir aussi complètement qu'une forte fièvre coupe l'appétit] (III:164–5).
Nursing his sorrow and pain, Marcel gradually grows indifferent to his grandmother's death. In a forecast of the stages
through which he will pass after Albertine's death later on,
Marcel begins by tolerating her company briefly, then finds
that he positively desires it, although at first not erotically
(II:810; III:179). The emotive sequence runs as follows: erotic
desire → unexpected grief → indifference → desire for happiness. The latter will soon metamorphose into erotic desire (for
Albertine), and the sequence will be repeated once more – as
indeed it has been repeated often already, both in Marcel's life
and in Swann's. Canonically, this cycle of desire leading to
disappointment producing yet more desire will only come to an
end with Marcel's discovery of his vocation to write a novel
about his life.[23] Whether this traditional reading of the final
episode can be sustained need not detain us here, since the
question posed in this section is not whether or not Marcel will
become a writer, but how he displaces his guilt and pain over
his grandmother's death. The obvious answer lies in his
growing erotic attraction to Albertine, the full complexity of
which we must now consider.

The great theme of *Sodome et Gomorrhe* II through the end of
Albertine disparue is, as is well known, jealousy. Marcel's desire
for Albertine is inextricably linked to his anxieties concerning
her possible lesbianism, anxieties that are aroused almost
immediately upon his resuming relations with her. First
Cottard plants the seed of doubt when he notices how closely
Albertine and Andrée are dancing in the casino (II:823–4;
III:191). Marcel himself then notices how Albertine eyes Mlle.
Bloch and her cousin (the latter reputed to be a lesbian) in a

mirror (II:830–1; III:197–8). Marcel asserts that his jealousy derives from his knowledge of Odette's infidelities to Swann (II:832; III:199–200), and everything in the narrative points to this source of Marcel's discomfort. Yet the differences between the two affairs are more striking. While Swann had indeed queried Odette about possible lesbian tendencies, these latter would appear to be Marcel's sole preoccupation in Albertine's case.[24] Well, not quite.

As Marcel observes some pages later: "my jealousy, caused by women whom Albertine perhaps loved, was abruptly to cease" (II:883). [ma jalousie causée par les femmes qu'aimait peut-être Albertine allait brusquement cesser] (III:248). Marcel will prove equally – if but momentarily – jealous of men. Here the supposed rival is Saint-Loup, whom he and Albertine encounter at the Balbec train station and with whom Albertine openly flirts. This curious little episode is followed immediately by Charlus's appearance and his initial encounter with Morel. From this moment to the end of *La prisonnière*, the Marcel–Albertine and Charlus–Morel relationships will be regularly counterpointed. Each illuminates the other, while complicating our understanding of the sex/gender system that operates in the novel. The *Recherche* narrates a complex game in which jealous lovers (Swann, Saint-Loup, Marcel, Charlus) attempt to dominate their beloveds (Odette, Rachel, Albertine, Morel) by manipulating desires the latter are believed to possess. In each instance, the wish for total mastery runs up against the contingency of the beloved's actual desires. The situation is also complicated by the lover's lack of lucidity about his own motives and feelings. The dialectic of jealousy is therefore, in principle, interminable.[25]

What is at stake, narratively and thematically, in these episodes? In a brilliant extended comparison of Freud and Proust, Malcolm Bowie cites the *Introductory Lectures on Psychoanalysis* to illustrate a fundamental tie between Freud's model of desire and that which is elaborated in the *Recherche*. Both, Bowie argues, presume the "'plasticity' or 'free mobility'" of libidinal energy (Bowie, *Freud*, p. 9). Nothing is more plainly indicated in the Balbec section of *Sodome et Gomorrhe* than this restless, uncontrollable quality of desire. It is presumed by Marcel to govern Albertine's every action, for he believes her perpetually to be seeking out new opportunities for pleasure, and is exemplified in Charlus, who appears here to be constantly on the prowl. But it is also manifested in Marcel's entire amorous history, even if he does not recognize this fact. The forward progress of the *Recherche*'s narrative has been motivated from the first by the series of the Narrator's love objects, from his mother to Gilberte to the Duchesse de Guermantes to Mlle. de Stermaria to Mme. Putbus's chambermaid and now finally to Albertine. This infinitely variable libidinal cathexis acts as a narrative goad, driving the story relentlessly onward, even as it appears to detain the Narrator and prevent his reaching that goal which the text has projected for him from the very first: to become a writer.

Jealousy is the condition or structure produced by the mobility of desire, by desire's incapacity to rest or be confined to a single object. In Deleuze's words: "Jealousy is the very delirium of signs."[26] Marcel's torment in Balbec and throughout *La prisonnière* and *Albertine disparue* derives from his inability to control or command desire (figured in Albertine), but this very wish is produced by his systematic misrecognition of desire's true nature. In attempting to master desire absolutely, Marcel ensures his own enslavement to it. What Marcel cannot comprehend (indeed, what men in this novel regularly fail to understand) is that libidinal energy, which is characteristically coded as female, can be non-exclusive, even (one might say especially) in its gender preferences.[27] This debility is poignantly illustrated in Marcel's hypothesis about Albertine and Saint-Loup: "I felt, since she had appeared to desire Saint-Loup, nearly cured for a time of the idea that she loved women, which I imagined to be irreconcilable [with loving men]" (II:894). [Je me sentais, puisqu'elle avait paru désirer Saint-Loup, à peu près guéri pour quelque temps de l'idée qu'elle aimait les femmes, ce que je me figurais inconciliable] (III:258). Like so much else in the *Recherche*, this is an error of which Marcel will only be disabused after long and painful experience.[28]

WHAT'S LOVE GOT TO DO WITH IT?

Marcel's education in desire's reality, which presumes the mobility of libidinal cathexis, continues virtually to novel's end. To anticipate what he learns, it may be useful to diagram (3.3) the sex/gender/sexual preference system that the *Recherche* ultimately exhibits. The system's complexity derives not only from the numerous positions that individuals may occupy, but also from the potential ambiguity in several positions that renders certain characters' sexual identity utterly indeterminate.

Before drawing any conclusions from this chart, it is necessary to note a few apparent anomalies. Moving from left to right, we notice that Charlus is at once a gay man who has been a faithful husband and is now a promiscuous lover. This is, on the evidence available, absolutely true. Charlus's devotion to his dead wife's memory is patent; we have no evidence that he indulged his homoerotic tastes before her death. But once he pursues men, he is utterly promiscuous and insatiable (although there is some indication that he may for a time be more or less faithful to Morel). Swann is heterosexually promiscuous both as husband and as lover, i.e., his sexual appetites remain more or less constant before and after his marriage to Odette. The same is true of Odette, who could possibly be included among the "many" promiscuous lesbians as well, at least prior to her marriage. The evidence of her lesbianism is ambiguous at best.

What generalizations does the chart reveal about sexuality and gender in the *Recherche*? First, promiscuity is more common among gay men and lesbians than among heterosexual men and women, the notable exception being, unsurprisingly, the prostitutes (Odette and Rachel).[29] Among the heterosexual males and females, affairs tend to be serial (as with Swann, the Duc de Guermantes, Odette after her marriage, and of course Marcel), while gay men and lesbians appear in the novel to be utterly faithless.[30] Charlus and Albertine are the prime, but hardly the only, examples. Second, *pace* Malcolm Bowie's discounting the presence of bisexuality in the *Recherche*, it is a more

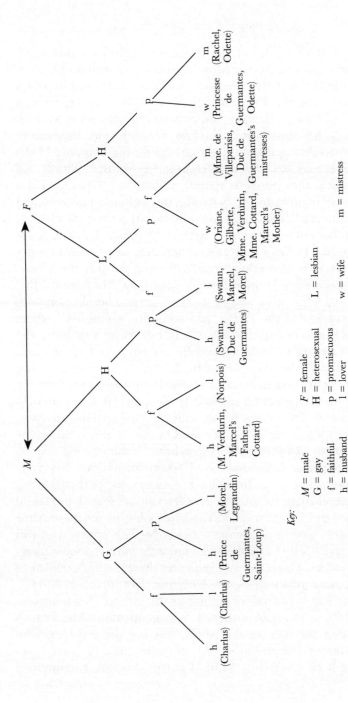

Diagram 3.3

Key:

M = male   F = female

G = gay   H = heterosexual   L = lesbian

f = faithful   p = promiscuous

h = husband   l = lover   w = wife   m = mistress

widespread sexual orientation than one might have imagined. Among major characters, Morel, Saint-Loup, and possibly the Prince de Guermantes (we don't know the exact nature of his relations with the Princess) all swing both ways at various times. Albertine certainly consents to relations with Marcel, although her tastes may incline primarily to lesbianism. Odette, while vigorously heterosexual during the time of the narrative, may have been different in her youth.[31] Third, and related to the previous point, lesbianism remains comparatively opaque to the Narrator throughout. The very fact that we never know for certain whether Albertine (or Odette) is a lesbian contrasts sharply with the intimate knowledge we acquire of Charlus's and others' homosexuality. Lesbians are nearly as numerous as gay men, including possibly the following women: Léa, Andrée, Mlle. Vinteuil and her friend, Mlle. Bloch and her cousin, and of course Albertine herself. But with the exception of the rather odd scene in "Combray" where Marcel observes Mlle. Vinteuil and her friend profaning the father's portrait, lesbian sexuality remains a hypothesized entity throughout the novel. Finally, try as one might to find one, the chart reveals no clear or consistent alignment with the class system. Aristocrats and bourgeois appear indiscriminately throughout. This is not to say that the two systems are completely autonomous of each other. On the contrary, the whole labor of the *Recherche* is to show how character and society articulate, how individuals and social formations are overdetermined in the Althusserian/Freudian sense of the term.

A miniature of the novel's overdetermined sexual and social relations can be glimpsed in the letter Charlus writes to Aimé in the last section of *Sodome et Gomorrhe*. The occasion of this characteristically Charlusian document is narrated some pages earlier, when Marcel clearly indicates the situation's relevance to his own relations with Albertine (see II:1019; III:375). Charlus has appeared for dinner at the Grand Hotel, accompanied by a footman outfitted as a gentleman. The latter's dress fools the men of the world, but not the servants, who easily pierce the disguise and recognize one of their own. Having been greeted by M. de Charlus, Marcel is summoned by Aimé, who inquires about the Baron's identity. Marcel's revelation produces a profound effect on the waiter, and he asks Marcel to interpret an odd letter he had received from this very Baron de Charlus, whom Aimé professes (truthfully it turns out) not to have known previously. The letter (II:1023–5; III:380–2) mobilizes all the novel's major motifs associated with sexual and social relations: erotic attraction punctuated (and in many respects motivated) by class differences; overweening pride mingled with abject shame; the desire for social improvement (to which Charlus appeals to seduce Aimé); the dissimulation of forbidden sexual tastes. Charlus has approached Aimé obliquely (he had twice summoned the waiter to undertake specific tasks that Aimé had failed to perform), but Aimé has missed the signals, perhaps in part because he is heterosexual. Charlus construes Aimé's response as an insult and out of wounded vanity writes the waiter a dissembling letter filled with vituperation.

The episode is all the more significant in that it repeats much the same pattern as Marcel's earlier encounter with Charlus after the dinner at the Duc and Duchesse de Guermantes's, when Charlus had offered to make Marcel his protégé. Charlus's inability to interest Aimé produces the same result as his previous failure with Marcel: it liberates the most violent passions. Marcel's commentary on the entire episode is worth quoting at length:

[Charlus's letter to Aimé] was, because of the anti-social love which was that of M. de Charlus, a more striking example of the insensible and powerful force that these currents of passion possess and because of which the lover, like a swimmer caught up in them without perceiving it, quickly loses sight of land. Doubtless the love of a normal man can also – when the lover by the successive invention of his desires, regrets, deceptions, projects, constructs an entire novel about a woman whom he does not know – allow us to register an equally noticeable separation of the two legs of the compass. All the same, such a separation was singularly enlarged by the character of a passion that is not generally shared and by the difference in ranks [*conditions*] between M. de Charlus and Aimé. (II:1026)

[Elle était, à cause de l'amour antisocial qui était celui de M. de Charlus, un exemple plus frappant de la force insensible et puissante

qu'ont ces courants de la passion et par lesquels l'amoureux, comme
un nageur entraîne sans s'en apercevoir, bien vite perd de vue la
terre. Sans doute l'amour d'un homme normal peut aussi, quand
l'amoureux par l'invention successive de ses désirs, de ses regrets, de
ses déceptions, de ses projets, construit tout un roman sur une femme
qu'il ne connaît pas, permettre de mesurer un assez notable écartement de deux branches de compas. Tout de même un tel écartement
était singulièrement élargi par le caractère d'une passion qui n'est pas
généralement partagée et par la différence des conditions de M. de
Charlus et d'Aimé.] (III:382)

The explicit comparison between "normal" and "anti-social"
types of love unites homosexuality and heterosexuality under a
single heading, while enforcing a distinction in the degrees of
irrationality – or, in the terms of the passage, irresistible and
imperceptible force – evident in each. The figure of the
compass recalls the famous conceit in Donne's "A Valediction:
Forbidding Mourning," where the compass legs symbolize the
two lovers. Here, however, the figure denotes not the relationship between two more or less equal human entities, but the
distance separating fiction from reality, or understanding from
the truth, that characterizes the representation of love
throughout the *Recherche*. The force of the figure shows that
passion – even "normal," i.e., heterosexual (and preeminently
male), erotic attraction – produces an aberrant epistemological
structure. The text names this structure, not incidentally, "un
roman." This general condition of misunderstanding, which is
part and parcel of any passion, is further exacerbated ("such a
separation was singularly enlarged") when the passion "is not
generally shared," or is "anti-social." Charlus's homosexuality
is just that. Homosexuality is typically represented throughout
the *Recherche* in the same manner. Bad enough to be straight
and in love (as both Swann and Marcel attest), but worse yet
to be gay and therefore subject to the sort of mad outbursts
instanced by Charlus's letter to Aimé.

But the passage goes one step further. In addition to the
increased mystification consequent upon homoerotic attraction, even greater confusion results when the lovers occupy
different social stations. The French "condition" is deliber-

ately ambiguous. While the primary meaning would seem to be "social position" or "rank," it may refer as well to sexual proclivity. By this point in the novel, sexual preference could easily be thought of as a "condition" in both the biological and the sociological senses of the term. One can be said to be homosexual in the same way that one can be said to be suffering from a hereditary and incurable disease. The opening pages of *Sodome et Gomorrhe* say so explicitly. But the novel also asserts, again in the same passage, the complex variation in homosexual types such that the system of homoerotic relations appears as highly differentiated as the finely graded world of the upper classes. The passage refers immediately to the difference in rank between Charlus and Aimé, but the same strictures apply equally to Charlus's relations with Morel, which are riven by powerful social tensions (see II:1096–7; III:449).

Nor is Marcel's erotic life exempt from this aspect of social determination. What Marcel fails to recognize at this point – although his mother sees it quite clearly – is Albertine's desire to make a good marriage. He scarcely guesses that social ambition (her own, but even more that of her aunt, Mme. Bontemps) has brought her to him. She appears in Balbec unexpectedly, having originally planned to stay away this season. It is precisely this social desire that enables her to endure the most appalling behavior on Marcel's part. In brief, erotic attraction and social distinction are inseparable in the *Recherche*. Lovers frequently occupy the position of servants. The attempt to enforce fidelity is invariably an expression of social power – a power that is perpetually contested, as the cases of Odette, Rachel, and Albertine amply illustrate.[32]

It may now be possible to schematize the system of values structuring the relations among the four principal lovers in *La prisonnière*. The Greimassian rectangle relating Marcel, Albertine, Charlus, and Morel projects their relations as in diagram 3.4.

Identifying Marcel as the figure for jealousy is unproblematic enough. So much is obvious on even a superficial reading of *La prisonnière*. As for Albertine, she is for the most part, until her final flight, pliable and unresistant to Marcel's wishes, not only

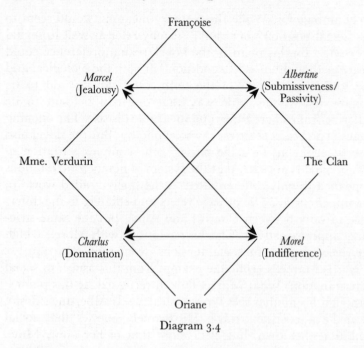

Diagram 3.4

sexually but in response to his highly arbitrary and often changeable commands concerning her daily activities. Her utter abnegation before his will is revealed at the very outset of their living together in his parents' house. In a striking passage that exposes the tyrannical character of Marcel's passion, we are told:

[Albertine's] somewhat inconvenient charm was, in fact, of behaving like a domestic animal which comes into a room and goes out again and is to be found wherever one least expects to find it, and she would often – something that I found profoundly restful – come and lie down beside me on my bed, making a place for herself from which she never stirred, without disturbing me as a person would have done. She ended, however, by conforming to my hours of sleep, and not only never attempted to enter my room but would take care not to make a sound until I had rung my bell. (iii:7)

[Son charme un peu incommode était ainsi d'être à la maison moins comme une jeune fille que comme une bête domestique qui entre dans une pièce, qui en sort, qui se trouve partout où on ne s'y attend pas et qui venait – c'était pour moi un repos profond – se jeter sur mon lit à côté de moi, s'y faire une place d'où elle ne bougeait plus, sans gêner comme l'eut fait une personne. Pourtant elle finit par se plier à mes heures de sommeil, à ne pas essayer non seulement d'entrer dans ma chambre, mais, à ne plus faire de bruit avant que jeusse sonné.] (III:525)

Marcel treats Albertine like a pet, a role to which she willingly submits until the very end. Even her flight, which takes Marcel by surprise, seems an act performed to comply with his deepest desire, as her farewell note intimates (III:427; IV:5).[33]

Charlus will of course undergo a profound transformation in *Le temps retrouvé*, but prior to his humiliation at the Verdurins', his sexual relations are closely allied to his desire (and ability) to dominate his beloved. In the case of Morel, this is most evident in the Baron's promotion of the violinist's career, but it extends to his constantly supervising Morel's life and loves. As for Morel himself, his cynicism with respect to Charlus's attentions is boundless, something he reveals to Marcel on numerous occasions. He is merely using Charlus, and when the Verdurins convince him that relations with the Baron are an encumbrance rather than an advantage, he summarily and brutally dismisses his patron. Morel's brief tirade, which leaves Charlus uncharacteristically speechless, even intimates that the two have never had carnal relations: "'Leave me alone. I forbid you to come near me,' Morel shouted at the Baron. 'You know what I mean all right. I'm not the first person you've tried to pervert!'" (III:321) ["Laissez-moi, je vous défends de m'approcher," cria Morel au baron. "Vous ne devez pas être à votre coup d'essai, je ne suis pas le premier que vous essayez de pervertir!"] (III:820)[34] Unconcerned about Charlus's sexual infidelities, Morel is eager only to preserve his position as the Baron's protégé (see the episode of Charlus's interest in Bloch at Balbec [II:1140–4; III:489–93]). Morel's indifference extends even to disdaining Charlus's offer to assume one of the aristocratic titles the Baron has at his disposal, although Morel's recalcitrance derives in part from class resentment (II:1044; III:400).

Mme. Verdurin's character and function are readily explained, since she has never wavered in the desire to establish her salon's exclusiveness from the first moment we encounter her in "Un amour de Swann." Tyrannizing over the members of the "little clan," she remains perpetually suspicious about their loyalty and jealously guards her self-created right to arrange their social life. It is just this threat to her power over the "faithful" that leads to the plot to humiliate and banish Charlus. The appearance of his social circle at the musical evening showcasing Morel's talent has, she fears, weakened her capacity to command her guests' time. Her polar opposite is the very "clan" over whom she rules, that passionless, indifferent circle of old (and some newer) acquaintances who submit to her every whim and allow her to dictate where and in whose company they will spend their evenings.[35]

That the Duchesse de Guermantes should crop up in this diagram at all may seem surprising at first. She scarcely appears in this volume, save to counsel Marcel concerning Albertine's wardrobe. But as always, her power is felt quite as much – perhaps more – in her absence as when she is present and given a speaking part. From the first, Oriane's position in the Faubourg Saint-Germain has rested in large measure on her appearing to be indifferent to its customs and regulations. Because she feigns to ignore its taboos – by inviting artists and intellectuals to her dinners, by speaking in the accents and vocabulary of a peasant, and by steadfastly refusing to acknowledge any social obligation – she maintains her position of utter exclusivity.[36] While she plays no special role in this volume's action, her importance to its ideological structure remains. She represents that which is in imminent danger of being usurped by Mme. Verdurin and her ilk.

Immediately after the revelation of Mme. Verdurin's grievances against Charlus (and thus against the Faubourg as a whole, whose principal representative he clearly is during the musical evening he has organized), we learn about the effect the Dreyfus Affair has had upon society:

Nobody will accuse the Dreyfus case of having premeditated such dark designs against fashionable society. But there it certainly broke down barriers. Society people who refuse to allow politics into their world [the Narrator has just observed that the Duchesse de Guermantes is among them] are as far-sighted as soldiers who refuse to allow politics to permeate the army. It is the same in society as in sexual taste, where one never knows to what perversions it may advert when once aesthetic considerations are allowed to dictate its choices. The reason that they were Nationalists gave the Faubourg Saint-Germain the habit of entertaining ladies from another region of society; the reason vanished with Nationalism; the habit remained. (III:236–7)

[On n'accusera pas l'affaire Dreyfus d'avoir prémédité d'aussi noirs desseins à l'encontre du monde. Mais là certainement elle a brisé les cadres. Les mondains qui ne veulent pas laisser la politique s'introduire dans le monde sont aussi prévoyants que les militaires qui ne veulent pas laisser la politique pénétrer dans l'armée. Il en est du monde comme du goût sexuel, où l'on ne sait pas jusqu'à quelles perversions il peut arriver quand une fois on a laissé des raisons esthétiques dicter ses choix. La raison qu'elles étaient nationalistes donna au faubourg Saint-Germain l'habitude de recevoir des dames d'une autre société, la raison disparut avec le nationalisme, l'habitude subsista.] (III:740)

The language here is highly overdetermined, condensing the political/military matter of the Dreyfus case, the conventions of high society, and the dangers of sexual deviance in a taut image of the first breaches in caste distinctions that will ultimately be rendered nugatory during the war and after, as the culminating episode of the Prince and Princesse de Guermantes's *matinée* will demonstrate. Oriane constitutes this volume's neutral term because the text forecasts the demise of her (and her class's) social power in Charlus's humiliation by the Verdurins. What then of the complex or ideal term? In what sense can it be said that Françoise, the peasant-born servant to Marcel and his family, represents the solution to the basic tension in values that the narrative mobilizes? It is not difficult to see how she combines jealousy and submissiveness. She is exceedingly put out by Albertine's intrusion into her masters' world, yet she remains entirely obedient to Marcel's will. But what is the value that she herself incarnates and that stands as the ideal projected by the narrative? It can only be servitude, which submits (as Marcel occasionally will do) to the irresistible force of one's own desire, combining the passivity of the beloved who allows herself to be used with the active passion of the lover who exploits his dominance to gratify her wishes and satisfy her tastes. Such a seemingly odd combination of qualities will ultimately enable, in the final volume, the aesthetic awakening Marcel experiences.[37]

If one is inclined to be skeptical about such a proleptic reading of this volume's action, it may be well to recall two signal facts. First, Françoise's culinary skills have consistently been dignified as a form of artistry, from the first descriptions of the Combray lunches prepared for Marcel's family (1:76–7; 70–1), to the dinner she concocts for M. de Norpois when he dines with Marcel and his family in Paris (1:493–4; 449–50).[38] On the latter occasion she is dubbed "the Michelangelo of our kitchen." Second, the matter of art, never far from the action at any moment in the *Recherche*, is especially prominent when Marcel attends the musical evening at the Verdurins'. There he hears Morel play an unpublished work by Vinteuil that contains elements of the famous sonata (which latter he himself had played while awaiting Albertine's return from the Trocadero that afternoon; see III:154–5; 664). The performance spurs him to lengthy reflections on art, igniting the spark of aesthetic inspiration that will continue to smolder until it finally bursts into flame at the end of *Le temps retrouvé* (III:250–65; 753–67). In this final episode, as is well known, Vinteuil's music once again provides the model for the aesthetic representation of those experiences Marcel believes hold the key to his happiness – and therefore to his vocation as a writer (see III:899; IV:445). The long detour of Marcel's grief, which ensues immediately upon his return from the Verdurins' and occupies virtually the whole of *Albertine disparue*, proves in the end to have been necessary to awaken his aesthetic vocation. Indeed, all the incidents, passions, distractions, and so forth about which we have read turn out to have been instrumental in creating the artist Marcel has resolved to become at novel's end. Here, the example of Vinteuil, particularly the reconstruction of his entire posthumous corpus through his daughter's lover's labor, both chastens and inspires Marcel. He recognizes that without this unlikely scribe's devotion, "what is for us his true work would have remained purely potential, as unknown as those universes to which our perception does not reach, of which we shall never have any idea" (III:265) [ce qui est pour nous son œuvre véritable fût resté purement virtuel, aussi inconnu que ces univers jusqu'auxquels notre perception n'atteint pas, dont nous n'aurons jamais une idée] (III:768). The pathos of such a passage in the light of what we know about Proust's own career is too powerful to ignore. The final volume will only augment it, as the Narrator's physical frailty increases and his acute consciousness of his mortality and the difficulty of completing his work occupy his mind almost totally.

As the diagram has illustrated, the ideological structure of *La prisonnière* takes us to the threshold of the novel's final movement. Its ultimate semantic opposition, Françoise/Oriane de Guermantes, anticipates the principal ideologemes in the *Recherche*'s final scene. But the novel has far to travel – to Venice and back, to Combray once more, and through the long, indispensable detour of the First World War – before it can overcome the various ideological tensions it has set in motion. Above all, the Narrator must resolve his feelings about Albertine, for nothing could be more plain than that he is far from realizing the combination of passivity and passion the narrative projects as its ideal term. It remains to account for the insane jealousy Marcel experiences in response to Albertine's putative lesbianism. To that end, I shall inquire more closely into the structural position lesbianism occupies in the novel's system of sexuality.

THAT OBSCURE OBJECT OF DESIRE

In the first diagram of sexual relations in *Sodome et Gomorrhe*, it will be recalled, male homosexuality was prohibited, male heterosexuality was prescribed, female homosexuality was not-prescribed, and female heterosexuality was not-prohibited. Whatever heuristic utility this schema may have for illuminating sex roles in the early sections of *Sodome et Gomorrhe*, the

complications introduced in the ensuing episodes make such a
straightforward valuation of different sexual practices patently
insupportable. Above all, bringing lesbianism to center stage
(it had hitherto been marginal, confined to Swann's suspicions
about Odette's previous life and the single scene between Mlle.
Vinteuil and her lover at Montjouvain) has shifted the ground
from a more or less exclusive focus on male eros to an obsessive
concern with female sexuality. From the end of *Sodome et
Gomorrhe* through much of *Albertine disparue*, the *Recherche* insist-
ently poses the infamous Freudian question: what do women
want?

It is worth reflecting a bit on why lesbianism would play
such a significant role in Proust's novel. The easy answer – that
Proust's guilt about his homosexuality led him to transpose his
hero's lover's gender in order to write about his own erotic
jealousy – evades the fundamental problem: why would
someone of Proust's background and socialization write about
this subject at all? It is doubtful that his choices were exclusively personal. Moreover, Proust could certainly write quite
openly – if not unambiguously – about male homosexuality in
Sodome et Gomorrhe and succeeding volumes. There is little
warrant for the commonplace about his incapacity to "come
out of the closet" in his fictional representations, however
reticent he may have been to do so in his own life.

In his study of nineteenth-century French representations of
prostitutes, Charles Bernheimer hints at the ideololgical nexus
Proust's novel tries to unravel:

Male fantasy now [in the last third of the nineteenth century]
becomes obsessed with what is unknowable about female sexuality,
with what resists dissection and positive identification. The power
behind this resistance is fantasized as a lack, gap, or fissure, most
specifically in the place of the genitals. That lack is felt to motivate
female desire, indeed to create woman as the subject of desire.[39]

Bernheimer notices this transformation in the arts, but he gives
no explanation for why it should have occurred at this period.
Antony Copley points in general to the restrictions imposed by
the Victorian morality governing bourgeois households, and in
particular to the retrograde divorce laws that prohibited

divorce altogether until 1884, and only allowed it on grounds of "matrimonial fault" prior to 1975.[40] Alain Corbin, attempting to account for the observed increase in prostitution from mid-century onwards, gives three principal causes: first, the simultaneous idealization and degradation that constituted bourgeois sexual ideology, so that the increasing sterility of their domestic life drove male bourgeois to frequent prostitutes in ever greater numbers; second, the medicalization of sexuality, in particular the belief that limitations had to be placed on female copulation, producing frustration among husbands, who were told (and quite likely accepted) they needed to have sex more frequently than their wives could safely sustain; and, third, the increasing numbers of celibate *petits bourgeois* who were attracted to the cities by better job opportunities but whose wages remained too low to contemplate matrimony and raising a family (Corbin, *Filles*, pp. 287–94). As Corbin writes elsewhere, the changing nature of sexuality was part and parcel of a general crisis in bourgeois domesticity, with this class growing in size and having to confront the contradictions inherent in its moral ideals:

The contemporary history of sexuality began around 1860. Dull rumblings shook the traditional culture; the imagery of the erotic was transformed. Locked in the private sphere, the bourgeoisie began to suffer from its morality. The myth of a bestial and liberated lower-class sexuality made escape from the confines of bourgeois morality an enticing prospect. The dark allure of prostitution increased. (Corbin, "Backstage," p. 549)

Frequenting prostitutes in greater numbers, bourgeois men discovered a whole new range of sexual practices unavailable in their conjugal relations. Above all, the changing sites for prostitutional procuring (Corbin notes the emergence of *femmes de café*, *magasins-prétextes*, and flower girls as characteristic of the new dispensation) altered the old system prevalent in the *maisons closes*, where men had been allowed simply to choose a partner who was required to provide them with their desired pleasures. In the novel environs prevailing after mid-century, the game of seduction was much more complicated: "all these new forms of conduct among prostitutes imply that *the woman give her client the impression that she could be seduced* and that she is no longer simply an animal deprived of the liberty of refusing herself" (Corbin, *Filles*, p. 249; emphasis in the original).[41] Generalizing broadly, Corbin characterizes the changing patterns in male bourgeois sexuality as part of a general social process in which the bourgeoisie more and more aped aristocratic sexual habits and practices (Corbin, *Filles*, p. 297).

One interesting new wrinkle that is directly relevant to the present topic was the taste for lesbian scenes staged in the brothels for their clients' benefit. Jill Harsin notes this phenomenon and attributes it primarily to the needs and desires of the prostitutes themselves and to the shrewd manipulations of bordello proprietors.[42] Corbin refers to the same development in *Les filles de noce* (Corbin, *Filles*, pp. 185–7). Elsewhere he interprets it less functionally than Harsin:

We ... know a great deal about the fascination that the lesbian exerted on the male imagination, a fascination that can be read as yet another symptom of the morbid character of male desire in the nineteenth century. The discussion of sapphism was very different from the discussion of pederasty. If male fantasies medicalized the latter, they poeticized the former. The nineteenth century invented the "lesbian," that paragon of gentleness, delicacy, and cleanliness ... (Corbin, "Backstage," p. 644)

Given this cultivation of lesbian sexuality among bourgeois men, why is lesbianism represented so phobically in the *Recherche*?

Corbin's further speculations hint at an answer and set the stage for a more detailed consideration of Marcel's obsession with Albertine's putative infidelities:

Men were fascinated by women's enormous capacity for pleasure; at the same time they feared any pleasure that women experienced in their absence ... Convinced of their sexual inferiority, men dreamed of the insatiability of women left to govern their own desires. In pursuit of satisfaction, they imagined, frantic lesbians pulled out all the stops. It was this fantasy, quite evident in *La Fille aux yeux d'or*, that drove Fourier as well as the voyeurs who frequented brothels later in the century to delight in tableaux vivants in which all the roles were filled by women. As in the theatrical display of hysteria at the Salpêtrière, men found this exhibition of female bodies somehow therapeutic. (Corbin, "Backstage," p. 645)

WHAT DO WOMEN WANT?

As the *Recherche* shifts focus from Sodom to Gomorrha, male sexuality gives place to female sexuality as the object of the novel's investigations. In line with this reorientation, it is necessary to reconfigure as in diagram 3.5 the Greimassian rectangle proposed earlier (see diagram 3.2, p. 125).

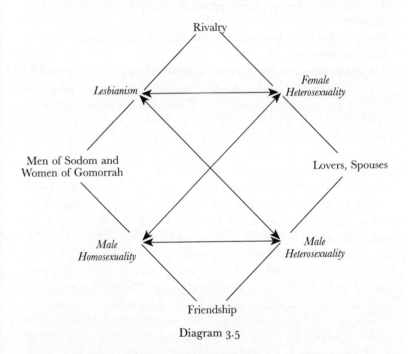

Diagram 3.5

By the end of *Sodome et Gomorrhe*, Marcel's exclusive concern is with Albertine and the mystery of her sexual nature. The horror he experiences at the thought of her lesbianism indicates that this latter is now absolutely prohibited. By comparison, female heterosexuality is now the most desirable quality and hence is specifically prescribed. Male homosexuality is certainly not prescribed, but now it is less threatening, since gay men do not immediately endanger Marcel's domination of Albertine. That male heterosexuality is neither prohibited nor prescribed indicates Marcel's continuing ambivalence towards Albertine's potential for heterosexual infidelity. Better that Albertine sleep around with men than that she have female lovers (which latter are, in Marcel's fevered imagination, potentially limitless).[43] It would also be possible to reverse the positions of male and female heterosexuality, since the former might still be prescribed (for Marcel), the latter not-prohibited (as a requirement for Marcel's relationship to Albertine). The complex and neutral terms would remain the same, although their gender codings would alter. These latter terms require some explanation.

What is signified by the combination of male homosexuality and male heterosexuality producing friendship? The novel has thrown up numerous examples of gay and straight men who are close friends: Charlus and Swann, Swann and the Prince de Guermantes, and at this point Charlus and the Narrator (whose friendship can emerge once it has become clear that the latter is not homoerotically inclined). But the most interesting revelation produced by the diagram concerns the relationship between Marcel and Saint-Loup. The latter's homosexual tastes will not be revealed until much later, but it can be supposed that a crucial component in their friendship has always been Saint-Loup's recognition of Marcel's univocal sexual inclination. Marcel's heterosexuality prevents his being an object of Saint-Loup's erotic interest. We shall have occasion to return to this question in the final chapter below. If, however, the not-prohibited value is female heterosexuality, other possibilities arise. We know that Charlus and Odette have been friends for many years. Of course, this may have derived from Odette's lesbianism (if indeed she actually indulged in it), so that Charlus–Odette would then instance the pact between the men of Sodom and the women of Gomorrha posited in *Sodome et Gomorrhe*'s opening section. But by this point in the novel, Odette's exclusively heterosexual tastes can be safely presumed. More provocative is the light shed on

Marcel's relations to Albertine. The letter she writes to explain her reasons for fleeing (III:427; IV:5) addresses him as "Mon ami" and insists on their close friendship. Structurally, this relationship would only be possible if Albertine were straight and Marcel gay. Leaving aside the endless speculations about the impact of Proust's own sexuality upon Marcel's militant heterosexism, the truly scandalous possibility concerns Albertine's gender. Is she the inverse of Charlus, i.e., a man hiding in a woman's body? If so, her lesbianism would be a form of heterosexual desire. Or, insofar as she is "virile," is her desire for Marcel a species of homoerotic attraction? Does she, in effect, love Marcel as a man, herself attracted to the manliness he represents? Or is she in fact a heterosexual female who projects into Marcel the qualities of a gay man, thereby foreclosing the erotic and liberating the amicable potential in their relations?

Albertine's sexual identity has been much debated, but no one has put the matter more lucidly and engagingly than Eve Sedgwick in commenting on Albertine's parapraxis about getting buggered:

the one way in which the narrator, in his broodings over it, does *not* (explicitly) interpret Albertine's remark is as a requisition of a specific sexual act, something they could actually do together. Instead, it occasions in him only "horror!" "despair," "rage," "tears"; his level of paranoid charade and anticipatory rejections is catapulted to a critical, indeed terminal, height by Albertine's seemingly far from cryptic ejaculation. This is rather unaccountable. He remarkably manages to interpret her expressed desire to get buggered as a sign of her essential *lesbianism*, hence of her inaccessibility to himself . . . the narrator may really hear Albertine's desire as terrifying, not because it isn't directed toward him, but because it is, her desire registering on him as a demand for a performance he fears he cannot give . . . If one cannot say with the utopian readers [Rivers and Bersani] that either within or around Albertine there are erotic possibilities that mark a potentially regenerative *difference from* the spectacularized Charlus plot, neither, in this fearful, shadowy blur of desiring too little, desiring the always wrong thing from the always wrong kind of person, can an intelligible *similarity to* Charlus be allowed to become visible. The chalky rag of gender pulled across the blackboard of sexuality, the chalky rag of sexuality across the blackboard of gender:

these most create a cloudy space from which a hidden voice can be heard to insist, in the words of a contemporaneous manifesto of male homosexual panic, "That is not what I meant at all. That is not it at all."[44]

Sedgwick's point, I take it, is that Albertine's expressed wish to have anal intercourse – even though it's not clear whether this indicates a desire for pleasure or disgust at the thought – horrifies Marcel just because of its powerful associations with male homosexuality. But of course it is nothing of the sort. Marcel's revulsion, it may be inferred (and as I believe Sedgwick intends), is in response to a sexual act that cannot be thought of as univocally male or female, gay or straight; hence the scandal of Albertine herself.[45] Her lesbianism (or, as Rivers hypothesizes, her androgyny) disrupts the smooth functioning of the sex/gender system that otherwise, even in the case of male homosexuality, operates with comparative rigor. Within the terms established by the *Recherche*, lesbianism is an unassimilable value.[46]

To recognize how this is so, we must turn now to the complex term projected in the diagram. If the prescribed value be female heterosexuality, then the combination with lesbianism producing rivalry is perfectly obvious. So much is made explicit by Marcel:

Next to the suffering I was feeling, what was the jealousy that I had experienced on the day when Saint-Loup had encountered Albertine with me at Doncières and when she had been so provocative towards him? Or that I had experienced in thinking again of the unknown initiator to whom I was indebted for the first kisses she had given me in Paris, the day when I was waiting for Mlle. de Stermaria's letter? That other jealousy, provoked by Saint-Loup, by some young man, was nothing. I would have had, in that case, at most to fear a rival whom I would have tried to remove. But here the rival was not my fellow-creature; his weapons were different; I couldn't struggle on the same terrain, give Albertine the same pleasures, nor even imagine them exactly. (II:1157–8)

[Qu'était à côté de la souffrance que je ressentais, la jalousie que j'avais pu éprouver le jour où Saint-Loup avait rencontré Albertine avec moi à Doncières et où elle lui avait fait des agaceries? celle aussi que j'avais éprouvée en repensant à l'initiateur inconnu auquel j'avais pu devoir les premiers baisers qu'elle m'avait données à Paris, le jour où j'attendais la lettre de Mlle. de Stermaria? Cette autre jalousie, provoquée par Saint-Loup, par un jeune homme quelconque, n'était rien. J'aurais pu dans ce cas craindre tout au plus un rival sur lequel j'eusse essayé de l'emporter. Mais ici le rival n'était pas semblable à moi, ses armes étaient différentes, je ne pouvais pas lutter sur le même terrain, donner à Albertine les mêmes plaisirs, ni même les concevoir exactement.] (III:504–5)

Unlike male homosexuality, which Marcel professes to understand (though he will continue to precise this knowledge virtually to the novel's end, notably by discovering Saint-Loup's proclivities and Charlus's descent into masochism), lesbianism will forever remain opaque to him. We may surmise that lesbianism here stands not only for female homoeroticism, but for female sexuality in general. When Marcel asserts his capacity to deal with that jealousy originating in heterosexual rivalry, he does so by claiming knowledge of what men can offer to women. He understands what men do and thus can simply do likewise – and presumably better. What he fails to comprehend – or even imagine – here and throughout *La prisonnière* and *Albertine disparue*, is what women themselves desire, what they are. What do women want? Marcel will never know, since before he discovers the truth about Albertine, she dies, thereby creating the possibility for his deliverance, not from ignorance, but from what the passage calls "suffering."[47]

THE PERMANENCE OF IDEOLOGY

It is high time to draw together the various strands I have woven into a narrative of the *Recherche*'s concept of ideology. To do so, I shall recall a much-neglected distinction proposed by Louis Althusser in his still seminal essay, "Ideology and Ideological State Apparatuses." In brief, Althusser distinguishes between what he terms "ideology in general" and particular historical ideologies. In the *Recherche*, one encounters many examples of the latter, the most prominent of which are probably nationalism and antisemitism. As we have seen, these ideologies were inflected by sexual attitudes. This connection suggested the possibility that in addition to the more obviously class-coded prejudices motivating characters' actions, sexual preferences also lead people to act in determinate ways. *Sodome et Gomorrhe* opens with the revelation of Charlus's homosexuality. For the rest of the novel it becomes the prime factor dictating his behavior, causing his ultimate fall from social power and respectability. Proust's treatment of male homosexuality thus functions to complicate his story about the class struggles between bourgeoisie and aristocracy without undermining its fundamental cognitive certainties. The Narrator may at first be naive about society and male homosexuality (indeed, part of his naïveté about the former derives from his ignorance of the latter), but in time he comes to know the truth about both. Nothing in principle prevents his mastering the codes for each and giving a perspicuous accounting of the laws governing them.

Female sexuality is an altogether different matter. Marcel's success in society, which reaches its apogee in the first half of *Sodome et Gomorrhe*, is succeeded by his utter failure with Albertine. Horrified by the prospect of her lesbianism, he attempts to wrench her violently back into a realm where, he supposes, he can control or channel her desire, thereby alleviating his own suffering and jealousy. Famously, his strategy flounders. It does so precisely because he can never know what she is and what she truly wants: "for if her body was in my power, her thought escaped the grasp of my thought" (III:395) [car si son corps était au pouvoir du mien, sa pensée échappait aux prises de ma pensée] (III:888). Marcel's jealousy and suffering thus express, as Paul de Man once observed, "an anxiety ... of ignorance, not an anxiety of reference ..."[48] They are a structural characteristic of Marcel's relationship to a particular object. Thematically, they instance a general condition that is far from resolved at novel's end.

Consider the following passage, which immediately precedes Marcel's admission that he has not succeeded in keeping Albertine captive:

Yet perhaps, [had I been] entirely faithful, I would not have suffered from infidelities that I would have been incapable of imagining. But what tortured me to imagine in Albertine was my own perpetual desire to please new women, to begin new romances; it was to attribute to her that look which I had been unable the other day, even while by her side, to prevent casting on the young cyclists seated at tables in the Bois de Boulogne. Because there is no knowledge, one can almost say there is only jealousy of oneself. Observation counts for little. It is only from the pleasure felt by ourselves that we can draw out knowledge and sadness. (III:392-3)

[Et peut-être pourtant, entièrement fidèle, je n'eusse pas souffert d'infidélités que j'eusse été incapable de concevoir. Mais ce qui me torturait à imaginer chez Albertine, c'était mon propre désir per-pétuel de plaire à de nouvelles femmes, d'ébaucher de nouveaux romans; c'était de lui supposer ce regard que je n'avais pu, l'autre jour, même à côté d'elle, m'empêcher de jeter sur les jeunes cyclistes assises aux tables du bois Boulogne. Comme il n'est de connaissance, on peut presque dire qu'il n'est de jalousie que de soi-même. L'ob-servation compte peu. Ce n'est que du plaisir ressenti par soi-même, qu'on peut tirer savoir et douleur.] (III:887)

Jealousy is not a relationship in which one stands to objects, but a condition one must endure in relation to oneself. Although it appears here under the sign of erotic attraction, its significance extends to the more general epistemological problem posed throughout the *Recherche*: how is it possible to know the truth about oneself (or indeed about anything)? Eros refers not only to one's longing for sexual attachments, but to the whole restless, irresolvable quest for self-knowledge that the novel dramatizes. Thus, one could legitimately (and quite literally) translate the phrase "d'ébaucher de nouveaux romans," as "to sketch out new novels." Each fresh start along a narrative itinerary holds out the promise of enlightenment. Yet each tale ultimately proves as much an *ignis fatuus* as the last, a lesson amply illustrated in *Albertine disparue* by Marcel's fruitless efforts to confirm the truth about Albertine's suspected lesbian liaisons. Jealousy acts as a narrative goad, propelling the construction of new hypotheses that can never be estab-lished beyond the shadow of a doubt (see Bowie, *Freud*, p. 58). In the *Recherche*'s thematic lexicon, jealousy names that permanent feature of human consciousness which historical materialism calls ideology.

Is Proust's novel, then, what Paul de Man and Malcolm Bowie suggest it is: a testimony to the interminable and impossible search for scientific certainty? Is error the irremediable condition of our cognitive activity? Mystification the unavoidable outcome of all our investigations? Does Marcel, in effect, learn nothing from all he has experienced and reflected upon? More globally, does the *Recherche* repeat the currently fashionable view that science is nothing but the bad faith of certain determinate historical ideologies?

Albertine's death does not immediately deliver Marcel from his grief, but by the end of *Albertine disparue*, he no longer stands in the same relation to her memory. He calls his state of mind at that point "indifference" and attributes his transformation to the capacity to forget, to situate his relationship with Albertine in a now distant historical epoch. Earlier, in *La prisonnière*, he had described this relationship somewhat differently:

our jealousy, rummaging through the past to extract from it some clues, finds nothing there; always retrospective, it is like a historian who has to write a history for which there are no documents; always belated, it hastens like a mad bull to that place where it fails to find the proud and dazzling creature who irritates it with his pricks and whose magnificence and cunning the cruel crowd admires. (III:143)

[notre jalousie fouillant le passé pour en tirer des inductions n'y trouve rien; toujours rétrospective, elle est comme un historien qui aurait à faire une histoire pour laquelle il n'est aucun document; toujours en retard, elle se précipite comme un taureau furieux là où ne se trouve pas l'être fier et brillant qui l'irrite de ses piqûres et dont la foule cruelle admire la magnificence et la ruse.] (III:653)

How is it that Marcel comes to forget Albertine? How is the obsessively jealous lover transmuted into the dispassionate Narrator? How, in short, does Albertine cease to be the subject of desire and become an object of disinterested contemplation? The answer lies in the metaphor Proust has carefully chosen to represent this relationship. The lover is like a historian, one who excavates materials from the past and recovers their meaning. Two conditions must obtain for this process to be carried forward: first, there must be materials (documents) to recover in the first place, i.e., one must have access to objects that testify to events and allow one to interpret what has happened; second, one must stand in a dispassionate relation to the object of one's inquiry, a relation requiring the historian to be in some sense outside of the history he or she studies. To be free of one's jealous concern is precisely to be able to stand beyond the ideological field that obscures understanding. If jealousy/ideology is a relation of consciousness to its own contents, the condition for authentic scientific inquiry, which I have been claiming all along is that to which the *Recherche* aspires, is to displace the object of understanding from consciousness to the world. Famously, this displacement cannot be accomplished by an effort of the will. Nor can it guarantee that one's hypotheses are in every respect valid, one's knowledge total. The reign of ideology does not come to an end with the emergence of science. But neither is the possibility of scientific knowledge forever banished by the unavoidable fact of ideological conditioning. Ideology and science name two permanent potentials of human consciousness.[49] The time has come to test the limits of each in the *Recherche*'s final volume.

CHAPTER 4

Revolution

> The social revolution of the nineteenth century can only create its poetry from the future, not from the past. It cannot begin its own work until it has sloughed off all its superstitious regard for the past ... in order to arrive at its own content the revolution of the nineteenth century must let the dead bury their dead. Previously the phrase transcended the content; here the content transcends the phrase.
>
> (Marx, *The Eighteenth Brumaire of Louis Bonaparte*)

From the outset, I have taken the *Recherche* at its word, maintaining that the dominant instance of class struggle during the first half-century of the Third French Republic was that between the bourgeoisie and the titled nobility as portrayed in Proust's novel. The laboring classes played only a subordinate role in this historical process, for which reason they remain marginal to the narrative. Such a judgment patently ignores the manifest instances of working-class militancy chronicled, for example, in Zola's *Germinal* (set at the end of the Second Empire, but obviously motivated by the famous Anzin strike in 1884), and amply documented by historians.[1] I have no intention of filling in this lacuna here, although I shall indicate below why working-class self-organization and its political and social effects need to be factored into one's final estimate of Proust's analysis of French society. I only wish to maintain that, appearances to the contrary, neither Proust's own class position nor the ideological horizons of his text are totally at odds with a licit construal of the fundamental social relations in France at this period.

This assessment of the *Recherche's* historical perspicacity squares with some recent marxist historiography on the Third Republic. The late Sanford Elwitt's two studies of class relations in pre-First World War France take as read the marxist axiom that the decisive structure in bourgeois societies is the labor–capital relation. In *The Making of the Third Republic* he contends: "an alliance of capitalists and petty producers, mobilized under the banner of republican democracy, developed the ideological perspective and social policies that expressed the essential nature of the Republic."[2] He goes on to argue that up to the Seize Mai crisis, the republicans considered the aristocratic right its principal enemy; thereafter, the primary antagonist was the workers.[3] But over the remainder of the book, Elwitt's ostensibly orthodox view of the struggle between labor and capital is complicated by his account of intra-class struggle between finance capital on one side and agrarian and industrial capital on the other. Moreover, from the 1880s onwards, Elwitt maintains that another party was added to the republican alliance: namely, a fraction of the titled nobility, who cooperated with the Freycinet Plan and broadly supported the economic policies of the republican majority.[4]

In *The Third Republic Defended*, the sequel to *The Making of the Third Republic*, the picture of class struggle is tempered even further. Despite the emergence of organized working-class resistance and socialist politics, the bourgeoisie was by and large able to manage class conflict under the banner of "solidarism," promoting class cooperation on both the economic and the ideological level. Elwitt sums up the effect of this programmatic strategy as follows: "It may be that whatever the limitations of reform to contain actual or potential working-class militance, the organized forces of the labor movement were relatively weak (compared with, say, the SPD in Germany). If so, then the goal of preserving and extending bourgeois hegemony did not require scuttling democratic political forms and even allowed occasional if fitful bouts of 'radicalism' (Emile Combes and to a less extent Clemenceau and Briand)."[5] Strikes there were, and working-class self-organization did manifestly grow between the 1880s and 1914, but the decisive feature of labor–capital relations in this period was labor's comparative weakness, its incapacity to exert significant social or political pressure on a republican polity committed to promoting bourgeois interests.[6] Unlike the nobility, who could periodically provoke severe political and ideological crises, the working class never seriously challenged the bourgeois state between the suppression of the Commune and the strike wave of 1917. For all its limitations of focus and emphasis, the *Recherche* presents an image of French society that is broadly in line with the historical record of class struggles during the period 1871–1914.

The war would change the political and social equation entirely. Beginning in 1917, liberal capitalism would lose its purchase on French – and not only French – society. The Clemenceau government instituted repressive measures and inaugurated a cycle of nationalism and conservatism extending well beyond the cessation of hostilities with the Central Powers. The French working class was, of course, no stranger to the ruthlessness of the repressive state apparatus, but in the run-up to the war, it lacked effective organizational unity. The Section Française de l'Internationale Ouvrière (SFIO) and the Confédération Générale du Travail (CGT), its principal political and trade union expressions, respectively, pursued distinct, and for the most part opposed, strategies as a result of their different histories.[7] In the war's aftermath, this historic split became these organizations' Achilles heel, producing the conditions under which a new political form, a Bolshevized political party (the Parti Communiste Française [PCF]) directly allied to a trade union federation (the CGT–Unitaire [CGTU]), would prosper. Of this new historical actor, the author of the *Recherche* was but dimly aware.

THE MUSE OF HISTORY

When *Du côté de chez Swann* was published by Grasset in 1913, Proust planned to bring out the remainder of his novel in two more volumes. The architecture of the whole was by then clearly laid out. When the war intervened, suspending publication, Proust would expand the existing manuscript enormously, adding new material and rearranging episodes already drafted. The war would alter the *Recherche* significantly, but it would leave its thematic and structural unity intact. What effect did the war have on Proust's text? How was Proust's analysis of the class struggles between the bourgeoisie and the aristocracy inflected by this unforeseen historical intervention? To begin to answer these questions, it is necessary to consider the trajectory of the novel's final volume, *Le temps retrouvé*, parts of which could be written only after the war had run its course.

An initial difficulty presents itself. Proust's manuscript gives no clear indication of where *Albertine disparue* ends and *Le temps retrouvé* begins. In the 1954 Pléiade edition (on which the Kilmartin translation is based), the break comes shortly after Marcel's return to Paris, with the revelation of Saint-Loup's infidelity to Gilberte and the Narrator's projected visit to Tansonville. *Le temps retrouvé* commences with the narration of this latter episode. The new Pléiade edition puts the division somewhat later, with Marcel already in residence at Tansonville and immersed in Gilberte's recollections of their mutual past. Without any clear-cut indication to the contrary, I shall propose that *Albertine disparue* comes to an end with Marcel's sudden departure from Venice with his mother, so that the break between the two volumes cleanly separates what we might call "Albertine" from "Combray" (or "Tansonville"). This division, however, leaves a long transitional section recounting the train journey from Venice to Paris suspended between the two volumes. On this journey, Marcel and his mother discuss the alterations in upper-class society consequent upon the various marriages that have recently occurred.

What is the historical period in which the "Venice" to "Tansonville" sections are situated? References to external events make this most uncertain – very much in the way that the external chronology of "Du côté de chez Swann" makes dating the fictional narrative a tenuous business. Gérard Genette situates this section in 1902–3; Gareth Steel places it in either 1904 or 1906, or, in a more speculative vein, possibly as late as 1913.[8] The general era of these events, however, is clear: they occur after the conclusion of the Dreyfus Affair and are meant broadly to signify the *belle époque*. The period was considered by many at the time – and certainly seemed even more so after the war – to be one of tranquility, prosperity, and social peace (albeit not for all classes, as I observed at the outset of this study). But as Proust's narration here indicates in several ways, beneath the surface of this apparently stable society, powerful currents of historical and social change continued to flow. Those crucial shifts in the structure of upper-class society that will be driven home to Marcel at the Guermantes reception which ends the novel have already begun to occur even before the war's outbreak.

Consider, for example, the Narrator's reflections on Gilberte's new social position as Saint-Loup's wife:

... Gilberte had been for only a short time the Marquise de Saint-Loup (and soon after, as we shall see, Duchesse de Guermantes) when, having attained that which was most striking and most difficult, thinking that the name Guermantes was now embodied in her like a glowing enamel and that, whatever the society she frequented, she would remain for all the world the Duchesse de Guermantes (which was an error, for the value of a noble title, like that of stocks and shares, rises with the demand and falls when it is on offer. Everything that seems to us imperishable tends towards decay; a position in society, like anything else, is not created once and for all, but, just as much as the power of an Empire, is rebuilding itself at every moment by a sort of perpetual, continual creation, which explains the apparent anomalies in social or political history in the course of half a century ...)

[... Gilberte n'était que depuis peu de temps marquise de Saint-Loup (et bientôt après, comme on le verra, duchesse de Guermantes) que, ayant atteint ce qu'il y avait de plus éclatant et de plus difficile, pensant que le nom de Guermantes s'était maintenant incorporé à elle comme un émail mordoré et que, qui qu'elle fréquantât, elle resterait pour tout le monde duchesse de Guermantes (ce qui était une erreur, car la valeur d'un titre de noblesse, aussi bien que de Bourse, monte quand on le demande et baisse quand on l'offre. Tout ce qui nous semble impérissable tend à la destruction; une situation mondaine, tout comme autre chose, n'est pas créée une fois pour toutes mais aussi bien que la puissance d'un empire, se reconstruit à chaque instant par une sorte de création perpétuellement continue, ce qui explique les anomalies apparentes de l'histoire mondaine ou politique au cours d'un demi-siècle . . .)][9]

The major motifs that have been the focus of this study coalesce in this passage. At stake here is not only the individual social reputation of Gilberte, Marquise de Saint-Loup, *née* Swann but more recently Mlle. de Forcheville. Equally at issue are the general processes that now govern life among the upper classes and cause social position to fluctuate in value, like stocks and shares in a capitalist economy or political power in the global political economy during the age of imperialism. At stake, in short, is the very concept of history, which has never been far from the Narrator's consciousness throughout the *Recherche* but which surfaces explicitly some few pages after this passage in the guise of "the Muse who has gathered up everything that the more exalted Muses of philosophy and art have rejected, everything that is not founded upon truth, everything that is merely contingent, but that reveals other laws as well: that is history" (III:692–3). [la Muse qui a recueilli tout ce que les Muses plus hautes de la philosophie et de l'art ont rejeté, tout ce qui n'est pas fondé en vérité, tout ce qui n'est que contingent mais révèle aussi d'autres lois: c'est l'histoire] (IV:254). Just this relationship between the contingency of historical events and the laws that nonetheless govern them will dominate the remainder of the novel. For the sake of convenience, the two long sections to follow, the war episode and the Guermantes reception, can be kept analytically separate, even though, as I'll be claiming at the end, they are thematically and structurally linked. Against the grain of much commentary, I shall insist that Proust's concept of history cannot be relegated to subordinate status in the hierarchy of his concerns. Put somewhat differently, one can say that the Proustian theme of time was never anything but a means for staging and comprehending the historical transition through which he and his society lived.

LA GUERRE EST FINI

The war episode intervenes between "Tansonville" and
Marcel's final sojourn in society – as it had in fact intervened
during the novel's composition itself, which existed in draft by
1912, although at that point it was but a third of what we now
know as the *Recherche*.[10] Marcel returns to Paris for a brief
period in 1914, then again permanently "at the beginning of
1916 when the sanatorium where I had been comfortably
lodged could no longer get medical staff. I returned then to a
Paris entirely different from that to which I had already
returned once before . . ." (III:743). [je passai à me soigner, loin
de Paris dans une maison de santé, jusqu'à ce que celle-ci ne
put plus trouver de personnel médical, au commencement de
1916. Je rentrai alors dans un Paris bien différent de celui où
j'étais déjà revenu une première fois . . .] (IV:301).

The dominant concern in the section dealing with the First
World War is Charlus's decline. Why does Proust tell this story
through this vehicle? The section marks the finale of the text's
long second movement, which had commenced with *Sodome et
Gomorrhe*. Charlus's history during the war closes that aspect of
the narrative written under the sign of eros (the latter will be
effectively absent from the Guermantes *matinée*). A second
strand is also woven into the war section, and it can fairly be
labelled "Saint-Loup." While the latter is implicated in many
of the same sexual practices that precipitate Charlus's fall, his
patriotism and his heroism on the field of battle stand in stark
contrast to his uncle's defeatism. But the decisive narrative fact
is the linking of Charlus's decadence with Saint-Loup's death.
Taken together they symbolize the demise of the French aristocracy as a whole, which has ceded its social power to the likes
of Mme. Verdurin and Mme. Bontemps.

The war episode is the most explicitly and programmatically
historical section in the *Recherche*. But how, precisely, does
history appear there? This narrative bloc opens with Marcel's
impressions of war-time Paris, from which he has been absent
for many years, save for a brief visit in August 1914. What has
changed? Among other things the hegemonic political ideol-

ogy. Its fulcrum has shifted from the secular republicanism that had ultimately won the day in the Dreyfus Affair to a patriotic nationalism that has broken down the last barriers between the older social castes, uniting even former Dreyfusards like M. Bontemps with the "party of social order, of religious tolerance, of military preparedness" (III:747). [le parti de l'ordre social, de la tolérance religieuse, de la préparation militaire] (IV:305). The principal figure for this shift in society's hierarchy is the Verdurin salon, which is now the locus of the most extreme nationalism, although it had once been a gathering place for Dreyfusards.

This and other perturbations in the socio-political climate lead Marcel to reflect on the historicity of ideologies, at the same time that he draws explicit comparisons between earlier periods in French history and the present: first the Directory (III:743–9; IV:301–6), then 1793 (III:744; IV:302), later the Congress of Vienna (III:784; IV:339), and finally the Paris of 1815 after the defeat of Napoleon at Waterloo (III:786; IV:342). The Directory was, of course, the first properly bourgeois oligarchy in French history; it replaced the radical republicanism of the Jacobins that had self-immolated in the Terror. Although a slight anachronism – since the events described here take place in 1916 – the reference is probably to the Clemenceau government formed in November 1917. But the object of these several, seemingly conflicting historical analogues, is to recall the period of France's preeminent national glory, the Napoleonic era, and to suggest that the spirit of national unity that bound France together as a nation from 1793–1815, also characterized patriotic support for the war. The point is made perfectly explicit in the passage cited above on the transmutation of Dreyfusism into nationalism (see III:747–8; IV:305–6). Proust asserts – and recent historiography confirms[11] – that the war produced an ideological consensus cutting across political and even class lines, at least prior to the defeats of 1917. This is well illustrated in the conversation between some ordinary soldiers in Jupien's male brothel (III:849–50; IV:399–400).

The most important moment signifying the breadth and

strength of this patriotic consensus comes with the death of Saint-Loup. Throughout the war episode, Saint-Loup is said to revive an older conception of "la patrie," showing that he is

more profoundly a Frenchman of Saint-André-des-Champs, more in conformity with all that at this moment was best in the Frenchmen of Saint-André-des-Champs, lords, citizens and serfs respectful of lords or in revolt against lords, two divisions equally French of the same family, the Françoise sub-branch and the Morel sub-branch, from which two arrows were launched, to be reunited anew [in their flight] towards a single target, which was the frontier. (III:760)

[plus profondément français de Saint-André-des-Champs, plus en conformité avec tout ce qu'il y avait à ce moment-là de meilleur chez les Français de Saint-André-des-champs, seigneurs, bourgeois et serfs respectueux des seigneurs ou révoltés contre les seigneurs, deux divisions également françaises de la même famille, sous-embranche-ment Françoise et sous-embranchement Morel, d'où deux flèches se dirigeaient, pour se réunir à nouveau, dans une même direction, qui était la frontière.] (IV:317)

His death, along with Charlus's final degradation, will mark the absolute limit of the aristocracy's purchase on social power. Focusing the episode of the war on these two figures is surely meant to indicate a break in the narrative temporality separating all that has preceded this episode and the *dénouement* of the Guermantes *matinée*. Proust thereby clinches the *Recherche*'s historical argument, that henceforth class struggles in France will assume new forms.

Charlus never participates in the patriotic nationalism embraced by his nephew and the new ruling strata. He remains ambivalent about the war to the end. More significantly, Morel, who is called up and sent to the front at the same time as Saint-Loup, exhibits none of the collective solidarity or patriotism characteristic of the vast majority of characters depicted in this episode. He shamelessly pursues his own self-interest and self-gratification, deserts the army, and when caught he betrays both Charlus and M. d'Argencourt, leading to their arrest. But in the end he is returned to the front and acquits himself bravely (III:883–4; IV:431–2). What does the novel intend in this brief vignette on the principal representa-tive of the working class?

In the first instance, and in contrast to the general respect shown for the aristocratic officer corps among the soldiers in Jupien's brothel, Morel's lack of patriotic fervor indicates a well-known aspect of working-class participation in the war effort: it was often half-hearted and generally unreliable, punctuated by periodic strikes that threatened the war effort. But the strikes were characteristically launched for immediately economic, rather than anti-patriotic reasons. Most were for higher wages, some few for shorter hours. The only link between working-class militancy, such as it was, and anti-patriotic attitudes was through workers' fear of being dispatched from secure and generally well-paid employment in the factories to hazardous duty at the front. Certainly the major working-class organizations, the CGT and the SFIO, were not at this period united in any anti-militarist political program.[12] On Proust's account, as in history itself, the French working class may not have embraced the war wholeheartedly, particularly as it wore on and the body count mounted, but its sporadic resistance was decidedly nonrevolutionary.

There are many more nuances in attitudes towards the war indicated throughout this section, but the major values can be grouped in the standard four-fold relation proposed in the Greimassian schema of diagram 4.1.

Most of the values and their *actants* in the diagram are uncontroversial, e.g., Charlus's defeatism, the Larivières' selflessness (see III:876–7; IV:424–5), Morel's selfishness, and the patriotism of the Verdurins and the Bontemps. What is termed "the Françoise branch" of the French people in the passage cited earlier is explicitly contrasted to the less worthy "Morel branch"; the former is characterized by that combination of selflessness and patriotism proposed here. The butler is Françoise's chief antagonist and tormentor during the war, exhibiting the combination of defeatism and selfishness that the diagram ascribes to him: "He waited for pieces of bad news as eagerly as if they had been Easter eggs, hoping that things would go badly enough to terrify Françoise but not badly enough to cause him any material suffering" (III:874–5; IV:423).

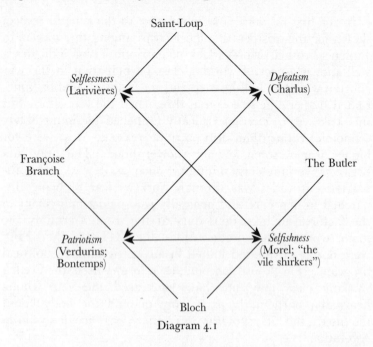

Diagram 4.1

The complex and neutral terms, Saint-Loup and Bloch, respectively, are perhaps more controversial. That the two are polar opposites becomes clear in a long passage in which Marcel describes his meeting them "less than a week after the declaration of the war" (III:758; IV:315). Bloch at first expresses the most vulgarly chauvinist sentiments about the war so long as he is convinced that his feeble eyesight will keep him from serving in the army:

But Bloch completely changed his mind about the war a few days later, when he came to see me in a state of frenzy. Although short-sighted, he had been passed fit for service. I was accompanying him home when we met Saint-Loup ... Bloch left us outside his house, overflowing with bitterness against Saint-Loup and saying to his face that men of his sort, privileged dandies who strutted about at head-quarters, ran no risks and that he, as a plain private soldier, had no wish to "get a hole in his skin just because of William." (III:760–2)

[Mais Bloch avait complètement changé d'avis sur la guerre quelques jours après, où il vint me voir affolé. Quoique "myope" il avait été

reconnu bon pour le service. Je le ramenais chez lui quand nous
rencontrâmes Saint-Loup ... Bloch nous quitta devant sa porte,
débordant d'amertume contre Saint-Loup, lui disant qu'eux autres,
"beaux fils" galonnés, paradant dans les états-majors, ne risquaient
rien, et que lui, simple soldat de deuxième classe, n'avait pas envie de
se faire "trouer la peau pour Guillaume."] (IV:317-8)

Bloch is a patriot so long as this position does not personally
inconvenience or threaten him. Saint-Loup, as is well known,
is made of sterner stuff.

That the slot for the complex term would be filled by
Saint-Loup scarcely requires argument. No reader will fail to
recognize in his character the hero of the war episode. But how
can it be that Saint-Loup represents some impossible combination of defeatism and selflessness; and how are these terms,
rather than patriotism, sublated in the ideal solution to the
ideological tensions generated by the war? In the first place,
while Saint-Loup is undoubtedly courageous and eager to do
his duty for France, he does so resignedly, conscious, it would
appear, that he had always been a doomed man:

Robert had often said to me sadly, long before the war: "Oh! my life,
don't let's talk about it, I am a condemned man from the start." ...
Perhaps this exaggeration ... came partly from the still unfamiliar
idea of sin [viz., Saint-Loup's homosexual inclinations], partly from
the fact that an entirely novel sensation has an almost terrible force
which later will gradually diminish. Or had he really, justifying it if
need be by the death of his father at an early age, a presentiment of
his own premature end? Such a presentiment would seem, no doubt,
to be impossible. Yet death appears to be obedient to certain laws ...
And may it not be possible that accidental death itself – like that of
Saint-Loup, which was perhaps in any case linked to his character in
more ways than I have thought it necessary to describe – is somehow
recorded in advance, known only to the gods, invisible to men, but
revealed by a peculiar sadness, half unconscious, half conscious (and
even, insofar as it is conscious, proclaimed to others with that complete sincerity with which we foretell misfortunes which in our heart
of hearts we believe we shall escape but which will nevertheless take
place) to the man who bears and forever sees within himself, as
though it were some heraldic device, a fatal date? (III:880-1)

[Robert m'avait souvent dit avec tristesse, bien avant la guerre: "Oh!
ma vie, n'en parlons pas, je suis un homme condamné d'avance." ...

Peut-être cette exagération tenait-elle pour Saint-Loup comme pour les enfants, ainsi qu'à l'idée du péché avec laquelle on ne s'est pas encore familiarisé, à ce qu'une sensation toute nouvelle a une force presque terrible qui ira ensuite en s'atténuant. Ou bien avait-il, le justifiant au besoin par la mort de son père enlevé assez jeune, le pressentiment de sa fin prématurée? Sans doute un tel pressentiment semble impossible. Pourtant la mort paraît assujettie à certaines lois … Et ne serait-il pas possible que la mort accidentelle elle-même – comme celle de Saint-Loup, liée d'ailleurs à son caractère de plus de façons peut-être que je n'ai cru devoir le dire – fût, elle aussi, inscrite d'avance, connue seulement des dieux, invisible aux hommes, mais révélée par une tristesse à demi inconsciente, à demi consciente (et même, dans cette dernière mesure, exprimée aux autres avec cette sincérité complète qu'on met à annoncer des malheurs auxquels on croit dans son for intérieur échapper et qui pourtant arriveront), particulière à celui qui la porte et l'aperçoit sans cesse, en lui-même, comme une devise, une date fatale?] (iv:428–9)

His fate, as the passage subsequently makes plain (iii:881–2; iv:429), is less personal and individual than that of his "race," the feudal military caste of which he is the principal representative throughout the novel. Saint-Loup is not a defeatist in the sense that Charlus is; rather, Saint-Loup expresses the consciousness of his class that in August 1914, it was marching into its final act on the stage of history. Nor is the Marquis a patriot either, in the Verdurin–Bontemps sense of loudly proclaiming one's devotion to the cause, less still in the vulgar, dishonest manner of the Bloc National that assumed parliamentary control in 1919 and on which the Narrator heaps scorn (iii:884–5; iv:432–3). Whatever the limits of Proust's own politics, the *Recherche* is under no illusions about the difference between patriotism and chauvinism, true courage and bluster, honorable conduct and self-aggrandizing rhetoric. If the *Recherche* is to some extent burdened with nostalgia for the past, the heaviest weight lies here, in the novel's heroization of Saint-Loup, above all in its comparison between the residual nobility manifested by his class during the war and the bourgeoisie's tawdry self-promotion on the morrow of the armistice.

A further dimension of Saint-Loup's idealization in this final episode surely hinges on the Narrator's attempt to come to

terms with the Marquis's newly discovered sexual tastes. It will
be recalled that the entire episode in Jupien's brothel turns on
Saint-Loup's presence there and on his mislaying his *croix de
guerre*. Moreover, as the conversation of the ordinary soldiers
makes plain, Saint-Loup's death in battle cannot be easily
divorced from his homoerotic tendencies. Heroism is a consequence, the text avers, of an especially powerful male
bonding between officers and enlisted men. On this reading, it
is now possible to cash out one of the implications of diagram
3.5 in the previous chapter: to wit, that the condition of true
friendship, which is consistently represented in the relationship
between Marcel and Saint-Loup throughout the novel, is male
bisexuality. With Saint-Loup dies the flower of aristocratic
patriotism and all the virtues with which it is associated, and
also the potential for non-antagonistic personal and social
relations. On all levels – sexuality, politics, ideology – Saint-
Loup's death gives the quietus to the utopian possibilities for
which the Narrator has perpetually been searching.

The war episode does not end with Saint-Loup's death and
the contrast between his admirable character and the hollow
nationalism of post-war politics, however. The final sentences
allude to the demise of another, more distant, *ancien régime*, as if
to reinforce the parallel already drawn with the revolutionary
upsurge that had inaugurated this 125-year process in France:

All this tomfoolery [the political and moral corruption of the
post-war period] was not exactly popular, but there was less disposition to blame the National Bloc when suddenly there appeared
on the scene the victims of bolshevism, those Grand Duchesses in
tatters whose husbands had been assassinated in carts, while their
sons after being left to starve and then forced to work in the midst of
abuse, had finally been thrown into wells and buried beneath stones
because it was believed that they had the plague and might pass it on.
Those of them who succeeded in escaping suddenly turned up in
Paris. (III:885)

[Tant de niaiserie agaçait un peu, mais on en voulut moins au bloc
national quand on vit tout d'un coup les victimes du bolchevisme, des
grandes-duchesses en haillons, dont on avait assassiné les maris dans
une brouette, les fils en jetant des pierres dessus après les avoir laissés
sans manger, fait travailler au milieu des huées, jetés dans des puits

parce qu'on croyait qu'ils avaient la peste et pouvaient la commu-
niquer. Ceux qui étaient arrivés à s'enfuir reparurent tout à coup ...
(IV;433; ellipsis in the original)[13]

What is one to make of this rather surprising reference to the
Bolshevik Revolution? On the one hand, it would seem to
participate in conventional Western European attitudes
towards the fledgling regime, depicting it as barbarous, the
aristocracy it overthrew as victims. Yet this standard view is
not that of the Narrator himself; it is attributed to public
opinion at large in an impersonal construction: "there was less
disposition to blame the National Bloc [*on en voulut moins au bloc
national*] ..." What was Proust's view of the major revolutionary transformation in his lifetime, and of the socio-political
effects it would have in France – notably the creation of the
French Communist Party?[14] I shall postpone this question,
which in any event admits of a speculative answer at best, until
the final pages of this study, in order to consider first the
ideology of art as this emerges in its fully elaborated form at the
Guermantes *matinée*. For Proust, as for Schiller, the path that
leads to solving political problems must necessarily pass
through the domain of the aesthetic.[15]

FIN DE L'HISTOIRE

The canonical view of *Le temps retrouvé* has held that with this
volume the *Recherche* comes full circle, uniting the two "ways"
initially posited as opposed and irreconcilable in "Combray"
and thus fusing Marcel's aesthetic desire with his social
ambition. He thereby attains that liberation from illusion
which he himself proclaims to be the mark of genuine bliss:
"Happy are those who have encountered truth before death,
and for whom, however close they may be to one another, the
hour of truth has struck before the hour of death" (III:948;
IV:488–9).[16] It would be foolish to deny or dispute this view
outright; too much in the text supports it, from the title
onwards. The recovery of the past is written in nearly every
line, from the visit to Tansonville with which, on the authority
of the 1954 Pléiade editors, the volume opens, to the final entry

into the Prince and Princesse de Guermantes's drawing room, where Marcel is able to recognize beneath the altered physiognomies of the guests so many of the figures whom he had known as a young man. Moreover, the famous occurrences of the uneven paving stone, the stiff napkin, and the tap of a spoon against a plate are exactly analogous, as Marcel himself observes, to that earlier and even more famous incident of the madeleine, which symbolizes for the narrator the past's persistence in certain sensory impressions capable of recapturing all its emotive and ideational significance.

At the same time, one must insist that regaining or recapturing or re-encountering ("retrouvé" can have all these senses) the past does not leave its object unaltered. When Marcel re-experiences moments from his earlier life, he is reconfiguring the material world, comprehending it in a new way. If what is at stake is Marcel's understanding of the past, then it may be hazarded that *Le temps retrouvé* is above all a meditation on history (and therefore society) and on the means for producing knowledge of it. Proust calls this means "art," but it is far from obvious what is entailed by this concept.

The complexity of the aesthetic theory in *Le temps retrouvé* would in principle demand a detailed exegesis of the long passage that commences with Marcel's tripping over the uneven paving stone and ends with his entry into the drawing room after the first piece of music is concluded (III:898–957; IV:445–96). But in this very passage, we are abruptly warned against taking at face value just such theoretical disquisitions as the text itself presents: "Whence the enormous temptation for the writer to write intellectual works. A great impropriety. A work in which there are theories is like an object on which the price tag has been left" (III:916; IV:461).[17] Rather than focusing on this "intellectual" aspect of the narrative, it may be more appropriate to consider the sequence of incidents in this final volume. Our aim is to discover how the structure of the plot – only the most naive or inattentive reader can believe that Proust's text lacks one – enforces certain conclusions concerning the nature of art and its relationship to historical understanding.

As I have maintained, one can legitimately take *Le temps retrouvé* to commence with Marcel's long visit to Tansonville, during which occur some of the nocturnal reflections with which the *Recherche* had opened. Ostensibly concerned with Marcel's disillusionment about his past, including his admiration for Saint-Loup, the episode closes on the final evening of Marcel's stay, when he reads a passage from the Goncourts' Journal describing the Verdurin salon. (This is of course a fictionalized pastiche, done by Proust in the manner of his earlier critical experiments in the *Contre Sainte-Beuve*.) The net effect, which Marcel records prior to "transcribing" the passage, is to deter him from his pursuit of literature. Writing no longer seems an exalted calling but merely the most commonplace reproduction of ordinary life's mundane details:

And when, before putting out my candle, I read the passage that I transcribe below, my lack of talent for literature ... appeared to me something less regrettable, since literature did not reveal any profound truth; and at the same time it seemed sad to me that literature was not what I had believed. On the other hand, less regrettable to me appeared the state of ill-health that was going to confine me in a sanatorium, if the beautiful things of which books speak were no more beautiful than what I had seen. But by a bizarre contradiction, now that the book spoke of them, I desired to see them. (III:728)

[Et quand, avant d'éteindre ma bougie, je lus le passage que je transcris plus bas, mon absence de dispositions pour les lettres ... me parut quelque chose de moins regrettable, comme si la littérature ne révélait pas de vérité profonde; et en même temps il me semblait triste que la littérature ne fût pas ce que j'avais cru. D'autre part, moins regrettable me parraissait l'état maladif qui allait me confiner dans une maison de santé, si les belles choses dont parlent les livres n'étaient pas plus belles que ce que j'avais vu. Mais par une contradiction bizarre, maintenant que ce livre en parlait j'avais envie de les voir.] (IV:287)

See them he shall, but not for many years. By then all will have changed dramatically in the world evoked to this point, including Marcel's hopes of realizing his vocation as a writer. This latter, postponed for so many years, seems now forever beyond his grasp.

The reception at the Prince and Princesse de Guermantes's is justly famous, a magnificent *tour de force* that reprises Proust's considerable stylistic and satiric skills and functions as a long coda to the novel's major thematic strains concerning time and art. Returning to society after a gap of nearly a decade,[18] Marcel is struck above all by the material decay that now permeates the faces and figures of the men and women he had known in his youth. At first, Marcel has difficulty recognizing his host and the assembled guests, who have all, he surmises, "donned wigs, generally powdered" (III:960) ["fait un tête," généralement poudrée] (IV:499). Gradually he realizes that age has altered each of their figures, and he proceeds to catalogue the successive shocks to his sensibility administered by the sight of his old acquaintances all fallen into decrepitude. The only exception is Odette (now Mme. de Forcheville), whose "appearance seemed a more miraculous defiance of the laws of chronology ..." (III:990) [son aspect ... semblait un défi plus miraculeux aux lois de la chronologie ...] (IV:526). But even she will eventually succumb, albeit more slowly: not three years hence, Marcel will encounter her at a party given by her daughter, where she will be verging on senility (III:994; IV:529).

As Marcel himself observes, the shock of seeing all these people so deeply etched by time is perhaps less astonishing than the transformation in society's hierarchy, which has fallen prey to the same irresistible force as its members' physiques. The exclusiveness of the Guermantes set is now permanently a thing of the past, as is the knowledge of the codes and taboos that constituted this social form's very essence:

And yet the sensation of time vanished and of the annihilation of a small part of my past was conveyed to me less vividly by the destruction of this coherent ensemble (which had been the Guermantes salon) than by the annihilation even of the knowledge of the thousand reasons, of the thousand nuances which made it such that one who was still to be found there now was so completely natural and in his place, while another with whom he rubbed shoulders there presented an aspect of suspect novelty. This ignorance was not only of society, but of politics, of everything. (III:1000)

[Encore la sensation du temps écoulé et d'une petite partie disparue de mon passé m'était-elle donnée moins vivement par la destruction de cet ensemble cohérent (qu'avait été le salon Guermantes) que par l'anéantissement même de la connaissance des mille raisons, des mille nuances qui faisait que tel qui s'y trouvait encore maintenant y était tout naturellement indiqué et à sa place, tandis que tel autre qui l'y coudoyait y présentait une nouveauté suspecte. Cette ignorance n'était pas que du monde, mais de la politique, de tout.] (IV:535–6)

Nowhere is the total reorganization of society more evident than in the altered positions of Mme. Verdurin and the Duchesse de Guermantes. The former, we learn, has now become Princesse de Guermantes (and is therefore the hostess of the reception Marcel is now attending; see III:998; IV:533), while the latter has fallen from her perch atop the Faubourg Saint-Germain and is now considered by the new *femmes du monde* as a "Guermantes from an inferior cask, of a less good vintage, a Guermantes *déclassé*" (III:1057) [une Guermantes d'une moins bonne cuvée, d'une moins bonne année, une Guermantes déclassée] (IV:582). To be a "Guermantes *déclassé*," it hardly needs repeating, is no longer to be a Guermantes at all. The impregnable social position that Oriane once occupied rested on nothing less than the incorrigible belief in the purity of her class background.

For the Narrator, then, the signal discovery enforced by the war and its aftermath is the fluidity of social (as well as political) power attendant on the final elimination of those barriers that had hitherto separated classes and fractions within a class from each other. The distinctions evident to him and to his family in the Combray of his youth, and jealously defended in the Paris of his early manhood, have now passed into oblivion. Society has become thoroughly permeable; the social order is now forever a site where social reputation fluctuates. Put in the classical terms of materialist theory, capitalism has now definitively displaced feudalism as the dominant principle of social structure.[19]

It is well known that these reflections on the transience of social distinction are the efficient cause of the Narrator's resolve to undertake the work he has postponed up to this moment in his life. Synthesizing his earlier speculations on art, and realizing at last that the subject of his text will be his own life and his experiences in that world which he has just dis-

covered to have vanished, Marcel projects the form this work
will take, and also its great theme of time (see especially
III:1088–91,1105–7; IV:609–12,623–5). It is thus plausible to
assert – and indeed is in broad accord with the conventional
view of the *Recherche* – that the final volume rests on the
opposition between the contrary poles of society and art.[20]
Beginning from this basic intuition, a Greimassian semantic
rectangle can be generated to map the ideological field governing the action in *Le temps retrouvé* (see diagram 4.2).

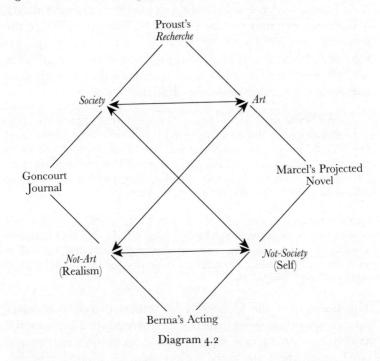

Diagram 4.2

The logical contradictories, Society/Not-Society, are so
apparent in this text – and in the canonical image of Proust – as
scarcely to require demonstration. They are evident, for
instance, in the Narrator's decision to abandon society altogether and pursue a solitary life in order to write his novel
(III:1034; IV:564). But their most rigorous opposition comes in
the concept of reading that has been among the novel's recur-

ring themes since "Combray." As Marcel observes: "For
between us and other beings there is a border of contingencies,
as I had understood during my days of reading in Combray
that there exists one in perception and which impedes the
absolute coming into contact of reality and the mind."
(III:1023) [Car il y a entre nous et les êtres un lisère de
contingences, comme j'avais compris dans mes lectures de
Combray qu'il y en a un de perceptions et qui empêche la mise
en contact absolue de la réalité et de l'esprit.] (IV:553)[21]

As for the other two logically opposed terms, Art/Not-Art,
that Proust equated the latter with realism no reader of the
Recherche, or of the series of texts that led up to it from *Les plaisirs
et les jours*, to the Ruskin translations, to the *Contre Sainte-Beuve*,
is likely to doubt. In any event, the opposition of realism to
authentic art is made perfectly explicit:

I was reassured in this conclusion [that habitual experience is an
impediment to the discovery of genuine aesthetic apprehension] of
the very falsity of presumedly realist art, which would not be so
deceitful if we had not acquired the habit in life of giving to what we
feel an expression so altogether different from, and which we take
after only a short time for, reality itself. (III:915)

[Je m'en assurais par la fausseté même de l'art prétendu réaliste et qui
ne serait pas si mensonger si nous n'avions pris dans la vie l'habitude
de donner à ce que nous sentons une expression qui en diffère
tellement, et que nous prenons au bout de peu de temps pour la
réalité même.] (IV:459–60)

The position of the Goncourt Journal is therefore obvious,
since it was precisely its realism that drove Marcel years earlier
to abandon his literary career, just as its subject matter was
none other than the very society Marcel himself had frequented. Whatever else the novel he projects here might
become, it could never resemble the false example set by the
Goncourts. It would be a work of art, but one, as Marcel avers
over and over again, that would grow out of himself; it would
present his own experience and would be an amalgamation of
the various epochs in his life (III:935–6; IV:477–8). Moreover,
the utterly personal, individual character of this work – Proust

had continually insisted on the importance of individual style to artistic greatness[22] – is such that, with his passing, all possibility of its realization will have been lost:

I knew perfectly well that my brain was like a rich basin to be mined, wherein lay vast and extraordinarily diverse precious beds. But would I have time to exploit them? I was the only person capable of doing it. For two reasons: with my death would disappear the only miner capable of extracting these minerals; but, even more, the bed itself [would disappear] ... (III:1094)

[Je savais très bien que mon cerveau était un riche bassin minier, où il y avait une étendue immense et fort diverse de gisements précieux. Mais aurais-je le temps de les exploiter? J'étais la seule personne capable de le faire. Pour deux raisons: avec ma mort eut disparu non seulement le seul ouvrier mineur capable d'extraire ces minerais, mais encore le gisement lui-même ...] (IV:614)

Not merely his own artistic skill, but the very materials out of which the work is to be constructed, reside inside him.

As the diagram has made plain, the novel Marcel plans to write cannot be the one we have nearly finished reading when we reach this point in the Narrator's development – all indications in the text to the contrary. But before proceeding to this, surely the most insistent interpretive puzzle in any reading of Proust (characteristically posed as the relationship between the Narrator and the author himself), one must account for the so-called "neutral" term in the Greimassian rectangle, the slot here occupied by the great actress Berma's art.

It will be noticed that all the combined terms in the diagram are versions of "art," as that term has been figured throughout the novel. In previous volumes, Elstir's paintings and Bergotte's writings have also served, along with Vinteuil's music, to indicate the lineaments of an aesthetic theory that the text could conscionably affirm. But none of these plays a significant role here; only Berma appears, somewhat surprisingly, from among the earlier pantheon of the Narrator's artistic exemplars to show that the trails he has pursued until now have been false ones. The digression on Berma's ultimate fate can have no other purpose than to enforce this point: that just as the path from life to art cannot but yield bad art, so that from art to life is equally disastrous. Berma's tragedy is to be now living out the roles she has played in the past (III:1068; IV:592).

I have been claiming from the outset that the signal achievement of Proust's *Recherche* is to have mapped or theorized with considerable perspicacity the dominant social structures and their transformation during the first half-century of the Third French Republic, that, in fine, this is a novel about the class struggles in France. It thus comes as no surprise when the resolution of the antinomy between society and art that motivates *Le temps retrouvé* can only be this very text. But what exactly is Proust's *Recherche* such that it incarnates the resolution between society and art, and in what ways does it differ from the novel Marcel has resolved to write (and may have already begun) at narrative's end? I begin with the second question, since it is somewhat easier to approach.

Close examination of Marcel's references to the work he describes in the closing pages of *Le temps retrouvé* reveals that, virtually without exception, they are in the future and the conditional,[23] indicating that this novel is at the moment of writing an unfulfilled project. It cannot therefore coincide with the text we are reading, logically speaking, since obviously the latter has already been written. The proof is that we have read it.[24] Of course, Marcel might possibly live to write something like the novel Proust has already composed, but this is unlikely on other grounds. Speaking in his own voice, the Narrator announces his intention to overcome the ravages of time, to immortalize various figures in his work to come. It is impossible to miss the optimistic tone in which he predicts the fulfillment of his aesthetic ambition:

I came to understand why the Duc de Guermantes, about whom, while looking at him seated in a chair, I had marvelled how little he had aged even though he had so many more years under him than I, as soon as he got up and tried to stand, had wavered on legs as shaky as those of old archbishops – about whom there is nothing more solid than their metallic crucifix [and] towards whom rush some vigorous young seminarists – and had only advanced with difficulty, trembling like a leaf, upon the scarcely practicable summit of his eighty-three years ... if enough time were allowed me to accomplish my work, I would not fail from the first to describe men (were this to make them resemble monstrous beings) as occupying a place so considerable, next to the one so restrained that is reserved for them in space, a place on the contrary prolonged without measure – since they touch simultaneously, like giants plunged into the years, epochs so distant, between which so many days have come to be placed – in Time. (III: 1 106–7)

[Je venais de comprendre pourquoi le duc de Guermantes, dont j'avais admiré en le regardant assis sur une chaise, combien il avait peu vielli bien qu'il eut tellement plus d'années que moi au-dessous de lui, dès qu'il s'était levé et avait voulu se tenir debout, avait vacillé sur des jambes flageolantes comme celles de ces vieux archevêques sur lesquels il n'y a de solide que leur croix métallique et vers lesquels s'empressent des jeunes séminaristes gaillards, et ne s'était avancé qu'en tremblant comme une feuille, sur le sommet peu praticable de quatre-vingt-trois années ... si elle m'était laissée assez longtemps pour accomplir mon œuvre, ne manquerais-je pas d'abord d'y décrire les hommes, cela dût-il les faire ressembler à des êtres mons-trueux, comme occupant une place si considérable, à côté de celle si restreinte qui leur est réservée dans l'espace, une place au contraire prolongée sans mesure puisqu'ils touchent simultanément, comme des géants plongés dans les années à des époques, vécues par eux si distantes, entre lesquelles tant de jours sont venus se placer – dans le Temps.] (IV:624–5)

Doubtless one must concede the potential pathos that insuffi-cient time may be allowed him (he expresses just such a fear in the lines omitted from the citation). But what the Narrator manifestly does not lack is confidence about his artistic project itself, about its power to preserve that which is transient in life, to, as another high modernist has it, gather it into the artifice of eternity. Art is, in Marcel's conception of it, the means for mastering time or history; it is that which can triumph over the otherwise irresistible force of material decay. Marcel's aes-thetic, and thus the novel he would produce, is ineluctably, and quite conventionally, idealizing.

The same cannot be said of the *Recherche* itself, which, as I've been arguing, is the record of an epoch and its social structures that, even at the moment of its composition, has already passed. In their different ways, Charlus and the Duchesse de Guermantes had attempted to master the contingencies of

social life, to order and preserve them in the way Marcel
suggests he will the materials of his novel. But the text shows,
and in at least one passage explicitly states, the failure of this
aestheticizing strategy to arrest the forces of historical change:

> Thus, in the Faubourg Saint-Germain, these three apparently
> impregnable positions of the Duc and Duchesse de Guermantes and
> of Charlus had lost their inviolability ... Thus changes the shape of
> things in this world; thus the center of empires, the survey of fortunes,
> the charter of social prestige, all that seemed definitive is perpetually
> remodelled, and the eyes of a man who has lived can contemplate the
> most complete change just there where it would have appeared to
> him most impossible. (III:1072)

> [Ainsi, dans le faubourg Saint-Germain, ces positions en apparence
> imprenables du duc et de la duchesse de Guermantes, du baron de
> Charlus, avaient perdu leur inviolabilité ... Ainsi change la figure
> des choses de ce monde; ainsi le centre des empires, et le cadastre des
> fortunes, et la charte des situations, tout ce qui semblait définit est-il
> perpétuellement remanié, et les yeux d'un homme qui a vécu
> peuvent-ils contempler le changement le plus complet là où jus-
> tement il lui paraissait le plus impossible.] (IV:596)

Whatever else society may be in this novel, it is not an object
that can be mastered and delivered from history in the putative
eternity of art. This is to say that the theory of art embraced by
Marcel and projected for the work he intends cannot be the
benchmark for judging the *Recherche*'s achievement. Proust's
aim is to represent the very object that the text itself proclaims
to be most resistant to aesthetic idealization.

One can make the same point in another way by recalling
Althusser's stipulative definition of ideology as "the (imaginary) relationship of individuals to the relations of production
and the relations that derive from them. What is represented in
ideology is therefore not the system of the real relations which
govern the existence of individuals, but the imaginary relation
of those individuals to the real relations in which they live."[25]
Posing the relationship between knowledge and ideology in
this manner, we can say that, for the characters in the *Recherche*,
the events in the plot and the ideas and actions of the figures

who populate the fictional world express their various ideologies. Marcel, one of the principal characters, is no different in this respect. One could even say that certain readers of this text – those who identify the *Recherche* with the novel Marcel is writing – occupy much the same position as the characters within it: all are inside ideology, specifically the aesthetic ideology that asserts the capacity of art to deliver one from historical contingency. For Proust (and possibly for readers of this study), by contrast, the imaginary world of the *Recherche* discloses, in its deconstruction of a variety of historical ideologies (snobbism, antisemitism, nationalism) the real, underlying relations of social existence that are the authentic causes of action and thought. My exposition to this point goes no further than Proust's (or the text's) own knowledge of its conditions of existence. It is possible, however, to know more than the novel discloses about itself, although we would not have been able to reach this point without first working through its labyrinthine presentation. Such will be my ultimate hypothesis about the *Recherche* as a work of art.

LES LENDEMAINS QUI CHANTENT

The *Recherche* shares with Marcel's novel one significant dimension: an orientation towards the future. This may seem peculiar in light of what has been said about the novel's militant refusal to be delivered from the inexorable processes of history. It is nevertheless possible, I think, to recognize in the passage cited above something of the transhistorical imperative about historical change that it has been the special task of marxism, as a science of the history of social formations, to establish. We can glimpse the distinctiveness of Proust's concept of history by looking at two contrasting accounts of the *Recherche*'s orientation towards the future: Fredric Jameson's and Walter Benjamin's.

Jameson's discussion intervenes in his essay on Ernst Bloch, whose *Principle of Hope* Jameson explicates by referring both to the *Recherche*'s plot and its materials (viz., the manners and mores of the leisured aristocracy). Of the latter he observes:

When we turn now to the actual social content of Proust, the hidden significance of such passions as snobbery and social climbing is at once revealed: so many the mystified figures of that longing for perfection, of an as yet unconscious Utopian impulse. At the same time, such social raw material, with its eternal receptions and drawing rooms and its pronounced class limitations, and the deliberate intention of Proust to paint a nobility in decay and on the point of vanishing into nothingness – all these things come to seem not so much reactionary as anticipatory. For it is precisely the leisure of this class, given over completely to interpersonal relationships, to conversation, art, and social planning (if one may so characterize the energy that goes into the building of a salon), fashion, love, which reflects in the most distorted way the possibilities of a world in which alienated labor will have ceased to exist, in which man's struggle with the external world and with his own mystified and external pictures of society will have given way to man's confrontation with himself.[26]

On Jameson's account, the political allegory in Proust posits the declining aristocracy of the Third Republic as a figure, however distorted, for that future classless society towards which, on a certain reading of Marx's texts, history is inevitably tending. This concept of history envisions a future utterly different from "the history of all hitherto existing society," one in which alienations, social strife, and mystification will no longer obtain. A world so constituted resembles nothing so much as the work of art Marcel himself has predicted at the novel's end, a world built along the lines of the "ästhetischer Staat" Schiller envisioned in his *Aesthetic Letters*.[27]

Nothing can prevent one's taking the *Recherche* in just this way, the more so if we accept Proust's lapidary statement about the effect of reading upon character: "In reality, each reader is, when he reads, the actual reader of himself" (III:949; IV:489). Moreover, there is some evidence in the very passage where Marcel remarks the permanent alteration in society's structure that the violence of historical change may contain a utopian dimension:

if individuals change their social situation, the most deeply rooted ideas and customs (just like the fortunes and alliances and hatred of nations) also change, among them even [the idea] of only receiving *chic* people. Not only does snobbishness change in form, it might one day disappear, like war itself; radicals and Jews would be received in the Jockey. (III: 1003)

[si les personnes changent de situation, les idées et les coutumes les plus indéracinables (de mêmes que les fortunes et les alliances de pays et les haines de pays) changent aussi, parmi lesquelles mêmes celles de ne recevoir que des gens chic. Non seulement le snobisme change de forme, mais il pourrait disparaître comme le guerre même, les radicaux, les juifs étre reçus au Jockey.] (IV:537)

Is this a vision of the classless society of the future? Hardly. The very image chosen to figure a social form from which invidious distinctions of status or rank have disappeared – radicals and Jews admitted to the Jockey Club – betrays the utopian force of its projection. The Narrator (and arguably Proust himself) can only imagine an egalitarian society in terms of upward mobility; the utopian moment evoked here remains inscribed within the concept of an already existing bourgeois society and its institutions. Surely a more authentic utopianism would have envisioned a world where organizations like the Jockey Club do not even exist.

That the novel's attitude towards the future might be construed differently, however, can be shown by referring to Walter Benjamin's seminal essay, "The Image of Proust," which, as I have had occasion to observe already, has provided much of the inspiration for the present project. The decisive passage from Benjamin is as follows:

Proust describes a class which is everywhere pledged to camouflage its material basis and for this very reason is attached to a feudalism which has no intrinsic economic significance but is all the more serviceable as a mask of the upper middle class. This disillusioned, merciless deglamorizer of the ego, of love, of morals – turns his whole limitless art into a veil for this one most vital mystery of his class: the economic aspect. He did not mean to do it a service. Here speaks Marcel Proust, the hardness of his work, the intransigence of a man who is ahead of his class. What he accomplishes he accomplishes as its master. And much of the greatness of this work will remain inaccessible or undiscovered until this class has revealed its most pronounced features in the final struggle.[28]

It is of course difficult to know exactly what Benjamin meant by this moment of "the final struggle." But given the date of this essay (1929), and the ongoing political confrontation in Germany between the bourgeoisie (along with its aristocratic and *lumpen* allies) and proletariat (tragically divided between social democratic and communist parties), it is certainly tempting to interpret it as the time just beyond the endpoint of the *Recherche* itself.[29]

To recapitulate, Proust's novel portrays post-war society as the ravaged remnant of a generally stable and prosperous world now irretrievably lost. Such was the dominant conception of the relationship between the pre- and post-First World War world among the European middle and upper classes. The chronic financial instability of the early 1920s was most spectacular in Germany, but it was palpable in France as well. Currency speculation might be curbed, but the value of the franc would never approach its pre-war levels against the dollar and sterling. In addition, the 1920s saw French industrial development, so long maturing from the early nineteenth century, come into full blossom. Even agriculture would be modernized in some areas. In virtually every sphere, the years 1919–22, when Proust wrote the final sections to be incorporated in the *Recherche*, can be seen in much the way Proust evokes them. The period was one of politically conservative bourgeois rule, of economic uncertainty, and of social dislocation. With one signal exception.

Nowhere in the novel we have is there any indication that Proust registered the increasing working-class militancy that would dominate the political scene in the years just following the time when its last episode occurs (i.e., in 1926 or 1927). Nothing about the birth of the French Communist Party and the conversion of the CGT from syndicalism to revolutionary socialism. We glimpse nothing, in short, of the deepening class war between workers and bourgeois that would lead in the end to the Popular Front government, the rise of fascism – not a negligible force in inter-war France – and the ultimate weakening of the republican polity to the point that it would collapse precipitously and unexpectedly after yet another German invasion in 1940.

Is it fair to tax the *Recherche* with this absence of prophetic power? Yes and no. To reach the text's ideological limits, it was first necessary to delineate its historical diagnosis of pre-war French society. Proust's understanding of this period has proven remarkably durable when compared to subsequent historiographic explanations. The text recognizes not only that the aristocracy has made its final exit, but that the era of liberal capitalism, when the ruling classes could rely on the general loyalty of those over whom they ruled, was equally a thing of the past. What it fails to register, save in the most attenuated and allusive manner, is the emergence of the bourgeoisie's new and potent class enemy. One can only speculate what Proust would have made of the challenge to bourgeois hegemony posed by the Communist Party. He did not, in any event, live to see its emergence as the dominant expression of working-class resistance. The *Recherche* anatomizes the underlying social contradictions of the *belle époque*; it cannot foresee their transformation into a wholly new configuration.[30]

The ideological limits of Proust's text are plain enough to historians, especially those with an eye to the post-war history of French socialism. As Robert Wohl writes:

> For those who cared to look, the signs of collapse [of liberal capitalism] were clear enough in the years before '14. The great protagonists of prewar French fiction – Rolland's Jean-Christophe, Proust's Swann, Martin du Gard's Jean Barois – all felt the crumbling of the world around them. Moral codes no longer seemed to correspond to feelings. Youth sought outlets in religious commitments of the revival of strange cults. Irrationalism was exalted. Imperialistic ventures attracted Europeans who found their native countries effete and boring. And new movements arose on both the Right and the Left that paraded their disdain for liberal values.[31]

Wohl deploys this hypothesis as a springboard to his ultimate judgment on the emergence of Bolshevism in Russia and France: communism was the working class's political reply to the crisis of liberal values and the inadequacy of social democratic solutions:

> The radical movements of prewar Europe, no less than the bourgeois movements they arose to combat, were victims of the liberal collapse. Their successors inherited everything but the dream of liberation that

made these movements tick. That dream died in the disappointments of 1919–23. Communism [by which Wohl means Stalinism], both in France and in Russia, was a product of the Revolution's failure, not its success.[32]

If Proust's text fails to project a social form beyond the bourgeois utopia of "careers open to talent," and if, as Benjamin opined, it generally occults the economic reality underpinning the leisured society it anatomizes, it nonetheless holds onto no illusions about the one ideology most often ascribed to it: the ideology of art, which, from Schiller to Marcuse and Adorno (and many lesser figures), has been offered either as compensation for or the means of deliverance from social alienation. In the conception of the *Recherche* as we have it, nothing is more certain than society's absolute resistance to aestheticization. The novel, if one can even use such a term to describe this most peculiar and unnovelistic of narrative texts, ceaselessly asserts the necessary and ongoing historicity of social life. The *Recherche* is a great work of art precisely to the degree that it refuses the temptation of aestheticizing history while demonstrating society's ineluctable entanglement in the material processes of historical change. Nothing would be less in keeping with Proust's fictional practice than to imagine a society that has been delivered from history, that is beyond or outside of time. As Althusser once observed: "Only an ideological world outlook could have imagined societies *without ideology* and accepted the utopian idea of a world in which ideology (not just one of its historical forms) would disappear without a trace ..."[33]

Proust's chronicle of the French aristocracy's final passing declares an end to the specific ideology expressing this class's position, at the same time that it asserts the permanence of ideology as such. If, as Althusser adds some lines after the sentence just cited, not even a future classless society will be able to do without ideology, then, *a fortiori*, neither could the fully bourgeois society of post-First World War France. Benjamin's brilliance was to have recognized that Proust's *Recherche* recorded both the aristocracy's exit from the stage of history and the bourgeoisie's consolidation, socially, politically, and above all ideologically.

Insofar as it makes sense to call our own world capitalist and bourgeois, we still have much to learn from Proust's novel, from its analysis of a now distant historical epoch certainly, but also from its dissection of certain historical ideologies that, it would seem, are far from moribund even today. The economic policies of the Reagan–Thatcher years made it appear to all and sundry that one could quite literally "get money for nothing." By the onset of the following decade, both economic and sexual life had assumed terrifying new forms, with the twin scourges of global recession and pandemic AIDS. As Proust understood perfectly well, someone must ultimately pay the price for the privilege exercised by the ruling classes not to engage in productive labor. And, to recall the second half of the line from Dire Straits, "chicks" are never entirely free.

Notes

INTRODUCTION

1 E. J. Hobsbawm, *The Age of Empire* (New York: Pantheon, 1987), p. 12.

2 Hobsbawm observes: "Economically, the shadows of the years of the Great Depression lifted, to give way to the brilliantly sunny expansion and prosperity of the 1900s. Political systems which did not quite know how to deal with the social agitations of the 1880s, with the sudden emergence of mass working-class parties dedicated to revolution, or with the mass mobilizations of citizens against the state on other grounds, appeared to discover flexible ways of containing and integrating some and isolating others. The fifteen years or so from 1899 to 1914 were a *belle époque* not only because they were prosperous and life was exceedingly attractive for those who had money and golden for those who were rich, but also because the rulers of most western countries were perhaps worried about the future, but not really frightened about the present. Their societies and regimes, by and large, seemed manageable" (*Empire*, pp. 276–7).

3 Arno J. Mayer, *The Persistence of the Old Regime: Europe to the Great War* (New York: Pantheon, 1981). In many ways, the present study is an elaboration of Mayer's thesis for the single social formation of the Third French Republic. While I shall differ from him in several matters of detail, my own understanding of Proust would have been all but unthinkable without the prior example of Mayer's magisterial synthesis.

4 If they do not lie deeper still in a more than twenty-year fascination with Proust that commenced when I was an undergraduate. A few years later, while continuing to read in – but not for many years all the way through – the *Recherche*, I was struck how my teachers in the university occupied much the same position in relation to the local gentry as did Swann and Marcel

in the Faubourg Saint-Germain. In Proustian fashion, only much later did I understand that I, too, was being recruited, however tactfully, to fulfill a comparable social function. Although I had not encountered it at that time, the following passage from *Le temps retrouvé* perfectly captures the congruence between the different milieux Proust and I were privileged to observe: "Moreover, the case that had presented itself for me to be admitted into the society of the Guermantes had appeared to me something exceptional. But if I got outside myself and the milieu that immediately surrounded me, I saw that this social phenomenon was not as isolated as it had appeared to me at first, and that from the basin of Combray where I had been born, quite a number in fact were the jets of water that, symmetrically with me, were elevated above the same mass of liquid that had nourished them. [D'ailleurs, le cas qui s'était présenté pour moi d'admis dans la société des Guermantes m'avait paru quelque chose d'exceptionnel. Mais si je sortais de moi et du milieu qui m'entourait immédiatement, je voyais que ce phénomène social n'était pas aussi isolé qu'il m'avait paru d'abord et que du bassin de Combray où j'étais né, assez nombreux en sommé étaient les jets d'eau qui symétriquement à moi s'étaient élevés au-dessus de la même masse liquide qui les avait alimentés.]" (*A la recherche du temps perdu*, ed. Jean-Yves Tadié et al., 4 vols. [Paris: Bibliothèque de la Pléiade, 1987–9], IV:547; my translation.) In another version, Proust had written, in place of "from the basin of Combray," "du bassin petit–bourgeois" (see ibid., p. 930).

5 I take as canonical in this regard the glancing blow hurled at Proust by Lukács in *The Meaning of Contemporary Realism* (London: Merlin Press, 1963). That the story of Proust's reception in marxist criticism and aesthetics is more complicated should perhaps go without saying, but those who doubt it can consult Ronald Thornton's excellent dissertation, "Marcel Proust and Marxist Literary Criticism from the Nineteen Twenties to the Nineteen Seventies" (Ph.D. dissertation, Indiana University, 1979). As Thornton shows, ambivalence towards Proust's work in the marxist tradition is already evident in his first marxist interpreter, none other than A. V. Lunachársky, one of the most powerful figures in the early Soviet Union's cultural apparatus. Lunachársky at one and the same time could condemn Proust as decadent and yet insist, as Engels did of Balzac, that his work was nonetheless realist in its accomplishment. Of Balzac, Engels wrote: "His great work is a unique elegy on the irrevocable decline of respectable society ... But despite this his satire was

~~nore~~ daring ... than when he dealt with the men and
~~n~~ with whom he deeply sympathized – the aristocracy"
~~d~~ in Georg Lukács, *Goethe and his Age*, trans. Robert Anchor
~~ndon:~~ Merlin Press, 1968], p. 125).

⌐ ~~e~~odor W. Adorno, *Negative Dialectics*, trans. E. B. Ashton (New York: Seabury Press, 1973).

7 Cited in Ortwin de Graef, *Serenity in Crisis* (Lincoln: University of Nebraska Press, 1993), p. 26.

8 That the underlying social stability evident in these texts is itself ideological, dependent upon repressing most of the signs of material inequities at home and imperial subjugation abroad, should go without saying – although typically it has just gone unremarked. See, for a critique of this ideology and its continuation in modern literary scholarship, Edward W. Said, "Jane Austen and Empire," in *Culture and Imperialism* (New York: Alfred A. Knopf, 1993), pp. 80–97.

9 Cf. Gene M. Moore, *Proust and Musil: The Novel as Research Instrument* (New York: Garland Publishing, 1985). Moore's understanding of this concept differs from the view advanced here in totally eschewing any reference to the available record of historical and sociological evidence on the Third Republic. His book charts the epistemological position established in Proust's narrative, without questioning or substantiating the validity of its hypotheses about French society. Moore's interest in the *Recherche* is exclusively formal, his explicit claims to the contrary notwithstanding.

10 Introduction to Marcel Proust, *Selected Letters (1880–1903)*, ed. Philip Kolb, trans. Ralph Manheim (Garden City, NY: Doubleday, 1983), xxiv–xxv.

11 This is the burden of Rosalind H. Williams's pioneering study, *Dream Worlds: Mass Consumption in Late Nineteenth-Century France* (Berkeley: University of California Press, 1982), which asserts: "in creating this new style of mass consumption the French were nearly as preeminent in the nineteenth century as they had been in developing the courtly model in earlier times. France pioneered in retailing and advertising, the twin pillars of modern consumer life. Its capital city became a sort of pilot plant of mass consumption ... If the North of England is the landscape that symbolizes the industrial revolution, the Île de France can well claim to serve as the emblem of the consumer revolution" (pp. 11–12).

12 See Jean-Paul Sartre, *What Is Literature?*, trans. Bernard Frechtman (1965; rpt. Gloucester, MA: Peter Smith, 1978), pp. 161–3,

where Sartre memorably evokes the generation of writers whose
careers began prior to the Great War and who "in their persons
and in their works ... opened the way to a reconciliation between
literature and the bourgeois public."

13 On Proust's aesthetic as a pointed rejection of literary history in
its then dominant mode in France (i.e., the scholarly and pedagogical methods of Gustave Lanson), see Antoine Campagnon, *La
Troisième République des lettres, de Flaubert à Proust* (Paris: Seuil,
1983).

14 *Against Sainte-Beuve*, trans. John Sturrock (Harmondsworth,
Middlesex: Penguin, 1988), p. 58.

15 Ibid., p. 61; ellipsis in the original.

16 Ibid., p. 81. The whole complex matter of Proust's relationship to
Balzac deserves more careful, sustained treatment. An appropriate point of entry is provided by Vincent Descombes's judgment that "... Proust's work does contain within itself the germ of
a perfect Balzacian novel ..." (*Proust: Philosophy of the Novel*,
trans. Catherine Chance Macksey [Stanford University Press,
1992], p. 153).

17 I might also have added Saussure, were it not for the existence of
Gilles Deleuze's excellent study, *Proust and Signs*, trans. Richard
Howard (New York: George Braziller, 1972), which thoroughly
corroborates the connection between Proustian representation
and Saussurean semiology. Mention of Saussure's name in con-
junction with Proust's will therefore come as no shock; Weber and
Durkheim are another matter, or so I surmise. But see Luc
Fraisse, "Une Sociologie transfigurée: Marcel Proust lecteur de
Gabriel Tarde," *Revue Historique de la Littérature française* (1988):
710–36, for a comparison of the *Recherche* to *fin de siècle* social
theory. Durkheim polemicized against Tarde, dooming the
latter's work to subsequent obscurity. But Tarde was an especially
acute commentator on the emergent structures of consumer
society in France; see Williams, *Dream Worlds*, pp. 342–84.

18 Cf. Descombes, *Proust*, pp. 157–94, for a brief treatment of the
social theory undergirding the *Recherche* (not only Durkheim but
Dumont), and pp. 294–8, for the novel's relationship to Weberian
sociology of religion.

19 *Cambridge Journal* 1 (July 1949): 613–22.

20 Cobban first essayed this line in his inaugural lecture to the chair
in history at University College, London: *The Myth of the French
Revolution* (London: H. K. Lewis, 1955). He later codified it in his
The Social Interpretation of the French Revolution (Cambridge University Press, 1964).

21 Cobban, "Historical Significance of Marcel Proust," p. 615.
22 Descombes, *Proust*, p. 160.
23 (New York: Institute for French Studies, 1936).
24 Ibid., p. 118.
25 (Paris: Nizet, 1986).
26 (Paris: Nizet, n.d.); and (New York University Press, 1971).
27 Wolitz, op. cit., p. 27.
28 On the same theme, cf. Albert Sonnenfeld, "Marcel Proust: Antisemite? I," *French Review* 62,1 (October 1988): 25–40; and idem, "Marcel Proust Antisemite? II," *French Review* 62,2 (December 1988): 275–82. Sonnenfeld handles the matter much less discreetly, without significantly advancing the case against Proust. Antisemitism is treated more extensively in chapter 3 below.

1 BASE AND SUPERSTRUCTURE

1 The conventional marxist characterization of the events of 1789–99 as a "bourgeois revolution" has been much criticized since the mid-1950s when Alfred Cobban started the revisionist log rolling. While vulgar versions of the marxist thesis have not fared so well (e.g., Soboul's later textbook redactions), the more detailed and sophisticated historiography (notably Lefebvre but also Soboul's earlier monograph on the *sansculottes*) has withstood the onslaught. E. J. Hobsbawm, *Echoes of the Marseillaise: Two Centuries Look Back on the French Revolution* (London: Verso, 1990), reprises the debates and offers a sober defense of the revolutionary social significance of 1789. Colin Mooers, in *The Making of Bourgeois Europe: Absolutism, Revolution, and the Rise of Capitalism in England, France and Germany* (London: Verso, 1991), chapter 2, "France: From Absolutism to Bonapartism," rescues the concept of bourgeois revolution from anachronism and argues persuasively that the outcome, if not the original intent, of the revolutionaries' overthrow of the Bourbon monarchy was to promote capitalist development. Cf. Alex Callinicos, "Bourgeois Revolutions and Historical Materialism," *International Socialism* 43 (1989): 143.
2 Jean-Marie Mayeur, "The Origins of the Third French Republic, 1871–1898," Part I of vol. IV in *The Cambridge History of Modern France*, trans. J. R. Foster (Cambridge: Maison des Sciences de l'Homme and Cambridge University Press, 1984), p. 46; hereafter cited parenthetically in the text as Mayeur. This view conforms in general to those of Guy P. Palmade, *French*

Capitalism in the Nineteenth Century, trans. Graeme M. Holmes (Newton Abbot: David & Charles, 1972), François Caron, *An Economic History of Modern France*, trans. Barbara Bray (New York: Columbia University Press, 1979), and Tom Kemp, *Economic Forces in French History* (London: Dennis Dobson, 1971); hereafter cited parenthetically in the text. The relevant sections in *The Cambridge Economic History of Europe*, vol. VII, ed. Peter Mathias and M. M. Postan (Cambridge University Press, 1978), chapters 5–7, take this comparative stagnation in French economic development as read, while arguing against prejudicial views concerning its particular causes (e.g., the Sawyer-Landes hypothesis about the backwardness of French entrepreneurs). Among the authorities I have consulted, only Jean-Charles Asselain significantly dissents from the consensus, but even he, at the outset of his study, admits the comparative "backwardness" of the French economy at the onset of the twentieth century: ". . . France at the beginning of the 20th century remained a semi-agricultural, semi-industrialized nation, midway between Great Britain or Germany on one side and Mediterranean Europe on the other; the very unequal industrialization of different French regions thus indicates, all things considered, the characteristic 'dualism' of incompletely developed countries" (*Histoire économique de la France du XVIIIe siècle à nos jours*, vol. I, De L'Ancien Régime à la Première Guerre mondiale [Paris: Seuil, 1984], p. 9).

3 The most vigorous case against mono-causal explanations in general has been put by François Caron, *Economic History*. Shepard B. Clough's "Retardative Factors in French Economic Development in the 19th and 20th Centuries," *Journal of Economic History*, Supp. III (1946): 91–102, is the most famous exposition of the coal deficiency thesis. It has been rebutted by Claude Fohlen, "Entrepreneurship and Management in France in the Nineteenth Century," in Mathias and Postan, eds., *Cambridge Economic History*, p. 348, and by Asselain, *Histoire économique*, p. 182. Demographic stagnation, while real, tended to be offset by immigration; see Yves Lequin, "Labour in the French Economy since the Revolution," in Mathias and Postan, eds., *Cambridge Economic History*, pp. 299–302. French banking practices were in some respects *en retard* in relation above all to Britain, but this seems not to have hampered capital formation and investment significantly; see Maurice Lévy-Leboyer, "Capital Investment and Economic Growth in France, 1820–1930," in Mathias and Postan, eds., *Cambridge Economic History*. The most thoroughgoing rebuttal of the regressive business mentality thesis has been given by Rondo

Cameron in his *France and the Economic Development of Europe,
1800–1914: Conquests of Peace and Seeds of War*, 2nd edn., rev. and
abridged (Chicago: Rand McNally, 1965); hereafter cited
parenthetically in the text as Cameron. But see also Fohlen,
"Entrepreneurship and Management."

4 "Thus the French economy entered the last quarter of the nineteenth century, which was to see a change in the international
conjuncture, with some, but only some, of the attributes of an
advanced industrial society ... French capitalism had taken on a
distinctive form which it was to conserve into the mid–twentieth
century" (Kemp, *Economic Forces*, p. 204). Even François Caron,
who is otherwise inclined to minimize the degree of French
stagnation during the nineteenth century, concedes the fact of
comparative disadvantage at this juncture. Stagnation was
evident in the declining profits of French industry during the
century's last quarter, due in part to France's inability to compete
in international markets: "The steadily-growing 'disharmony'
between the French economy and the international economy can
only be explained by this incompleteness in the structures of
French industry, the result of the factors underlying previous
industrial growth" (Caron, *Economic History*, p. 144).

5 The same point is made by Roger Price in *An Economic History of
Modern France, 1730–1914*, rev. edn. (London: Macmillan, 1981),
p. 225.

6 This in two ways. First, there was no general depopulation of the
countryside until the 1880s, thus necessitating the importation of
immigrant labor for industry; second, the level of workers' education (even after the much-vaunted Ferry reforms) remained
woefully inadequate to the needs of a modern industrializing
economy (see Lequin, "Labour," pp. 305, 309–18). Once
Europe's model for producing a technical intelligentsia (see
Cameron, *France*, pp. 36–43), France now lagged behind in educating both its technical cadres and, more egregiously, its laboring population.

7 Cameron confirms Kemp's view: "In France the revolutionary
land settlement, coupled with the legislation on inheritance,
actually retarded the progress of both agriculture and industry by
fostering an exaggerated individualism, providing motives for
reducing the birth rate, and contributing to the *morcellement* of
territory. In the hundred years following the Revolution the
number of agriculture proprietors doubled in France, while the
agricultural population remained stationary and the population
as a whole increased by less than 50 per cent. The average size of

these properties, while large enough to give the proprietor pride of ownership and hold him on the soil, was too small to permit the employment of much capital or the most efficient techniques. Thus agricultural productivity remained low and the growth of industry inhibited by inadequate labor supply and restricted markets" (Cameron, *France*, p. 22).

8 By comparison, Britain had attained a comparable reduction of its agricultural labor force by the middle of the eighteenth century, while Germany in 1913 employed less than 35 per cent of its available workers in agriculture (see Mathias and Postan, eds., *Cambridge Economic History*, pp. 141, 444).

9 See Madeleine Rebérioux, "A Radical Republic? 1898–1914," Part II of vol. IV in *The Cambridge History of Modern France*, p. 334; hereafter cited parenthetically in the text. Again for purposes of comparison, more than a decade on from the end of the war, France still lagged far behind Great Britain, Germany, and the Netherlands in agricultural productivity; see Philippe Bernard and Henri Dubief, *The Decline of the Third Republic, 1914–1938*, vol. V in the *Cambridge History of Modern France*, trans. Anthony Forster (Cambridge: Maison des Sciences de l'Homme and Cambridge University Press, 1985), p. 141.

It might be objected that the Second Empire was just as much a peasant-based society as the Third Republic, even more so in terms of sheer numbers. The point to bear in mind, though, is that the earlier regime fueled economic expansion through large public works projects, an option not so readily available during the Third Republic (with the notable exception of the Freycinet plan). Bonapartism floated on an increasingly fragile bubble of expansive state expenditures; the more fiscally conservative republic had to rely on growth in domestic markets, against which the rural economy acted as a brake.

10 Marc Bloch, *French Rural History: An Essay on its Basic Characteristics*, trans. Janet Sondheimer (Berkeley and Los Angeles: University of California Press, 1966), pp. 246–7. *Les caractères originaux de l'histoire rurale française* was originally delivered as lectures in Oslo in 1929; these were revised and published in 1931.

11 Cf. John McKay, "The House of Rothschild (Paris) as a multinational industrial enterprise: 1875–1914," in A. Teichova, M. Lévy-Leboyer, and H. Nussbaum, eds., *Multinational Enterprise in Historical Perspective* (Cambridge University Press, 1986), pp. 74–86.

12 Price, *Modern France*, pp. 229–30. Cf. Herman Lebovics, *The Alliance of Iron and Wheat in the Third French Republic 1860–1914:*

Origins of the New Conservatism (Baton Rouge: Louisiana State University Press, 1988). For a dissenting view on the retardant effects of the tariffs on the economy as a whole, see Asselain, *Histoire économique*, p. 181.

13 Asselain, *Histoire économique*, pp. 201, 207.

14 Cf. Lévy-Leboyer, in Mathias and Postan, eds., *Cambridge Economic History*, pp. 274–5; and David Higgs, *Nobles in Nineteenth-Century France: The Practice of Inegalitarianism* (Baltimore: Johns Hopkins University Press, 1987), pp. 113, 129.

15 Lévy-Leboyer, in Mathias and Postan, eds., *Cambridge Economic History*, pp. 264–6.

16 Certain inefficient industries were kept alive through captive colonial markets: textiles and steel, for instance; see Jacques Marsaille, *Empire colonial et capitalisme français: Histoire d'un divorce* (Paris: Albin Michel, 1984), pp. 50–4.

17 See Perry Anderson, "The Figures of Descent," *New Left Review* 161 (January–February 1987): 20–77; rpt. in idem, *English Questions* (London and New York: Verso, 1992). Anderson's interpretation of Britain's long-term economic decline has provoked a stormy debate. In the present context, however, there seems little evidence to undermine the basic claim that from the First World War to the rise of Thatcherism, France's economy modernized more rapidly and completely and as a result it out-performed Britain's by a large margin.

18 Stanley Hoffmann, "Paradoxes of the French Political Community," in Hoffmann et al., eds., *In Search of France* (Cambridge, MA: Harvard University Press, 1963), p. 3. Hoffmann's general view of the Third Republic's "immobilism" has been defended by Michel Crozier in *La Société bloquée* (Paris: Seuil, 1970).

19 Hoffmann, "Paradoxes," p. 15.

20 E. J. Hobsbawm, *The Age of Empire, 1875–1914* (New York: Pantheon, 1987), p. 238.

21 Cf. Theodore Zeldin, who concludes his chapter on the early republican state as follows: "The old authoritarian state survived, despite the Revolution. The deputies were representatives of liberty against it, but when they became ministers they were unhesitating in maintaining its power. The republic exhibited herself in public wearing liberal clothes, but one had grounds for suspecting that she was simply the old Napoleonic state disguised, not altered too fundamentally" (*France 1848–1945: Politics and Anger* [New York: Oxford University Press, 1979], pp. 239–40).

22 Arno J. Mayer, *The Persistence of the Old Regime: Europe to the Great War* (New York: Pantheon, 1981), p. 135.

23 Ibid., pp. 166–7; cf. Higgs, *Nobles*, p. 124.
24 Mayeur's formulation is somewhat imprecise. The truth is that the *industrial* working class was effectively excluded, not workers as a whole.
25 See Zeldin, *Politics and Anger*, p. 213.
26 On the government's relationship with the army between 1870 and the First World War, see chapter 3 below.
27 See Robert R. Locke, *French Legitimists and the Politics of Moral Order in the Early Third Republic* (Princeton University Press, 1974); and Jean-Denis Bredin, *The Affair: The Case of Alfred Dreyfus*, trans. Jeffrey Mehlman (New York: George Braziller, 1986), passim.
28 See also George Weisz, *The Emergence of Modern Universities in France, 1863–1914* (Princeton University Press, 1983), pp. 95, 115–17, 126, 128.
29 See Mayeur, "Origins," pp. 89–90, 109–16, from which much of this paragraph is drawn. The standard work on French education in this period is Antoine Prost, *L'Enseignement en France, 1800–1967* (Paris: Armand Colin, 1968), on which Mayeur's discussion is largely based. On the "pre-history" of the struggles for secular education, see Robert Anderson, "The Conflict in Education – Catholic Secondary Schools (1850–70): A Reappraisal," in Theodore Zeldin, ed., *Conflicts in French Society: Anticlericalism, Education and Morals in the Nineteenth Century* (London: George Allen and Unwin, 1970), pp. 51–93.
30 See Jo Burr Margadant, *Madame le Professeur: Women Educators in the Third Republic* (Princeton University Press, 1990), for a thorough treatment of the first generation of *normaliennes* who graduated from the newly created teacher training school at Sèvres.
31 See Weisz, *Emergence*. Cf. Theodore Zeldin, "Higher Education in France, 1848–1940," *Journal of Contemporary History* 1,3 (July 1967): 53–80, which presents a rather jaundiced view of the universities at this period.
32 Louis Althusser, "Ideology and Ideological State Apparatuses (Notes Towards an Investigation)," in idem, *Lenin and Philosophy and Other Essays*, trans. Ben Brewster (New York: Monthly Review Press, 1971), p. 157.
33 On history textbooks in the early Third Republic, see Régine Robin, "Essai sur la stéréotype républicaine: les manuels d'Histoire de la IIIe République jusqu'en 1914," *Littérature* 44 (Décembre 1981): 98–116.
   The republican myth has proven extremely tenacious. For a

recent example, see Perry Anderson's "Nation–States and National Identity," *London Review of Books* (9 May 1991): 3–8, a review of the late Fernand Braudel's *The Identity of France. Vol. II: People and Production*; rpt. in Anderson's *A Zone of Engagement* (London and New York: Verso, 1992). On Anderson's account, it would appear that Braudel in his final years took upon himself the patriotic duty to celebrate his native land by providing a material historical basis for its national cohesion. It is quite fascinating – and indicative of the continuing hold that republican ideology exercises over French intellectuals – to recognize that in reproducing the commonplaces of nationalist historiography, Braudel was relying on just that type of historical method which he and his *Annales* colleagues had done so much to undermine.

34 Cf. Paul Gerbod, "The Baccalaureate and its Role in the Recruitment and Formation of French Elites in the Nineteenth Century," in Jolyon Howorth and Philip G. Cerny, eds., *Elites in France: Origins, Reproduction and Power* (New York: St. Martin's Press, 1981), pp. 46–56.

35 Cf. Zeldin, "Higher Education," p. 80.

36 Cited in Ezra N. Suleiman, *Elites in French Society: The Politics of Survival* (Princeton University Press, 1978), p. 37. Some pages later, Suleiman quotes from Philippe Ariès, "Problèmes de l'éducation," concerning the position of the *grandes écoles* at the pinnacle of French higher education: "the grandes écoles, where one entered by competitive examination, which became more and more difficult, established within the powerful but fluid divisions of birth and fortune, a new social category, defined at once by its small size and by its merit. It carried a name, the 'elite.' The word is of the time. In an older language the word certainly existed, but it was always used as part of a phrase: the elite of the nation or of the country, and then simply the elite" (p. 42). The basic thesis of Suleiman's study, written in the wake of the post-'68 reforms in French higher education, is that the *grandes écoles* have maintained their monopoly on the reproduction of French bureaucratic and professional elites because of a consensus among the left and the right (meaning on the one extreme social democrats, and on the other the political representatives of the *haute bourgeoisie*) concerning their contribution to political stability and order. His evidence for this consensus boils down to observing that the Mitterand Parti Socialiste in the 1970s showed no inclination to overturn the system, and that the Ecole Nationale d'Administration originated during the Popular Front. One wonders whether he could have so sanguinely asserted the immortality of

these bastions of bourgeois privilege had his interviewees been the *enragés* of May '68, or included representatives of the French Communist Party, rather than being confined to those with access to the Elysée Palace. Suleiman's conclusion in this respect amounts to nothing more than the tautology that as long as France remains a bourgeois society its system of higher education will tend to reproduce bourgeois social relations.

37 Karl Marx, "The Civil War in France," in idem, *The First International and After*, ed. David Fernbach (New York: Vintage, 1974), p. 230. Marx is referring here to the brutal suppression of the Commune and to the French bourgeoisie's pretension to a monopoly over social power and justice, a modern equivalent to the *droit de seigneur*

38 Cf. Mayer, *Persistence*, chapter 3, "Political Society and the Governing Elites: Linchpin of the Old Regime." It should perhaps be added that the bulk of these elites came from Paris, a not incidental fact when one reflects on their portrayal in Proust's *Recherche*. Zeldin's figures on the composition of the Chamber (from 1881) confirm the point; see *Politics and Anger*, p. 213. He offers no comparable figures for the Senate, but asserts that it quickly "became one more bastion of the rule of politicians, for it was a chamber which essentially represented them. The people elected were largely retired deputies and civil servants" (p. 227).

39 See Lebovics, *Alliance*, and Judith F. Stone, *The Search for Social Peace: Reform Legislation in France, 1890–1914* (Albany: SUNY Press, 1985).

40 Eugen Weber, *France: Fin de Siècle* (Cambridge, MA: Harvard University Press, 1986), p. 240; cf. Bredin, *Affair*, pp. 517–20, for the press's significance in the Dreyfus Affair.

41 Hobsbawm, *Empire*, p. 238.

42 Mayeur, "Origins," p. 116; Weber, *Fin de Siècle*, p. 27.

43 P. Albert, et al., *Histoire générale de la presse française*, III, De 1871 à 1940 (Paris: Presses Universitaires de France, 1972); cited in Mayeur, "Origins," p. 117.

44 The great historian of this process is Eugen Weber, whose *Peasants into Frenchmen: The Modernization of Rural France 1870–1914* (Stanford University Press, 1976) is unrivalled in its account of how a backward, in many ways almost medieval, countryside was not only modernized (albeit slowly) during the first half-century of the Third Republic, but became part of a culturally, politically, economically, and (very important) linguistically unified nation. Of the three principal agents of this massive social transformation (roads and railroads, schooling, military service), only the army

could be said to have remained contested terrain for bourgeois hegemony. In virtually every other sphere, the dissemination of bourgeois values and the identification of *la patrie* with conservative republicanism can safely be presumed. On the creation of a national market for agricultural commodities and the modernization of French agriculture in the early twentieth century, counter-balanced by the resistance to incorporation in non-local markets throughout many regions outside the Paris Basin, see Hugh D. Clout, *The Land of France 1815–1914* (London: Allen & Unwin, 1983), pp. 137–53.

45 Weber, *Fin de Siècle*, p. 244.

46 See *Remembrance of Things Past*, trans. C. K. Scott Moncrief, Terence Kilmartin, and Andreas Mayor, 3 vols. (New York: Random House, 1981), 1:95–6; hereafter cited parenthetically in the text by volume and page number, followed by the French original, *A la recherche du temps perdu*, ed. Jean-Yves Tadié et al., 4 vols. (Paris: Bibliothèque de la Pléiade, 1987–9). This is the new Pléiade edition, which replaces the older three-volume text established by Clarac and Ferré; it contains a concordance to page numbers in the earlier edition. The passage referred to here comes at 1:87–8. Throughout, I have silently modified the standard English translation to highlight features that are pertinent to my argument. On the controversies over military service, see Locke, *French Legitimists*, pp. 198–201, 210–11; and Rebérioux, "Radical Republic," pp. 345–9.

47 On Chambord and the Orleanist pretender, the Comte de Paris, see Zeldin, *Politics and Anger*, pp. 34–7, 55–62

48 A role it was not infrequently called upon to play during the Third Republic, quelling working-class militancy when the government thought such repression necessary – as the government did, for example, systematically and without compunction during the Clemenceau ministry from October 1906 to July 1909.

49 On the Legitimists in the National Assembly, see Locke, *French Legitimists*, chapter 5.

50 The passage has been commented on by Antoine Compagnon in his superb exegesis of the Racine motif in the *Recherche*, "Proust on Racine," *Yale French Studies* 76 (1989): 45–9. Compagnon uses this little episode to illustrate Proust's relationship to Racine's shifting status in turn-of-the century academic criticism.

51 The Pléiade editors indicate that the examination in question was for the "superior primary" certificate, which came after the third form in the colleges (II:1467). Workers' children would not likely

have gone so far, and they certainly would not have been asked to write on Racine, as Giselle was; see Renée Balibar, *Les français fictifs: le rapport des styles littéraires au français national* (Paris: Hachette, 1974). On the Sée law and its impact on secondary education for women, the definitive study is Françoise Mayeur, *L'enseignement secondaire des jeunes filles sous la Troisième République* (Paris: Presses de la Fondation Nationale des Sciences Politiques, 1977), pp. 9–238.

52 One further indication about women's education prior to the Third Republic is that Mme. de Villeparisis and Marcel's grandmother were schoolmates at the Sacré Coeur (see 1:21; 1:20). No other evidence concerning this generation of women's formal education is given. The standard work on the situation of upperclass women in the nineteenth century, Bonnie G. Smith's *Ladies of the Leisure Class: The Bourgeoises of Northern France in the Nineteenth Century* (Princeton University Press, 1981), asserts the predominance of convent education through the early years of the Third Republic, although challenges to the Church's monopoly in this area began to emerge at the end of the Second Empire; see chapter 7, "Education: Innocence versus Enlightenment," pp. 165–86.

53 Differences between male and female secondary education, however, persisted until after the First World War; see Prost, *L'Enseignement*, pp. 261–5; Karen Offen, "The Second Sex and the Baccalauréat in Republican France, 1880–1924," *French Historical Studies* 13,2 (1983): 252–86; and Margadant, *Madame le Professeur*, chapter 8.

54 On the role presumed for women in sustaining the republic, see Margadant, *Madame le Professeur*, passim; and Linda L. Clark, *Schooling the Daughers of Marianne: Textbooks and the Socialization of Girls in Modern French Primary Schools* (Albany: SUNY Press, 1984), pp. 5–80.

55 Marcel Proust, *Selected Letters, 1880–1903*, ed. Philip Kolb, trans. Ralph Manheim (Garden City, NY: Doubleday, 1983), p. 343, and *Correspondance*, vol. III (1902–1903), ed. Philip Kolb (Paris: Plon, 1976), p. 383; hereafter cited parenthetically in the text as *Letters* followed by page references to English translation and French original, respectively.

56 In fact, while press freedom was guaranteed from 1881 onwards, various forms of censorship – having mostly to do with what one could and could not publish concerning officials – persisted under the republic. The *procès* Zola is probably the best remembered

instance, but there were others; see Zeldin, *Politics and Anger*, p. 232.

57 Much the same point is made about political opinion by Charlus in *Le temps retrouvé*: see III:811; IV:364.

2 CLASS AND CLASS STRUGGLE

1 Madeleine Rebérioux, "A Radical Republic? 1898–1914," Part II of vol. IV in *The Cambridge History of Modern France*, trans. J. R. Foster (Cambridge: Maison des Sciences de l'Homme and Cambridge University Press, 1984), p. 333.

2 Jean-Charles Asselain, *Histoire économique de la France du XVIIIe siècle à nos jours*, vol. I (De l'Ancien Régime à la Première Guerre mondiale) (Paris: Editions du Seuil, 1984), pp. 195–6.

3 On the former topic, see, for example: Erik Olin Wright et al., *The Debate on Classes* (London and New York: Verso/New Left Books, 1989), which draws upon a rich and extensive literature. On the latter, the debate between Edward Thompson and Perry Anderson is especially illuminating: see Thompson, Introduction to *The Making of the English Working Class* (New York: Vintage, 1963), and idem, *The Poverty of Theory and Other Essays* (New York: Monthly Review Press, 1978); and Anderson, *Arguments Within English Marxism* (London: Verso/New Left Books, 1980).

4 *Capital: A Critique of Political Economy*, vol. III, trans. David Fernbach (Harmondsworth, Middlesex: Penguin/New Left Review, 1981), p. 1025; hereafter cited parenthetically in the text by volume and page number.

5 Cf. *Grundrisse*: "Although capital can develop itself completely as commercial capital (only not as much quantitatively), without this transformation of landed property, it cannot do so as industrial capital. Even the development of manufactures presupposes the beginning of a dissolution of the old economic relations of landed property. On the other hand, only with the development of modern industry to a high degree does this dissolution at individual points acquire its totality and extent; but this development itself proceeds more rapidly to the degree that modern agriculture and the form of property, the economic relations corresponding to it, have developed. Thus England in this respect [is] the model country for the other continental countries" (Karl Marx, *Grundrisse: Foundations of the Critique of Political Economy [Rough Draft]*, trans. Martin Nicolaus [Harmondsworth, Middlesex: Penguin/New Left Review, 1973], p. 277).

6 See Karl Marx, *Capital: A Critique of Political Economy*, vol. I, trans. Ben Fowkes (Harmondsworth, Middlesex: Penguin/New Left Review, 1976), chapters 29 and 31, on the genesis of capitalist farmers and industrial capitalists, respectively.

7 This is the burden of the so-called Nairn–Anderson theses, put forward in *New Left Review* in the 1960s. The argument is reprised in Perry Anderson, *English Questions* (London and New York: Verso, 1992).

8 See Pierre Bourdieu, *Distinction: A Social Critique of the Judgement of Taste*, trans. Richard Nice (Cambridge, MA: Harvard University Press, 1984). Proust may not have provided the inspiration for Bourdieu's study, but his signature is clearly legible everywhere in the book – both in specific references to Proust's aesthetic opinions and in the overall conceptualization of upper-class life as an inscription of material struggles onto symbolic ones. The following lapidary observation nicely summarizes the worldview that dominates the *Recherche*: "Economic power is first and foremost a power to keep economic necessity at arm's length. This is why it universally asserts itself by the destruction of riches, conspicuous consumption, squandering, and every form of *gratuitous* luxury" (*Distinction*, p. 55; Bourdieu's emphasis).

9 Ibid., pp. 483–4; Bourdieu's emphasis.

10 In a long note appended to Marx's discussion of differential rents and rising production prices, Engels gives this process a characteristically economistic twist. He asserts that the very same tendency that has contributed to massively increased ground rents, and thus to the unrivalled prosperity of the large landowners, "explains why this vitality of the large landowner is gradually approaching its end." The sun was even then (1894) setting on the age of the great agricultural magnates because rising rents had made European grain uncompetitive on the world market. Engels somberly predicts the "ruin [of] European large-scale landownership completely – and small-scale ownership into the bargain" (*Capital*, III:859, 860).

11 George Weisz, *The Emergence of Modern Universities in France, 1863–1914* (Princeton University Press, 1983), p. 8. Even at the time Weisz wrote this sentence, more was known than his judgment allows.

12 See Ralph Gibson, "The French Nobility in the Nineteenth Century – Particularly in the Dordogne," in Jolyon Howorth and Philip G. Cerny, eds., *Elites in France: Origins, Reproduction and Power* (New York: St. Martin's Press, 1981), pp. 31–7; hereafter cited parenthetically in the text.

13 Philippe du Puy de Clinchamps, *La noblesse*, 3rd edn. (Paris: Presses Universitaires de France, 1968), p. 67.
14 See David Higgs, *Nobles in Nineteenth-Century France: The Practice of Inegalitarianism* (Baltimore: Johns Hopkins University Press, 1987), pp. 2–3; hereafter cited parenthetically in the text.
15 Theodore Zeldin, *France 1848–1945: Politics and Anger* (New York: Oxford University Press, 1979), p. 40; hereafter cited parenthetically in the text.
16 See Herman Lebovics, *The Alliance of Iron and Wheat in the Third French Republic, 1860–1914: Origins of the New Conservatism* (Baton Rouge: Louisiana State University Press, 1988), pp. 47–50.
17 See Michelle Perrot, ed., *A History of Private Life:* IV, *From the Fires of Revolution to the Great War*, trans. Arthur Goldhammer (Cambridge, MA: Belknap Press, 1990), p. 374.
18 Theodore Zeldin, "Higher Education in France, 1848–1940," *Journal of Contemporary History* 1,3 (July 1967): 69; hereafter cited parenthetically in the text.
19 See Michalina Vaughn, "The *Grandes Ecoles*," in Rupert Wilkinson, ed., *Governing Elites: Studies in Training and Selection* (New York: Oxford University Press, 1969), p. 85; cf. Paul Gerbod, "The Baccalaureate and its Role in the Recruitment and Formation of French Elites in the Nineteenth Century," in Howorth and Cerny, *Elites*, pp. 47–8.
20 See Karen Offen, "The Second Sex and the Baccalauréat in Republican France, 1880–1924," *French Historical Studies* 13,2 (1983): 252–86.
21 See Jo Burr Margadant, *Madame le Professeur: Women Educators in the Third Republic* (Princeton University Press, 1990).
22 See Jean-Jacques Becker, *The Great War and the French People*, trans. Arnold Pomerans (New York: St. Martin's Press, 1986).
23 George D. Painter, *Marcel Proust: A Biography*, 2 vols. (New York: Random House, 1959), 1:1–3; hereafter cited parenthetically in the text followed by volume and page number.
24 See *Remembrance of Things Past*, trans. C. K. Scott Moncrieff, Terence Kilmartin, and Andreas Mayor, 3 vols. (New York: Random House, 1981), III:654–5; hereafter cited parenthetically in the text by volume and page number, followed by the French original, *A la recherche du temps perdu*, ed. Jean-Yves Tadié et al., 4 vols. (Paris: Bibliothèque de la Pléiade, 1987–89). This is the new Pléiade edition, which replaces the older three-volume text established by Clarac and Ferré; it contains a concordance to page numbers in the earlier edition. The passage referred to here comes at IV:218–19. Throughout, I have modified the standard

English translation to highlight features that are pertinent to my argument.

25 Arno Mayer, *The Persistence of the Old Regime: Europe to the Great War* (New York: Pantheon, 1981), pp. 102–5; hereafter cited parenthetically in the text. Cf. Jerome Blum, *The End of the Old Order in Europe* (Princeton University Press, 1978), p. 422.

26 Cf. Blum, *Old Order*, p. 422. The obvious example of this phenomenon in the *Recherche* is Legrandin, the engineer and snob from Combray who one day begins calling himself "Legrandin de Méséglise," illegitimately usurping the title of a long-deceased noble family.

27 Walter Benjamin, "The Image of Proust," in idem, *Illuminations*, trans. Harry Zohn (New York: Schocken Books, 1969), p. 206.

28 Proust could be utterly contemptuous towards the aesthetic deficiencies of his aristocratic patrons. Writing to Reynaldo Hahn, he tartly observed, apropos of a lecture by the Marquis de Segur: "If the Rothschilds are the only people who don't know how to pronounce French, the aristocracy are the only ones who can neither speak nor write it" (Marcel Proust, *Selected Letters*, vol. III, 1910–1917, trans. Terence Kilmartin [London: HarperCollins, 1992], p. 50). On the other hand, when it could serve his purposes, his flattery knew no bounds – as in his extravagant notice of the poetry of his friend, Comtesse Anna de Noailles: see Painter, *Proust*, II:80–1, who largely concurs with Proust's assessment – a sentiment scarcely shared by posterity.

29 See Blum, *Old Order*, who calls the *Recherche* "the great obituary of the French nobility ..." (p. 424).

30 The Althusserian terminology here is deliberate – and, I hope, precise. Proust was "interpellated" as a subject because the discourses and practices of the classes that "hailed" him were pregiven, not invented by him; as Althusser remarks, "individuals are always already subjects." Proust's subjectivity was "overdetermined" insofar as his class affiliations were complex and not necessarily all of a piece: bourgeois identifications often conflicted with aristocratic aspirations, producing that characteristic combination of resentment and desire that Proust dubbed "snobbism."

31 The only two extended commentaries I have been able to locate are: Eric C. Hicks, "Swann's Dream and the World of Sleep," *Yale French Studies* 34 (1965): 106–16; and William Stewart Bell, *Proust's Nocturnal Muse* (New York: Columbia University Press, 1962), pp. 55–65. Neither takes up the text's political implications.

32 For a text that is so obsessively focused on memory and that dramatically invokes sleep from its opening pages, the *Recherche* presents precious few dreams. The length and detail of Swann's are therefore especially striking. The passage cries out for the commentary it has hitherto failed to receive.

33 On prolepsis in the *Recherche*, see Gérard Genette, *Narrative Discourse: An Essay on Method*, trans. Jane E. Lewin (Ithaca: Cornell University Press, 1980), esp. pp. 68–78. Somewhat hyperbolically – but not unjustifiably – Genette remarks: "The *Recherche du temps perdu* uses prolepsis to an extent probably unequalled in the whole history of narrative, even autobiographical narrative . . ." (p. 68).

34 The basic essay elaborating this model is A. J. Greimas and François Rastier, "The Interaction of Semiotic Constraints," *Yale French Studies* 41 (1968): 86–105; rpt. in Greimas, *On Meaning: Selected Writings in Semiotic Theory*, trans. Paul J. Perron and Frank H. Collins (Minneapolis: University of Minnesota Press, 1987), pp. 48–62. Often in the ensuing pages I shall draw upon this Greimassian schema to map various narrative structures in the *Recherche*. I put no particular stock in the strong structuralist version of the model, which claims that all narratives can be mapped according to the four-fold logical relations it projects. For my purposes, the semantic rectangle is merely a useful heuristic, or, in an older rhetorical terminology, a method of invention. I take my cue from the essay's epigraph from Destutt de Tracy: "One should beware of believing the inventive mind operates according to chance."

35 A slight over-statement, since there is one intimation – it is no more – that Swann may as a young man have had homosexual relations with Charlus. The source for this rumor is none other than Charlus himself. By the point in the novel at which the charge is made (the musical evening at the Verdurins' in *La prisonnière*), he can scarcely be termed a reliable informant (see III:304; 804). Marcel's sexuality – more precisely, his ideology of sex and gender – is treated in the next chapter.

36 William Languth comments on the dream's relationship to Swann's marriage: "through this dream of Odette's disappearance Swann comes to a revived memory of Odette as she originally was known in her humble reality. This is the mechanism which enables Swann ultimately to make the moves within himself that led to marriage, fusion, with the absent object of the dream" ("The World and Life of the Dream," *Yale French Studies* 34 [1965]: 126). Languth's view coincides with Bell's: "It seems likely that had it not been for this dream, Swann would not

have returned to Odette ..." (*Proust's Nocturnal Muse*, p. 62). A psychologically plausible reading that tends, however, to elide what is obviously the dream's most powerful feature: Swann's continuing anxiety.

37 The relevant texts by Willy Hachez, H. R. Jauss, and Georges Daniel discussing this problem are all cited by Genette (*Narrative Discourse*, p. 90 n. 7), who then posits an approximate chronological span for the novel's action from "Un amour de Swann" to the *matinée* at the Princesse de Guermantes's from 1877–1925. In his alternative chronology (*The Proustian Community* [New York University Press, 1971], p. 216), Seth Wolitz mentions an explicit reference in *A l'ombre des jeunes filles en fleurs* to Odette's having been painted by Elstir in October 1872 (see I:908; II:205). When some pages later Odette is identified as the model for this portrait, Proust leaves it deliberately ambiguous whether it was painted before or after her initial acquaintance with Swann (see I:920; II:215–16). We only know that she sat for it prior to her marriage. This somewhat earlier dating of "Un amour de Swann" is just plausible, even if we accept 1877–8 as the period of Marcel's birth, for the French text relating this event to Swann's affair reads: "car c'est vers l'époque de ma naissance que commença la grande liaison de Swann ..." (I:191). The editors of the new Pléiade edition suggest that evidence for the earlier date was undermined by Proust's corrections in 1912–13 (see I:1197 n. 1).

38 The latter date makes sense in light of the references at one of the early Verdurin dinners to Gambetta's death and to Grévy's presidency (see I:235–6; 212–13). Gambetta died in December 1882, so that the dinner can only have occurred during Grévy's second presidential term in the mid-1880s (he resigned in the wake of the honors scandal on December 2, 1887). Interestingly, an earlier reference to Gambetta's funeral tends to confirm one's conviction that "Un amour de Swann" must be situated in the mid-1880s at the earliest, since Proust had originally referred, not to Gambetta but to the funeral of Victor Hugo, which took place in 1885 (see the note to the 1954 Pléiade edition, I:961). This accords with Swann's comment to Cottard that he would be lunching with M. Grévy at the Elysée the following day (I:235; 212–13). Cf. Gareth H. Steel, *Chronology and Time in "A la recherche du temps perdu"* (Genève: Droz, 1979), p. 99. Steel's is perhaps the most detailed study to date of the discrepancies between internal chronology and external events. His work confirms one's sense that this problem is especially acute in "Un amour de Swann" (see pp. 68–9, 93).

39 Lebovics, *Alliance of Iron and Wheat*.
40 Cf. the following contemporary observation: "They are seam-stresses, or milliners according to what's posted. Inside the estab-lishment, the *mise en scène* is complete; there are fabrics, patrons, work in progress. In reality, it is a place of debauchery where often, under the pretext of a lucrative business, one takes in young women who quickly allow themselves to become perverted" (C. J. Lecour, *La Prostitution à Paris et à Londres* [1877]; quoted in Hollis Clayson, *Painted Love: Prostitution in France in the Impressionist Era* [New Haven: Yale University Press, 1991], p. 113). Accord-ing to Clayson, the major trades for "indecent" women in popular iconography were, in addition to the two mentioned above, laundress, flower girl, and chambermaid – i.e., all the occupations in which lower-class women could earn a meager living (pp. 115–17). Swann's mistress might have been a seam-stress, but as Proust's text indicates, she might more accurately be described simply as a "working girl," with all the ambiguity that phrase possesses in modern English.
41 T. J. Clark, *The Painting of Modern Life* (New York: Alfred Knopf, 1985), pp. 145–6. On prostitution in France during the second half of the nineteenth century, see Alain Corbin, *Les Filles de noce: misère sexuelle et prostitution (19e et 20e siècles)* (Paris: Aubier Mon-taigne, 1978); idem, "Backstage," in Perrot, *Private Life*, pp. 560, 589–90, 611–13; and Jill Harsin, *Policing Prostitution in Nineteenth-Century Paris* (Princeton University Press, 1985). Useful discuss-ions of the representation of prostitution in literature and the visual arts, in addition to Clark's superb treatment of Manet's *Olympe* in *The Painting of Modern Life*, chapter 2, can be found in Charles Bernheimer, *Figures of Ill-Repute: Representing Prostitution in Nineteenth-Century France* (Cambridge, MA: Harvard University Press, 1989); and Clayson, *Painted Love*. Prostitution and sexuality more generally are treated at length in chapter 3 below.
42 On the Third Republic's aligning itself with the legacy of 1789, even with some aspects of Jacobinism, see E. J. Hobsbawm, *Echoes of the Marseillaise: Two Centuries Look Back on the French Revolution* (London: Verso, 1990), pp. 70–1, 84–5. The definitive study of republican symbolism prior to the First World War is Maurice Agulhon's *Marianne au pouvoir: L'imagerie et la symbolique républi-caines de 1880 à 1914* (Paris: Flammarion, 1989). Agulhon's research generally supports the allegorical reading proposed here. He argues in conclusion that the central republican symbol, Marianne, was precisely allegorical in opposition to the personal-ized symbols of monarchical or dictatorial power, and, further

support for my thesis, that the former was programmatically feminine in opposition to the latter's resolute masculinity (*Marianne au pouvoir*, p. 349).

43 See John Rothney, *Bonapartism after Sedan* (Ithaca: Cornell University Press, 1969). Rothney puts the nadir of Bonapartism in 1879, a date that corresponds roughly with the moment of Swann's liaison, if we accept the customary chronology dictated by Marcel's birth. Nonetheless, Rothney calls the Boulanger Affair "the Bonapartists' last fling" (p. 280), a judgment that accords well with the way I see this episode figured in Swann's dream.

44 See Karl Marx, *The Eighteenth Brumaire of Louis Bonaparte*, in Marx and Engels, *Collected Works*, vol. xi (New York: International Publishers, 1979), pp. 99–197, especially pp. 170–82, 193–5. Cf. Alain Plessis, "The Rise and Fall of the Second Empire, 1852–71," vol. iii in *The Cambridge History of Modern France*, trans. Jonathan Mandelbaum (Cambridge: Maison des Sciences de l'Homme and Cambridge University Press, 1985). Plessis presents a less critical view of the regime than Marx but does not diverge significantly from him on this point (see p. 55).

45 Cf. the following contemporary assessment by Paul Cambon, friend of Jules Ferry, written in autumn 1885: "The general impression is that the Republic is at the end of its tether. Next year we shall have revolutionary excesses and then a violent reaction. What will emerge from all this? Some kind of dictatorship ... There is no government in France" (quoted in Jean-Marie Mayeur, "The Origins of the Third French Republic, 1871–1898," Part i of vol. iv in *The Cambridge History of Modern France*, trans. J. R. Foster [Cambridge: Maison des Sciences de l'Homme and Cambridge University Press, 1984], p. 126). Certain socialists agreed with this assessment, breaking with their Radical allies and supporting Boulanger. And the anarchists, disenchanted with the reformist programs of the Parti Ouvrier, promoted strikes in the late 1880s that contributed to the widespread belief that social order was crumbling; see Bernard H. Moss, *The Origins of the French Labor Movement 1830–1914: The Socialism of Skilled Workers* (Berkeley and Los Angeles: University of California Press, 1976), pp. 127–30.

46 Mayeur, "Origins," p. 132.

47 The best modern study of the episode confirms this view; see Frederic H. Seager, *The Boulanger Affair: Political Crossroad of France 1886–1889* (Ithaca: Cornell University Press, 1969): "The bulk of the General's votes in by-elections came not from

Boulangists, who were in fact latter-day Jacobins, but from embittered royalists and Bonapartists ... The General's hard-core support in the by-elections as in 1889, was drawn from artisans and industrial workers, who were not seeking a dictatorship, but rather a better sort of Republic, more responsive to their needs" (p. 4). It is thus difficult to accept P.-V. Zima's assertion that Boulangism was really the revolt of the petit bourgeoisie (see his *Le désir du mythe: Une lecture sociologique de Marcel Proust* [Paris: Nizet, n.d.], p. 272), much less his conjecture that the Third Republic should properly be compared with the Weimar Republic in the 1920s. What should be stressed, as I have been arguing throughout, is precisely the way in which the Third Republic was a stable polity that survived all threats to its existence. It is therefore the following that must be explained: by what means did the bourgeoisie ultimately enforce its political as well as its social hegemony in France? What made the class struggles in France at this period non–revolutionary?

48 See Hicks, "Swann's Dream," p. 114; and Bell *Proust's Nocturnal Muse*, p. 59.

49 See Michael Burns, *Rural Society and French Politics: Boulangism and the Dreyfus Affair, 1886–1900* (Princeton University Press, 1984), Part Two. Agulhon's concluding hypothesis is also relevant here: "in spite of certain appearances, the truly antagonistic myth to Marianne in France has perhaps not been the Christian but the Napoleonic myth, not the Holy Virgin but the soldier" (*Marianne au pouvoir*, p. 349).

50 Have I over-read this dream? In particular, is the historical allegory (revolution = Boulangism; Napoleon/Forcheville = the titled nobility) likely to have been perceived by a contemporary reader? The Boulangist episode scarcely carries the same thematic weight as, say, the Dreyfus Affair or the Battle of Verdun (the latter being the model for the Battle of Combray in *Le temps retrouvé*). Boulangism was, however, a far from negligible phenomenon; prior to the Affair – i.e., during the very period in which "Un Amour de Swann" is set – it was arguably the most significant political incident in the Republic's history. A condensation of aristocratic sentiment, it provides a convenient and historically pertinent referent for the generalized class anxieties that are easily recognizable in Swann's dream. As for Napoleon III, his presence here would be unaccountable without the political resonance that I have attributed to the dream figure. Proust was certainly not Dante, but neither was he uninterested in allegorical figuration, as the discussion of Giotto's frescoes in

"Combray" (1:87–9; 80–1;) amply illustrates. This important passage has been treated with great care by Paul de Man; see his *Allegories of Reading: Figural Language in Rousseau, Nietzsche, and Proust* (New Haven: Yale University Press, 1979), pp.73–8.

51 As Nelly Wolf cogently argues, Françoise is at once a type derived from classical comedy and the novel's principal figure for "the popular classes." She represents an archaic social order under threat from the democratizing tendencies of republican rule, which, on the level of economy, will render her occupation supernumerary, and, through education, will dispose of her linguistic heritage. She is, consequently, the last in her line: after her, the literature of the Third Republic will produce no more servant figures; "the people" will signify just workers or peasants. See Nelly Wolf, *Le peuple dans le roman français de Zola à Céline* (Paris: Presses Universitaires de France, 1990), pp. 134–40.

52 De Man's essay on Proust ends with the following gnomic sentence: "*A la recherche du temps perdu* narrates the flight of meaning, but this does not prevent its own meaning from being, incessantly, in flight" (de Man, *Allegories*, p. 78).

53 Leo Bersani reads the death as integral to Proust's "mortuary aesthetic," in which art redeems the damaged phenomenal goods of life; see his "'The Culture of Redemption': Marcel Proust and Melanie Klein," *Critical Inquiry* 12 (Winter 1986): 399–421. I shall consider whether this aesthetic ideology is the novel's last word in the final chapter below.

54 The relationship between Proust's (generally autobiographical and historical) treatment of the Affair in *Jean Santeuil* and the more complex view of it presented in the *Recherche* is discussed in Lynn R. Wilkinson, "The Art of Distinction: Proust and the Dreyfus Affair," *MLN* 107,5 (December 1993): 976–99.

55 See Genette, *Narrative Discourse*, p. 66–7.

3 IDEOLOGY

1 See Paul-Marie de la Gorce, *The French Army: A Military–Political History*, trans. Kenneth Douglas (New York: George Braziller, 1963), p. 9; Alistair Horne, *The French Army and Politics, 1870–1970* (New York: Peter Bedrick Books, 1984), p. 15; and Douglas Porch, *The March to the Marne: The French Army 1871–1914* (Cambridge University Press, 1981), p. 41; hereafter cited parenthetically in the text.

2 Porch here follows Eugen Weber's *Peasants into Frenchmen* (Stanford University Press, 1976), q.v.

3 See de la Gorce, *French Army*, pp. 20–3, and Horne, *Politics*, p. 16, for the view that aristocrats achieved a new prominence after 1870. Porch asserts, to the contrary, that aristocrats were no more numerous in the officer corps, much less the general staff, after 1870 than before (*March*, pp. 17–18).

4 See Arno Mayer, *The Persistence of the Old Regime: Europe to the Great War* (New York: Pantheon, 1981), p. 308; Horne, *Politics*, p. 17; and Jean-Denis Bredin, *The Affair: The Case of Alfred Dreyfus*, trans. Jeffrey Mehlman (New York: George Braziller, 1986), p. 17; hereafter cited parenthetically in the text.

5 Both Horne and de la Gorce make this point. Although writing from different vantage points and over two decades apart, they see the military history of the pre-war Third Republic through a similar lense: the subsequent history of the French armed forces in relation to the state, particularly during the Algerian War. As a result, they tend to be much more critical of military prerogatives than, for example, Porch.

6 Madeleine Rebérioux, "A Radical Republic? 1898–1914," Part II of vol. IV in *The Cambridge History of Modern France*, trans. J. R. Foster (Cambridge: Maison des Sciences de l'Homme and Cambridge University Press, 1984), pp. 194–5; hereafter cited parenthetically in the text.

7 Stephen Wilson, *Ideology and Experience: Antisemitism in France at the Time of the Dreyfus Affair* (Rutherford, Teaneck, Madison: Fairleigh Dickinson University Press, 1982), pp. 279–90, 319–78. On Madeleine Rebérioux's account, nationalism and antisemitism were fundamentally *petit bourgeois* phenomena; see Rebérioux, "Radical Politics," pp. 202–4.

8 See Eugen Weber, *Action Française: Royalism and Reaction in Twentieth-Century France* (Stanford University Press, 1962), pp. 23–43; René Rémond, *The Right Wing in France: From 1815 to de Gaulle*, trans. James M. Laux (Philadelphia: University of Pennsylvania Press, 1969), p. 253; and Bredin, *Affair*, p. 521.

9 Had Jaurès not been assassinated by a royalist fanatic in July 1914, things might have gone differently. Weber avers that no clear evidence points to collusion by Action Française, but he concedes that their ideological program and their support for violent political demonstrations in the years leading up to the war certainly encouraged such acts (*Action Française*, p. 91). Cf. Harvey Goldberg, *Life of Jean Jaurès* (Madison: University of Wisconsin Press, 1962), pp. 469–70. Goldberg speculates that Jaurès would probably have supported French mobilization once Germany invaded Belgium, but that in the aftermath of the

butchery in 1916, he would almost certainly have campaigned for a speedy armistice (see pp. 473–4, which relies on contemporary assessments by Jaurès' colleagues but finally endorses the subsequent judgment rendered by G. D. H. Cole).

10 The classic indictment of French nationalism, written by a former Dreyfusard, remains Julien Benda's *La trahison des clercs* (1927). But even Benda betrays an anti-Teutonic strain. For him, the origins of modern nationalism among the intellectuals were uniquely German; French traitors to the intellectual calling like Barrès, Maurras, and Péguy merely imitated their German forebears and masters. "Germanism" played a decisive role in the ideological class struggles over *la patrie* that were a more or less permanent feature of the Third Republic's political life until its demise in 1940, affecting, in the period relevant to Proust, intellectual figures as prominent as Renan and Durkheim; see the fascinating study by Martin Thom, "Tribes Within Nations: The Ancient Germans and the History of Modern France," in Homi K. Bhabha, ed., *Nation and Narration* (London and New York: Routledge, 1990), pp. 23–41.

11 Yet the matter remained extraordinarily troubled for Proust, who was a close friend of the Daudet family, a great admirer of Léon (co-founder with Maurras of Action Française and to whom *Le côté de Guermantes* was dedicated), and an equally enthusiastic fan of Barrès's literary writing. After the war, in an admiring essay on Daudet, Proust professed – how genuinely it is difficult to know; his capacity for socially useful flattery is well documented – to be a regular reader of the Action Française newspaper (see Marcel Proust, *Contre Sainte-Beuve* [précédé de *Pastiches et mélanges* et suivi de *Essais et articles*], ed. Pierre Clarac and D'Yves Sandre [Paris: Bibliothèque de la Pléiade, 1971], p. 603). One surmises that Proust shared at the very least the classicist biases of Maurras and his colleagues; whether he shared their ultra-royalism is another matter.

12 See *Remembrance of Things Past*, trans. C. K. Scott Moncrieff, Terence Kilmartin, and Andreas Mayor, 3 vols. (New York: Random House, 1981), II:693,734; hereafter cited parenthetically in the text by volume and page number, followed by reference to the French original, *A la recherche du temps perdu*, ed. Jean-Yves Tadié et al., 4 vols. (Paris: Bibliothèque de la Pléiade, 1987–89). The passages referred to here come at III:68,107. Throughout, I have modified the standard English translation to highlight features that are pertinent to my argument.

13 See Seth L. Wolitz, *The Proustian Community* (New York: New

York University Press, 1971), chapter v; and Albert Sonnenfeld, "Marcel Proust: Antisemite?," i and ii, *French Review* 62,1 (October 1988): 25–40; 62,2 (December 1988): 275–82.

14 George Mosse puts the point even more strongly: "Ever conscious of the stereotypes they shared with other outsiders – nervous, lacking restraint, slaves to the lower passions – Jews were often careful not to act or look 'Jewish.' Assimilation always included a flight from a former identity" (*Nationalism and Sexuality: Respectability and Abnormal Sexuality in Modern Europe* [New York: Howard Fertig, 1985], p. 187).

15 My general indebtedness to Gilles Deleuze's masterful discussion of the *Recherche*'s semiotic system, *Proust and Signs*, trans. Richard Howard (New York: George Braziller, 1972) will be obvious. I shall have occasion to refer to his analyses of jealousy and sexuality later on. Here, however, it needs to be emphasized that Deleuze's generally Platonic reading of the novel, privileging art as the locus where non-material signs provide access to truth, is undone by his own eighth chapter, "Antilogos, or the Literary Machine," which was added to the original text for the English edition.

16 On the medicalization of homosexuality in Proust's era, see J. E. Rivers *Proust and the Art of Love: The Aesthetics of Sexuality in the Life, Times, and Art of Marcel Proust* (New York: Columbia University Press, 1980), pp. 156–8, 208; Antony Copley, *Sexual Moralities in France, 1780–1980: New Ideas on the Family, Divorce, and Homosexuality (An Essay on Moral Change)* (London and New York: Routledge, 1989), pp. 135–72; and Alain Corbin, "Backstage," in Michelle Perrot, ed., *A History of Private Life*: IV, *From the Fires of Revolution to the Great War*, trans. Arthur Goldhammer (Cambridge, MA: Belknap Press, 1990), pp. 640–2; hereafter cited parenthetically in the text. Proust seems to have read Krafft-Ebbing, and he may also have had contact with Dr. Ambroise Tardieu, his father's medical colleague and a popular authority on homosexuality; see Copley, *Sexual Moralities*, p. 172.

17 Cf. Mosse, *Nationalism*, p. 189. The intimate relationship posited here between Judaism and homosexuality is elaborated in Naomi Diamant, "Judaism, Homosexuality, and Other Sign Systems in *A la recherche du temps perdu*," *Romanic Review*, 81,2 (1991): 179–92. Diamant valorizes homosexuality much more unequivocally than I feel is sustainable on a careful account of the sex and gender relations in the text.

18 *The Journals of André Gide*, trans. Justin O'Brien, 4 vols. (New York: Alfred A. Knopf, 1948), ii:409–10. See also pp. 276–7 and

369 in the same volume, for Gide's critical view of *Sodome et Gomorrhe*. That Proust was secretive about his homosexuality in life is beyond question; that his novel is similarly evasive is less certain. The whole matter is too complex for effective summary in a note. Suffice it to say that unilateral opinions like Gide's are probably misleading, a fact that the remainder of this chapter attempts to demonstrate.

19 Jean-Paul Sartre, *What Is Literature?*, trans. Bernard Frechtman (1965; rpt. Gloucester, MA: Peter Smith, 1978), p. 36.

20 These values for mapping the social ideology of sexual relations are the very ones Greimas and Rastier propose in their fundamental essay, "The Interaction of Semiotic Constraints"; see Algirdas Julien Greimas, *On Meaning: Selected Writings in Semiotic Theory*, trans. Paul J. Perron and Frank H. Collins (Minneapolis: University of Minnesota Press, 1987), pp. 53–6. On the pact between the men of Sodom and the women of Gomorrha, see II:646; III:25.

21 Rivers, who argues passionately for the androgynous ideal projected in the *Recherche*, notices that the true representative of male bisexuality is Morel (see *Proust and the Art of Love*, p. 201). Few readers of the *Recherche* are likely to concur in Rivers's celebration of Morel's character, on whatever grounds. The truth about him and about Proust's attitude towards that which he represents will only be fully realized in *Le temps retrouvé*, where he is explicitly contrasted with Saint-Loup. The latter is equally ambiguous sexually, but not morally in the end. A similar judgment of the creative artist's androgyny concludes Antoine Compagnon's otherwise impeccable examination of Racine's role in the *Recherche*; see "Proust on Racine," *Yale French Studies* 76 (1989): 56–8.

Malcolm Bowie argues the converse of Rivers and Compagnon. He denies that bisexuality plays any significant role in the novel, either theoretically or as a feature of character, partly on the basis of the word's complete absence from the *Recherche*. He does, however, hypothesize a certain bisexual tendency on the aesthetic level: "... Proust nevertheless endowed his narrator with an indefinite capacity for bisexual phantasy and repeatedly allowed a volatile sense of sexual indeterminacy into the fine textures of his writing" (*Freud, Proust and Lacan: Theory as Fiction* [Cambridge University Press, 1987], p. 81; hereafter cited parenthetically in the text). Less persuasive is Margaret Gray-McDonald's assertion that Albertine represents the eruption of *écriture féminine* within Marcel's controlling discourse; see her

"Marcel's *Écriture Féminine*," *Modern Fiction Studies* 34,3 (Autumn 1988): 337–52.

22 See Leo Bersani, "'The Culture of Redemption': Marcel Proust and Melanie Klein," *Critical Inquiry* 12 (Winter 1986): 399–421, esp. 399–402. While differing from Bersani in several crucial respects, what follows could scarcely have been written without his provocation. Bersani's reading is contested, albeit obliquely, by Angela Moorjani in her essay, "A Cryptanalysis of 'Les Inter-mittences du cœur,'" *MLN* 105,4 (September 1990): 875–88.

23 More sophisticated than most, Bersani still partakes of this stan-dard view of *Le temps retrouvé* in relation to the rest of the novel; see "'The Culture of Redemption,'" p. 406. In this respect, Bersani scarcely advances beyond the standard interpretation offered some thirty years ago by René Girard; see the latter's *Deceit, Desire, and the Novel*, trans. Yvonne Freccero (Baltimore: Johns Hopkins University Press, 1965), pp. 297–8. Malcolm Bowie's rather scathing remarks about the false simplicity that such a reading imposes on the *Recherche* as a whole are very much to the point (Bowie, *Freud*, pp. 46–8).

24 Bowie locates the asymmetry in the fact that Swann learns the truth about Odette, while Marcel never does about Albertine (*Freud*, p. 59). One can be less sanguine about Swann's know-ledge of Odette than Bowie, as I am, and still agree that Marcel's ignorance concerning Albertine seems by comparison virtually limitless. I am unpersuaded by Gisela Norat's unequivocal asser-tion that Odette has engaged in lesbian relations; see "*Swann's Way*: Path to the Other Gender's Domain," *Essays in Literature* 18,1 (Spring 1991): 122–31.

25 As Deleuze remarks: "The beloved's lies are the hieroglyphics of love. The interpreter of love's signs is necessarily the interpreter of lies" (*Proust*, p. 9). Cf. Bowie, *Freud*, p. 58.

26 Deleuze, *Proust*, p. 122.

27 See Eve Kosofsky Sedgwick, "Proust and the Spectacle of the Closet," in idem, *Epistemology of the Closet* (Berkeley and Los Angeles: University of California Press, 1990), pp. 213–51.

28 See Bowie, *Freud*, pp. 52–4, on the limits of the Narrator's binary model for hypotheses about Albertine. That this debility may derive from what Sedgwick terms Proust's "male homosexual panic" is a possibility that cannot immediately be dismissed; see Sedgwick, *Closet*. Deleuze puts much the same point in a char-acteristiclaly provocative manner: "All lies are organized around homosexuality, revolving around it as around their center. Homosexuality is the truth of love" (*Proust*, p. 78). Equally pro-

vocative, but hardly convincing, is Mark D. Guenette's claim that the most important of the *Recherche*'s secrets can be unlocked once we recognize the Narrator as a closeted homosexual and Saint-Loup as his sole love object (for whom all the women, from Gilberte and Odette to Albertine and Mme. de Guermantes, are screens); see "Le Loup et le Narrateur: The Masking and Unmasking of Homosexuality in Proust's *A la recherche du temps perdu*," *Romanic Review* 80,2 (1989): 229–46.

29 Far and away the best study of prostitution in the nineteenth and twentieth centuries is Alain Corbin's *Les filles de noce: misère sexuelle et prostitution (19e and 20e siècles)* (Paris: Aubier Montaigne, 1978); hereafter cited parenthetically in the text as Corbin 1978. More narrowly focused on state regulation, Jill Harsin's *Policing Prostitution in Nineteenth-Century Paris* (Princeton University Press, 1985) is also useful. I am also indebted in a general way to T. J. Clark's brilliant study of Manet's *Olympe*, "Olympia's Choice," in idem, *The Painting of Modern Life: Paris in the Art of Manet and His Followers* (New York: Alfred A. Knopf, 1985), pp. 79–146, which provided the initial inspiration to think about prostitution as a category integral to the nineteenth-century French bourgeoisie's self-understanding. His formulation of its indispensability is worth quoting: "The category 'prostitute' is necessary, and thus must be allowed its representations. It must take its place in the various pictures of the social, the sexual, and the modern which bourgeois society puts in circulation. There is a sense in which it could even be said to anchor those representations: it is the limiting case of all three, and the point where they are mapped most neatly onto one another" (*Painting*, p. 103; hereafter cited parenthetically in the text).

30 Thus, one would wish to modify the generality of Deleuze's otherwise shrewd judgment and note its heterosexist bias: "The true generality of love is serial, our loves are experienced profoundly only according to the series in which they are organized" (*Proust*, p. 79). It seems likely that Deleuze has more or less covertly adopted the Narrator's point of view in this instance.

31 Rivers reads the *Miss Sacripant* episode in *A l'ombre des jeunes filles en fleurs* as indicating something of the sort; see *Proust and the Art of Love*, pp. 231–2, 245.

32 Recall also Mme. Verdurin's various attempts to legislate love: Swann and Odette; Brichot and his mistress; and, most spectacularly, Charlus and Morel. In each case, social distinction – in the form of Mme. Verdurin's jealously guarding her prerogatives as hostess – is at issue.

33 A contradictory account is given much later by Andrée: that Albertine left at the behest of Mme. Bontemps, who was arranging her marriage with the Verdurins' nephew (see III:627–8; IV:193–4). It is not possible to reach any definite conclusions about Albertine's true motives, in this or any other instance.

34 Much earlier, Marcel had surmised as much: "Unfortunately for M. de Charlus, his lack of common sense, and perhaps, too, the probable chastity of his relations with Morel, made him go out of his way at this period to shower upon the violinist strange bounties which the other was incapable of understanding, and to which his nature, impulsive in its own way, but mean and ungrateful, could respond only by an ever-increasing coldness or violence which plunged M. de Charlus – formerly so proud, now quite timid – into fits of genuine despair" (II:1043–4) [Malheureusement pour M. de Charlus, son manque de bon sens, peut-être la chasteté des rapports qu'il avait probablement avec Morel, le firent s'ingénier dès cette époque à combler le violoniste d'étranges bontés que celui-ci ne pouvait comprendre et auxquelles sa nature, folle dans son genre, mais ingrate et mesquine, ne pouvait répondre que par une sécheresse ou une violence toujours croissantes, et qui plongeaient M. de Charlus – jadis si fier, maintenant tout timide – dans des accès de vrai désespoir] (III:399).

35 The occasion for the breach is somewhat more complicated than the summary indicates, issuing from two related causes: (1) Morel's refusal to play at the house of Mme. Verdurin's friend because Charlus would be unable to attend; (2) Charlus's imperiously excluding from the musical evening certain guests whom Mme. Verdurin wished to invite, in particular the Comtesse Molé (see III:229–36; 733–9). The point, however, stands: Mme. Verdurin is pathologically jealous of her social prerogatives, and Charlus represents a serious threat to her domination over the "clan."

36 Her failure to appear at Morel's performance, despite Charlus's invitation, perfectly exemplifies her characteristic social strategy.

37 Although one cannot be certain, it would seem that Marcel's sexual life with Albertine is exclusively masturbatory; so far as the text reveals, she is but the passive object of his desire, never a fully gratified partner.

38 The comparison is repeated in the Narrator's speculations about how he will construct his novel near the end of *Le temps retrouvé* (III:1091; IV:612).

39 Charles Bernheimer, *Figures of Ill Repute: Representing Prostitution in*

Nineteenth-Century France (Cambridge, MA: Harvard University Press, 1989), p. 271.

40 Copley, *Sexual Moralities*, pp. 108–24

41 Hollis Clayson casts a different light on these developments when she interrogates the Impressionists' ideology of representing prostitutes: "The works we have examined demonstrate that although the theme of lower-class urban female prostitution appealed to a wide variety of bourgeois artists, the subject of covert prostitution was especially appropriate to the avant-garde project of detached yet 'factual' art making. The lives and legends of the alleged insoumises, women working in various low-paying jobs, helped these painters ideologically to bridge the gap between the two seemingly antithetical qualities of modernity central to the Impressionists: the indeterminacy and fleeting quality of experience and the cold commodification of social relations" (*Painted Love: Prostitution in French Art of the Impressionist Era* [New Haven: Yale University Press, 1991], p. 152). Proust's relationship to this ideology is far from settled.

42 Harsin, *Policing*, pp. 283, 300–2.

43 Marcel's fantasies may have had some basis in historical fact. Corbin's description of the proliferating sites for sexual contact during the nineteenth century indicates that it would have been comparatively easy for Albertine to encounter like-minded women in her diurnal perambulations around the city: see Corbin, *Filles*, pp. 213–14. Or is this just the patriarchal ideology of neo-regulationism reasserting itself, as Hollis Clayson would have it? For our purposes, it scarcely matters. As in so much ideology, thinking makes it so. Marcel's fears are historically plausible, even if they are wildly exaggerated, since men of his class seemed to have believed in widespread female promiscuity.

44 Sedgwick, *Closet*, pp. 239–40; cf. Bowie, *Freud*, p. 73, for a somewhat different take on this same passage. Of course, everything is much less complicated if one presumes with Mark Guenette (see above, n. 28) that Marcel is gay, in love with Saint-Loup, and dissimulating the fact by presenting Albertine as a woman. Would that the *Recherche* could ever be so unambiguously univocal in its figural codings.

45 Or is Marcel's dismay a further expression of his creator's putative homophobia? Corbin's account of standard nineteenth-century views on the male homosexual would support such speculation: "The homosexual shared the characteristic vices of women: gossip, indiscretion, vanity, inconstancy, duplicity. Seeking to unmask him, forensic medicine painted a fantastic

portrait, which incorporated every one of the era's marks of infamy. In 1857 Dr. Ambroise Tardieu showed how the pederast violated the rules of hygiene and cleanliness, how he shunned purifying ablutions. He could be recognized by certain morphological signs, most notably the condition of the buttocks. A relaxed sphincter, an anus shaped like a funnel or adapted to accommodate an object the shape and size of a penis – these were unmistakable signs of belonging to the recently identified species" (Corbin, "Backstage," p. 640). We may recall once more that Tardieu was Proust's father's colleague.

46 Clark's surmise about the sexual scandal of Manet's *Olympe* is relevant here: "It is sometimes said – it was said already in 1865 – that Olympia is not female at all, or only partly so. She is masculine or 'masculinized'; she is 'boyish,' aggressive, or androgynous. None of these words strikes me as the right one, but they all indicate quite well why the viewer is uncertain. It is because he cannot easily make Olympia a Woman that he wants to make her a man ... that a woman has sex at all – and Olympia certainly has one – does not make her immediately *one thing*, for a man to appropriate visually; her sex is a construction of some kind, or perhaps the inconsistency of several" (Clark, *Painting*, p. 132).

47 Shari Benstock's peremptory judgment is too univocal, but it does highlight a prominent tendency in Proust's representation of female sexuality: "[Proust's] portrayal of lesbian women was particularly injurious, and the descriptions of Gomorrah constitute a homosexual male fantasy of the homosexual female's world – that is, constituted by Proust's hatred of and fascination with the 'woman' in himself, the spirit that accounted for his own homosexuality ... Proust's misreading of women's response to other women tended to confirm the suspicions the larger reading public had of lesbian practices and to fulfill the latent expectations and fantasies in which both homosexual and heterosexual men indulged" (*Women of the Left Bank: Paris, 1900–1940* [Austin: University of Texas Press, 1986], p. 56). Benstock interprets negatively what Rivers takes to be the sign of Proust's liberated sexuality.

48 Paul de Man, *Allegories of Reading: Figural Language in Rousseau, Nietzsche, Rilke, and Proust* (New Haven: Yale University Press, 1979), p. 19.

49 This is the import of Althusser's thesis on the permanence of ideology (on which see chapter 4 below). The clearest exposition of the science/ideology relation is given in his lectures on "the

spontaneous philosophy of the scientists"; see Louis Althusser, *Philosophy and the Spontaneous Philosophy of the Scientists and Other Essays*, ed. Gregory Elliott, trans. Ben Brewster et al. (London and New York: Verso, 1990), pp. 69–165.

4 REVOLUTION

1 On strikes during the Third Republic, see Bernard H. Moss, *The Origins of the French Labor Movement 1830–1914: The Socialism of Skilled Workers* (Berkeley and Los Angeles: University of California Press, 1976), pp. 63, 65–6, 85, 90, 99–100, 147–8, 153; and Madeleine Rebérioux, "A Radical Republic? 1898–1914," Part II of vol. IV in *The Cambridge History of Modern France*, trans. J. R. Foster (Cambridge: Maison des Sciences de l'Homme and Cambridge University Press, 1984), pp. 245–55. On the attempt to secure labor peace through welfare legislation during the quarter-century prior to the First World War, see Judith F. Stone, *The Search for Social Peace: Reform Legislation in France, 1890–1914* (Albany: SUNY Press, 1985). A famous case study of the origins and aftermath of a single strike in 1895 is Joan Wallach Scott's *The Glassworkers of Carmaux: French Craftsmen and Political Action in a Nineteenth-Century City* (Cambridge, MA: Harvard University Press, 1974).

2 Sanford Elwitt, *The Making of the Third Republic: Class and Politics in France 1868–1884* (Baton Rouge: Louisiana State University Press, 1975), p. 1.

3 Ibid., p. 14.

4 Cf. Herman Lebovics, *The Alliance of Iron and Wheat in the Third French Republic 1860–1914: Origins of the New Conservatism* (Baton Rouge: Louisiana State University Press, 1988).

5 Sanford Elwitt, *The Third Republic Defended: Bourgeois Reform in France, 1880–1914* (Baton Rouge: Louisiana State University Press, 1986), p. 297. The contrary view is argued in Moss, *French Labor*, which maintains that the key transformation in French working-class organization was from the cooperative movements of the pre-republican era to the revolutionary socialism that took hold from the 1880s onwards.

6 Joan Scott, *Glassworkers*, provides evidence for this claim in a single town in the Tarn. The classic work on the political force of industrial action in France is Edward Shorter and Charles Tilly, *Strikes in France 1830–1968* (Cambridge University Press, 1974). Their data indicate that the distinctive feature of pre-war versus post-war strikes was the latter's significantly greater size, i.e., in

numbers of workers involved (see pp. 51–5). The thesis about the
comparative weakness in working-class self-organization prior to
the First World War accords with standard accounts of the origins
of the French Communist Party: see especially Annie Kriegel, *Aux
origines du communisme français 1914–1920: Contribution à l'histoire du
mouvement ouvrier français*, Première Partie, "De la guerre à la
révolution" (Paris: Mouton, 1964); and Robert Wohl, *French
Communism in the Making, 1914–24* (Stanford University Press,
1966).

7 See Moss, *French Labor*, passim; and Wohl, *French Communism*,
pp. 29–38.
8 Gérard Genette, *Narrative Discourse: An Essay on Method*, trans.
Jane Lewin (Ithaca: Cornell University Press, 1980), pp. 91–2;
Gareth H. Steel, *Chronology and Time in "A la recherche du temps
perdu"* (Geneva: Librairie Droz, 1979), pp. 74, 93–4.
9 *Remembrance of Things Past*, trans. C. K. Scott Moncrieff,
Terence Kilmartin, and Andreas Mayor, 3 vols. (New York:
Random House, 1981): III:685; hereafter cited parenthetically in
the text by volume and page number, followed by the French
original, *A la recherche du temps perdu*, ed. Jean-Yves Tadié et al., 4
vols. (Paris: Bibliothèque de la Pléiade, 1987–89). The passage
quoted here comes at IV:247–8. I have silently modified the
standard English translation where a more literal rendering is
required.
10 See George Painter, *Marcel Proust: A Biography*, 2 vols. (1959; rpt.
New York: Vintage, 1978), II:183–4.
11 See Philippe Bernard and Henri Dubief, *The Decline of the Third
Republic, 1914–1938*, trans. Anthony Forster, vol. v in the Cambridge History of Modern France (Cambridge and Paris: Maison
des Sciences de l'Homme and Cambridge University Press, 1985),
pp. 39–45; and Jean-Jacques Becker, *The Great War and the French
People*, trans. Arnold Pomerans (New York: St. Martin's Press,
1986).
12 See Bernard and Dubief, *Decline*, pp. 6–7, 42, 54–6, 70–2;
Kriegel, *Aux origines*, pp. 52–233; and Becker, *Great War*,
especially chapters 1, 2, 3, 14, and 17.
13 The editors of the 1954 Pléiade edition indicate that Proust seems
to have planned further remarks on the Russian émigrés which he
did not live to complete (III:1132). The subject is originally
broached a couple of pages earlier apropos of the Duchesse de
Guermantes's devotion to the dispossessed Russian nobility
(III:883; IV:430–1) In a letter to Mme. Scheikévitch of January 21,
1918, Proust expressed his sympathy for her unhappy situation in
the wake of Lenin's coming to power, professing his devotion to

"the Russia of Tolstoi, of Dostoevski, of Borodino ..." Marcel Proust, *Correspondance*, ed. Philip Kolb, vol. xvii (Paris: Plon, 1989), p. 76.

14 Gilles Deleuze hints, if no more than that, at the truth of the Lenin-Proust relation. Still, his provocative observation is worth recalling because it is so much at variance with standard views of the *Recherche* as a wholly aestheticized text: "(In a series of famous pages, Proust analyzes the power of social forgetting in terms of the evolution of the Parisian salons from the Dreyfus Affair to the First World War. Few texts constitute a better commentary on Lenin's remark as to society's capacity to replace 'the corrupt old prejudices' by new prejudices even more infamous or more stupid)" (*Proust and Signs*, trans. Richard Howard [New York: George Braziller, 1972], p. 80).

15 The relevant passage in Schiller comes in the second of his *Aesthetic Letters*: "if man is ever to solve that problem of politics in practice he will have to approach it through the problem of the aesthetic, because it is only through Beauty that man makes his way to freedom" (*On the Aesthetic Education of Man*, trans. Elizabeth M. Wilkinson and L. A. Willoughby [Oxford: Clarendon Press, 1967], p. 9).

16 For the canonical view, see, among others, George Painter, *Proust*; Georges Poulet, *Proustian Space*, trans. Elliott Coleman (Baltimore: Johns Hopkins University Press, 1977); Poulet, "Proust and Human Time," in *Proust: A Collection of Critical Essays*, ed. René Girard (Englewood Cliffs, NJ: Prentice-Hall, 1962); and Roger Shattuck, *Proust's Binoculars: A Study of Memory, Time and Recognition in "A la recherche du temps perdu"* (1963; rpt. New York: Vintage, 1967). The view infects even Genette's and Deleuze's otherwise more careful and nuanced treatments. The contrary position, that no happy synthesis is ever achieved, and that the novel endlessly demonstrates this impossibility, has been most forcefully asserted by Paul de Man, who comments: "As a writer, Proust is the one who knows that the hour of truth, like the hour of death, never arrives on time, since what we call time is precisely truth's inability to coincide with itself. *A la recherche du temps perdu* narrates the flight of meaning, but this does not prevent its own meaning from being, incessantly, in flight" (*Allegories of Reading: Figural Language in Rousseau, Nietzsche, Rilke, and Proust* [New Haven: Yale University Press, 1979], p. 78). A post-de Manian reading that closely examines the madeleine episode is Kevin Newmark's "Ingesting the Mummy: Proust's Allegory of Memory," *Yale French Studies* 79 (1991): 150–77.

17 Proust's manuscript continues: "Yet, this latter only indicates a

value contrary to that in literature, which logical reasoning diminishes" (1954 Pléiade, III:1135).

18 Opinion differs on the precise date when the reception occurs. Willy Hachez gives 1919, taking the reference "thirty years after Boulanger" literally. Steel puts it in 1923–24 on the basis of internal chronology (*Chronology*, p. 75). Genette hypothesizes an even later date of 1925. Arguing from the evidence that the war episode is explicitly dated 1916 in the text, he speculates that Marcel's second withdrawal from society would have been of similar duration to the first (*Narrative Discourse*, pp. 91–2). But as with the uncertain chronology in "Un amour de Swann" and with the period of "Venice" and "Tansonville," it would seem that a more general designation is appropriate here. Let us designate the *Recherche*'s final moment, then, simply "post-war."

19 On the level of the economy, of course, this transition has long since been accomplished (see above, "Base and Superstructure"). But on the ideological level, and to some extent on the political, the landed nobility had managed to forestall the transition to bourgeois society a good while longer. The war puts paid to the aristocracy's last illusions of power – in Proust's mind, if not necessarily in that of all his characters.

20 See the notebooks of 1909–11, published as *Matinée chez la Princesse de Guermantes*, ed. Henri Bonnet and Bernard Brun (Paris: Gallimard, 1982), which show that in its original conception, the *Recherche*'s final volume would have been divided into two parts: "L'adoration perpétuelle" (an exposition of Proust's aesthetic theories); and "Le bal de têtes" (a short narrative text recounting Proust's recollections of a salon after an absence of some fifteen or twenty years).

21 In addition to Paul de Man's seminal text cited previously (see n. 16), one should consult the exhaustive consideration of Proust's theory of reading in relation to the knowledge and representation of society in David R. Ellison, *The Reading of Proust* (Baltimore: Johns Hopkins University Press, 1984). Both these studies amply demonstrate the irreconcilability of the two poles of this opposition, thus substantiating, if inadvertently, the point I have insisted upon here.

22 The programmatic statement comes in "The Method of Sainte-Beuve": "But in art there are no initiators or precursors (at least in the scientific sense). Everything is in the individual, each individual starts the artistic or literary endeavour over again, on his own account; the works of his predecessors do not constitute, unlike in science, an acquired truth from which he who follows

after may profit. A writer of genius today has everything to do. He is not much further advanced than Homer" (*Against Sainte-Beuve and Other Essays*, trans. John Sturrock [Harmondsworth: Penguin, 1988], p. 11). One could cite innumerable similar remarks in other essays, in Proust's letters, and in his notebooks. As Vincent Descombes points out, this is what marks Proust as a definitively modernist writer; see his *Proust: Philosophy of the Novel*, trans. Catherine Chance Macksey (Stanford University Press, 1992), p. 138.

23 Some few examples: "je bâtirais mon livre" (IV:610); "ne ferais-je pas mon livre" (612); "Ce serait un livre" (621). That this book is definitively in the future, the following passage would seem to confirm. Its indication of an unfinished project, constantly evolving, is never contradicted: "The organization of my memory, of my preoccupations, was related to my work, perhaps because, while the letters [I] received were forgotten a moment later, the idea of my work was in my head, always the same, in perpetual becoming" (III:1099). [L'organisation de ma mémoire, de mes préoccupations, était liée à mon œuvre, peut-être parce que, tandis que les lettres reçues étaient oubliées l'instant d'après, l'idée de mon œuvre était dans ma tête, toujours, la même, en perpétuel devenir] (IV:619). The complexity (and occasional inconsistency) of Proust's deployment of tenses is well known. To my mind, the most instructive discussion of this aspect of the novel is the chapter on "Frequency" in Genette, in particular the treatment of what he terms "iterative narrative" (*Narrative Discourse*, pp. 116–27).

24 Genette insists on a distinction between the Marcel about whom we have been reading and the Narrator (by convention also called "Marcel") who has told the story of the previous or other self. Genette's judgment on the significance of this distinction jibes with the point I am making here: "The subject of the *Recherche* is indeed 'Marcel becomes a writer,' not 'Marcel the writer': the *Recherche* remains a novel of development, and to see it as a 'novel about the novelist,' like the *Faux monnayeurs*, would be to distort its intentions and above all to violate its meaning; it is a novel about the future novelist" (*Narrative Discourse*, p. 227).

25 "Ideology and Ideological State Apparatuses (Notes towards an Investigation)," in Louis Althusser, *Lenin and Philosophy and Other Essays* (New York: Monthly Review Press, 1971), p. 165.

26 Fredric Jameson, *Marxism and Form: Twentieth-Century Dialectical Theories of Literature* (Princeton University Press, 1971), pp. 153–4.

27 See Schiller, *Aesthetic Letters*, Letter XXVII.

28 Walter Benjamin, "The Image of Proust," in idem, *Illuminations*, ed. Hannah Arendt, trans. Harry Zohn (1968; rpt. New York: Schocken Books, 1969), p. 210. A passage from Benjamin's "Proust-Papiere" confirms the general drift of this thought: "Marx showed how the class-consciousness of the bourgeoisie fell into an insoluble self-contradiction at the culminating point of its development. Georg Lukács (cf. *Geschichte und Klassenbewusstein*, Berlin, 1923, p. 73), concurs in this remark when he says: 'This situation of the bourgeoisie is historically reflected in this point, that it did not force down its predecessor, feudalism, even when the new enemy, the proletariat, appeared.' But the appearance of the proletariat removes the strategic situation to the battlefront against feudalism. The citizenry must here seek an agreement at any price to seek protection in feudalistic positions, less against the pressing proletariat than against the voice of their own class-consciousness. This is the position of Proust's work. His problems descend from a satiated society, but the answers at which he arrives are subversive" (*Gesammelte Schriften*, hrsg. Rolph Tiedemann and Hermann Schweppenhäuser [Frankfurt am Main: Suhrkamp, 1980], II.3:1054; cited in Ronald Thornton, "Marcel Proust and Marxist Literary Criticism from the Nineteen Twenties to the Nineteen Seventies" [Ph.D. dissertation, Indiana University, 1979], p. 72, whose translation I have adopted).

29 Benjamin's own study of emergent capitalism, the *Passagenwerk*, famously locates the crucial moment in capitalist development somewhat earlier than the period studied here, viz., in the Second Empire. For Benjamin, Baudelaire rather than Proust is the exemplary poet of high capitalism. Benjamin's study, only portions of which have been translated into English, has never been far from my mind while working on this project. In her excellent exposition of the *Passagenwerk*, Susan Buck-Morss, comments pertinently on Benjamin's achievement: "[Benjamin] compels us to search for images of sociohistorical reality that are the key to unlocking the meaning of his commentary – just as the commentary is the key to their significance ... Moreover (and this is the mark of his pedagogical success), he allows us the experience of feeling that we are discovering the political meaning of these phenomena on our own" (Susan Buck-Morss, *The Dialectics of Seeing: Walter Benjamin and the Arcades Project* [Cambridge, MA: MIT Press, 1991], p. x). Substitute "Proust" for "Benjamin" in this passage, and one comes close to my own sense of the sociohistorical essence of the *Recherche*.

30 Yet even here, one must take care. The passage on the appearance of the Russian émigrés cited in the previous section establishes the fundamental opposition between nationalism and Bolshevism, which, on the authority of Eric Hobsbawm, was the decisive contest at least through the Great War; see E. J. Hobsbawm, *Nations and Nationalism since 1870: Programme, myth, reality* (Cambridge University Press), pp. 122–3.

31 Wohl, *French Communism*, p. 449.

32 Ibid., p. 454.

33 Louis Althusser, *For Marx*, trans. Ben Brewster (1969; rpt. London: New Left Books, 1977), p. 232.

Index

Académie Française 48
Action Française 112
administrative bureaucracy 31, 35
Adolphe, Uncle (in *A la recherche*) 92
Adorno, Theodor W. 4, 184
aesthetic themes (in *A la recherche*) 4,
   11–12, 98–102, 169, 174–5, 177–9
agriculture, French 19–20, 24, 28, 50, 57
Aimé (in *A la recherche*) 93, 96, 132–5
Albertine disparue 124, 127, 129, 140, 149,
   151, 152, 157
Albertine (in *A la recherche*) 42, 62, 73,
   93, 96, 102, 117, 118, 119, 124–32,
   135–7, 139, 140–1, 144–53
Alsace and Lorraine 20, 28
Althusser, Louis 6, 33, 132, 178, 184
   "Ideology and Ideological State
      Apparatuses" 149
   Reading "Capital" 6
"Un amour de Swann" 66–84, 88–91,
   94, 138
anal intercourse 147–8
Andrée (in *A la recherche*) 127, 132
anti-clericalism 30, 43–6
anti-militarism 112
antisemitism 15, 43, 45, 87, 107, 111,
   112, 114–17, 123–4, 150
Anzin strike 154
d'Argencourt, M. (in *A la recherche*) 162
aristocracy 30, 40–1, 97, 168, 179–80,
   183
   see also bourgeoisie, and aristocracy
Aristotle 12
army, French 38–40, 43, 108–12, 113,
   117
art forms (in *A la recherche*) 48, 140
art, historicism and 98–102
Art/Not-Art, theme of 174
Asselain, Jean-Charles 25, 51

Austen, Jane
   Emma 8
   Mansfield Park 8
"Autour de Mme. Swann" 94–6

Balbec (in *A la recherche*) 42, 70, 91, 92,
   93, 96–8, 117, 118, 126, 128, 129,
   135, 137
Balzac, Honoré de 10, 12, 63
   La Comédie Humaine 1, 12
   Sarrasine 7
banks 21–2, 23
Banque de France 21
Barrès, Maurice 114
Barthes, Roland, *S/Z* 7
base and superstructure 4, 17–50
Bell, William Stewart 82
belle époque 3, 21, 25, 27, 35, 49, 51, 119,
   158, 183
Benjamin, Walter 7, 38, 61, 65, 100
   "The Image of Proust" 181–2, 184
Bergotte (in *A la recherche*) 48, 90, 94,
   175
Berma (in *A la recherche*) 48, 175–6
Bernheimer, Charles 142
Bersani, Leo 126, 147
"Biche" *see* Elstir
bisexuality 126, 132, 167
Bloc National 112, 166, 167–8
Bloch, Ernst 179–80
Bloch, Marc 20
Bloch (in *A la recherche*) 48, 65, 86–7, 93,
   113, 114, 137, 164–5
Bloch, Mlle. (in *A la recherche*) 126,
   127–8, 132
Bloch family (in *A la recherche*) 97, 104
Bolshevism 183
Bonapartists 17, 23, 29, 31, 79, 80, 91,
   95, 108, 109, 113

Radicals, French 31, 111
La Raspelière (in *A la recherche*) 126
Rebérioux, Madeleine 35, 59, 110
relationships (in *A la recherche*), chart
   135–6, 141, *diagram 3.4*
Rémond, René 29
Rennes trial 105
republicanism 56, 79, 87, 161
Restoration (of French monarchy) 58
revanchism 109
revolution 4, 154–85
Revolution, French *see* French
   Revolution
Revolution, Russian 168
Revue pédagogique 32
Riffaterre, Michael 7
Rivers, J. E. 147, 148
Rolland, Romain, *Jean-Christophe* 183
Roman Catholic Church 30, 32, 43–6,
   109, 111, 117
Rothschild, James 21
Rothschild, house of 22, 23, 95
Rousseau, Jean-Jacques 13
royalists 31, 56, 79
Ruskin, John 44, 174

Saint-Loup, Robert de (in *A la recherche*)
   97, 102, 164–7, 170
   death 38, 160, 162, 165, 167
   as Dreyfusard 114
   and Gilberte 157, 158–9
   personal wealth 49
   as representative of nobility 39–41,
      91, 108, 113
   sexuality 126, 128, 129, 132, 146,
      148–9, 157, 160, 167
Sainte-Euverte, Mme. de (in *A la
   recherche*) 89–91
salons 47, 48, 64, 65, 88–9, 116–18, 161,
   170–1
Sartre, Jean-Paul 4, 11
   What is Literature? 124
Schiller, Friedrich 168, 184
   Aesthetic Letters 180
Second Empire 21, 22, 23
Second International 2
Second World War 28
Section Française de l'Internationale
   Ouvrière (SFIO) 156, 163
Sedan, fall of 6, 17, 80
Sedgwick, Eve 147–8
Seine region 51–2
Seize Mai crisis 155

sexual preference (in *A la recherche*)
   130–2, *diagram 3.3*
sexuality 14, 118–53
   see also bisexuality; homosexuality;
   lesbianism
Simonet, Albertine *see* Albertine (in *A la
   recherche*)
"Ski" (in *A la recherche*) 88
Social Democrats (Germany) 2, 112,
   155
social relations 98, 145, *diagrams 2.2, 3.5*
Socialist Party (French), 60, 111
Society/Not-Society, theme of 173–4
Sodome et Gomorrhe 71, 91, 95, 104, 114,
   118–29, 132–6, 141–2, 145–51, 160
Sorel, Albert 12
Spagnoli, John J., *The Social Attitude of
   Marcel Proust* 14
Steel, Gareth 157–8
Stendhal, Henri 1
Stermaria, M. de (in *A la recherche*) 96–7
Stermaria, Mlle. de (in *A la recherche*)
   96–7, 129, 148–9
strikes 155–6, 163
Swann, Charles (in *A la recherche*) 94–6,
   98, 99, 107, 108, 119
   and antisemitism 115–16
   dream about Napoleon III 66–84
   diagram 2.1
   and Dreyfus Affair 114–16
   as Dreyfusard 39, 46, 104
   errotic attachments 47, 77–9, 83–4,
      90, 127, 128, 130, 134, 142
   essay on Vermeer 75
   father of 85–6
   friendships 146
   personal wealth 49, 62
   social position 53–4, 64–5, 86–7,
      89–91
Swann, Gilberte *see* Gilberte
Swann, Odette *see* Odette

Talleyrand, Charles Maurice de 40
Tansonville (in *A la recherche*) 14, 49, 74,
   157, 168, 169
"Tansonville" (in *A la recherche*) 157, 160
tariffs 36
Le temps retrouvé 39, 47–8, 65, 76, 93, 99,
   102, 113, 126, 137, 140, 157,
   168–77
Terror 161
Thiers, Louis Adolphe 17, 28–9
transport system, French 21

Cambridge Studies in French

General editor: Malcolm Bowie (*All Souls College, Oxford*)
Editorial Board: R. Howard Bloch (*University of California, Berkeley*),
Terence Cave (*St John's College, Oxford*), Ross Chambers (*University of
Michigan*), Antoine Compagnon (*Columbia University*), Peter France
(*University of Edinburgh*), Toril Moi (*Duke University*), Naomi Schor
(*Harvard University*)

Also in the series (* denotes titles now out of print)